BEATRICE LILLIE
The Funniest Woman in the World

BEATRICE LILLIE
The Funniest Woman in the World

BRUCE LAFFEY

WYNWOOD™

WYNWOOD™ Press
New York, New York

Library of Congress Cataloging-in-Publication Data

Laffey, Bruce.
    Beatrice Lillie : the funniest woman in the world / Bruce Laffey.
        p.   cm.
    ISBN 0-922066-22-1 : $18.95
    1. Lillie, Beatrice, 1898–   . 2. Actors—Great Britain—
Biography.   3. Comedians—Great Britain—Biography.
I. Title.
PN2598.L56L34   1989
792'.028'092—dc20
[B]   89-16745
                                                                  CIP

Copyright © 1989 by Bruce Laffey
Published by WYNWOOD™ Press
New York, New York
Printed in the United States of America

Preface

In the middle of the 1950s Beatrice Lillie and I were looking into the windows of a Doubleday Book Shop on Fifth Avenue in New York City. The newly published autobiography of a famous celebrity, an actress whom Bea knew well, was prominently displayed.

"You know, everyone is always after me to write a book about my life," she said, staring at the familiar face on the cover, "but I don't know if I could tell everything that's happened, about my family or my private affairs."

"You could do a whole volume on your affairs," I quipped.

"That's not what I meant and you know it," Bea retorted. She gathered her mink coat around her and we began to stroll down Fifth Avenue. "It's just that I don't think I'd be able to say it all."

"Tell you what, Trixie," I volunteered, "I'll write a book about your scandalous life, the men, the dogs, the parakeets!"

She stopped and looked up at me, not laughing, and said, "I really wish you would." She meant it. There were no cassette recorders in those days, but we talked endlessly walking Fifth Avenue in New York or Park Lane in London, in the car, in dressing rooms, and over drinks. Her never-ending optimism and vitality in the face of, in many instances, overwhelming unhappiness were an inspiration and a continuing source of amazement during our friendship over the years. I adored her, and this story is told with love, respect, and admiration.

THE AUTHOR GRATEFULLY ACKNOWLEDGES THE FOLLOWING CONTRIBUTORS:

Hartney Arthur, Kaye Ballard, Mrs. Palmer T. Beaudette, Carl Bell, Valerie Bettis, Hubert Bland, David Bolton, Tommy Brent, Douglas Byng, Thelma Carpenter, Pamela Clatworthy, Marc Connelly, Edmond Dante, Michael Davis, Shannon Dean, Charles DeForest, Carol Arthur DeLuise, Frank Derbas, Fritz and Eugenia DeWilde, Dorothy Dickson, Sir Anton Dolin, Shaun Duffy, Alan Duncan, H.R.H. Prince Philip, Duke of Edinburgh, John Ellis, Robert Feyte, Mike Filey, Maurice Ford, Arlene Francis, Harold French, Mr. and Mrs. Reginald Gardiner, Janet Gari, James Gavin, Sir John Gielgud, Mim Goloboff, Ellen Graham, Mr. and Mrs. Tony Gray, Margaret Hall, Nancy Hamilton, Margaret Harris: Grand Central Galleries, Radie Harris, Gladys Henson, Ted Hook, Gary Hunt, George Hunter, Al Jones, Christine Jorgensen, Austin Kane, Robert Lantz, Gordon Manzi, H.R.H. The Princess

9

ACKNOWLEDGMENTS

Margaret, Fran McClure, Donald J. McCurchy, Robert "Doc" McGunigle, Bruce Medville, Billy Milton, Susette I. Mitchell, Phyllis Monkman, Mary Tyler Moore, Philippa Moore, Richard Morris, Odette Myrtil, National Library of Australia, Virginia Obedin, Sir Laurence Olivier, Most Rev. Andre Penachio, Paul Phillips, Michael Pober, Wesley H. Poling: Yale University, Dr. John Prutting, Cyril Ritchard, Arthur Siegel, Bob Sidney, Lord Snowdon, Leonard Soloway, John Springer, W. Ray Stephens, Dorothy Swerdlove, Bill Thompson, Tom Toth, Peter Turgeon, Capt. and Mrs. James Tyler, Jose Vega, Scott Walters: Photography, Ronnie Waters, Alured Weigall, Hope Williams, Iva Withers, Iggie Wolfington,

and

Dr. Marvin Shapiro

The author has made every attempt to contact those holding the copyrights to all photographs used.

ONE

"I wasn't born, I was won on the playing fields of Eton," declared Bea Lillie. "It was 1898, 1900, or 1903 depending upon which *Who's Who* you happen to own. The American one says 1903 and that's the one I keep at home."

Eton is known to be a goodly distance from number 68 Dovercourt Road in Toronto, Canada, where the actual event took place. Dovercourt Road was situated in an area then referred to as "Cabbage Town" and was peopled by a number of Irish immigrants.

Bea's father, John Lillie, came to Canada from County Cork in Ireland where he was born in 1861. He served a hitch with Her Majesty's Service in India, and when he was honorably discharged he chose to emigrate to Toronto rather than return to Ireland. John Lillie was endowed with a gentle sense of humor and an abhorrence for the pretentious. When he wooed and ultimately married Lucy Ann Shaw, he inherited a great deal of the latter. Perhaps it was Lucy's independence and ambitions that first attracted him, although she was also a striking and well-bred woman ten years his junior whose erect carriage and haughty demeanor gave her the appearance of being taller than she actually was.

"My mother never went overboard," Bea once said to me. "She went overbred!"

Lucy Ann Shaw's family went to Toronto from Manchester in England. Her father was a clothier until he eventually bought a farm and retired. When John Lillie decided to marry Lucy, he courted her, won the blessings of her parents first and, finally, Lucy's detached consent. Lucy would, until the end of her days, remain convinced that she had wed beneath her station in life, a fact she never attempted to conceal from her husband. Lucy's ancestors were Portuguese and Spanish on the distaff side, which may explain her lifelong interest in music and her fiery temper. One thing seems certain: John was seldom bored.

In spite of her marital doubts, Lucy was an admirable wife. She was an excellent cook, a fine housekeeper, and a first-rate gardener. She and John, with his handlebar mustache and courtly manner, were an ideal couple, outwardly at least. Lucy was an accomplished pianist as well as a trained singer, and her powerful soprano voice graced the choirs of the Anglican and Presbyterian churches around Toronto for the next few years. Unhappily for Lucy, her hopes for a career via the concert halls of the world was a desire she would never fulfill. Lucy loved to sing and she sang everything, including daily conversations about the house. John, on his way to his job as a prison guard at the Toronto city jail, might have the daily grocery order sung to him from out the window, or Lucy might warble the latest news over the phone to her mother.

"She used to run straight up the scale just saying hello," said Bea. "A bit like Lily Pons doing 'The Bell Song.' "

John and Lucy Lillie became the parents of two daughters, Muriel first and then Beatrice Gladys eighteen months later on May 29, 1894. It was the year Toronto switched from horse-drawn streetcars to electrically powered transportation though not necessarily in celebration of Bea's arrival. Massey Hall, a red brick edifice with superb acoustics, opened in 1894 and became the home of the Toronto Choral Society and sponsored visiting musical artists. The Grand Opera House, completed twenty years earlier, provided Shakespearean productions or presented the latest hits from London or New York and enabled Toronto to become a leading theatre town on provincial and transborder circuits.

Bea was born at 68 Dovercourt Road but the family moved to

North Cote when she was three years old. She was a quiet, inquisitive child at first and, as she grew older, would favor her father in numerous ways. She would share his dislike for the highbrow and the pretentious, and this disdain for both became an integral element of her comedy. Muriel, on the other hand, was an impetuous and boisterous girl who dominated and took charge of her younger sister. She exhibited many of Lucy's qualities. She was quick-tempered, haughty, and strong-willed. Later she became quite adept in the kitchen and an adroit gardener as well, although her sudden outbursts of anger at the stove might send a pot of ruined gravy sailing through the back door and into her azaleas. Later in her life, Muriel's straight-out candor would cost her innumerable friendships. Bea had no particular affection for cooking or gardening and for most of her life employed cook and gardener to prove it. As they matured, Bea and Muriel cultivated extraordinary senses of humor which Muriel insisted they inherited from their father. Bea's early comedic outbursts probably stemmed from a need to be recognized or acknowledged by her mother, who, on the other hand, took herself and life very seriously.

Thrift, often bordering on tightfistedness, came to both girls through their mother. This they learned when they trailed behind Lucy on her shopping chores, emulating her as they delicately raised their skirts and stepped over puddles at the curbs. Lucy knew the value of a penny and made sure her daughters found out early in life. There was also a Victorian morality she instilled in Bea and Muriel that surfaced in both sisters now and then during the course of their careers, often at very odd times.

Beatrice and Muriel remained close friends as they developed, going to and from school together and spending leisure time with each other. Eventually Bea became "Bootie" and Muriel "Sister Anne," pet names they bestowed upon each other. Bea and Muriel played house in the afternoons under the freight cars on a railroad spur near their home until their father, fearing for their lives, forbade it. Together the Lillie family picnicked on the beaches of Lake Ontario in the summers or visited the elder Shaws on their farm. Bea enjoyed the farm animals and all of her life she was surrounded by dogs and cats and, on occasion, lovebirds and budgerigars. In the winter, there were evenings around the fire at home, tobogganing, and curling, a popular game similar to ice hockey, on the lake. Bea and Muriel ice-skated on the many large rinks scattered about the area. Chocolate ice cream was a customary treat after Sunday dinner. Through it all, presiding as head of the family, was Lucy, iron-willed, straight-laced, imperious, and unbending, her determination to "be somebody" uppermost in her mind. She constantly urged John to better himself financially. At one point he invested in an international employment agency designed to secure employment for the British, Irish, and Scottish immigrants arriving from the United Kingdom. Unfortunately, many of these arrivals were headed westward and into the United States. Toronto was fast becoming a national metropolis with expanding trade as Bea grew older, but Lillie's investment was not to prove fruitful.

When John Lillie moved his family to Gladstone Avenue, Lucy began to teach piano and voice. She also changed the spelling of her first two names to Lucie Anne which she felt added a touch of refinement to the endeavor. Muriel began studying piano, and Lucie was thrilled to discover that she possessed an unusual talent for music. She decided then and there that music would be her oldest daughter's career. This decision transformed Bea's life considerably. She was alone a great deal while her sister practiced. Muriel was no longer free to accompany her on various expeditions where she required a chaperone. Consequently Bea was forced to invent new diversions with which to while away the hours and, most important, attract some notice. Sliding down the banister, though a lovely attention getter, was forbidden and might end with Bea racing up the stairs and Lucie in hot pursuit. This could be followed by a severe lecture, or she might be remanded to her room with no dinner forthcoming. Rather than starve to death, Bea forwent the balustrade for the sidewalk, and clad in a red pleated skirt she loved, she wandered to such exotic places as High Park where the bluebells grew as high as her shoulders and where she could ogle the homes of the affluent, the elite of Toronto, whose families had settled in the city in the 1840s. Sometimes she coaxed a nickel from her father, an easy touch, and dashed off to a drug store on Yonge Street where she would indulge in ice cream covered with whipped cream, nuts, and cherries. To earn her own money, Bea would descend upon Mr. Lee, the local Chinese laundryman, and regale him with songs such as "Oh, for the Wings of a Dove," a favorite of her mother's, whom she emulated right down to the final note, and other equally entertaining ditties until Mr. Lee would toss in the towel, so to speak, and reward her. The greengrocer, on the other hand, was serenaded with less esoteric arias, and he, too, gave until it hurt. Early in life, Beatrice Lillie learned the wisdom of varying her program to suit her audiences! When Muriel could steal away from the piano, she and Bea would observe the cycling meets which were a fad in the 1890s or attend the yachting or rowing contests on the lake.

At the same time that the Lillies changed residences, Muriel and Bea switched to the George Street School. Muriel was a superior student to Bea, but Bea could invoke laughter from the other students. As a result she was invited on trips to the zoo, birthday parties, and various other gatherings and usually managed to entertain the crowd with antics such as imitations of her mother's singing or of Muriel at the piano. Bea found it less burdensome to withdraw into humor than to suffer the demands of general conversation on topics such as world affairs, books, or politics.

Lucie began including Bea in the music lessons, essentially to keep her out of trouble, but Bea centered her attention upon her mother's facial and vocal expressions. Over and over, as she was discovered staring, Lucie would sing in her high soprano, "Look at your book and not at me! Look at your book and not at me!"

John Lillie observed his family's activities with bemused interest, not really understanding it all. He lost most of his investment in the employment agency and then opened a cigar store with the little he had left over. Lillie's emporium was unique in that it boasted the first cigar store Indian in Toronto.

"He kept muttering, 'Call and see us, have a cigar,' " claimed Muriel. Bea and Muriel loved and respected their father but he would remain in the background as Lucie shaped their lives to meet her specifications.

Lucie was engaged as choir director for Cooke's Presbyterian Church on Queen's Street and their lives underwent another change. This time the family moved to Sherbourne Street. Lucie then decided to include her two daughters in her activities at Cooke's, since all the "right" people attended the Anglican or Presbyterian church in Toronto at the time.

Muriel, who was progressing rapidly as a pianist, suddenly found herself playing the organ for Sunday services. Bea was then enrolled in Sunday school, which convened in the church basement Sunday mornings. After an hour or two of fun and games, most of the children adjourned to their homes but Bea was required to sit through one, often two, long grown-up services as she waited for her mother and sister to take her home. Lucie grudgingly gave up her arguments to have John attend Cooke's with his family. Bea remembered for many years after the strong odor of naphtha clinging to her freshly laundered white gloves as she correctly folded her hands on her lap.

One day Lucie overheard Bea singing to herself in her room. The quality and the pitch were quite good. Lucie decided then and there that Bea would study voice. She was given little choice in the matter, but it gave her something to do. The lessons also gave her more time to spend with her sister, without whom she found it difficult to make decisions as to what to wear to school or how to occupy her time.

A new pair of black gloves, without lye, opened enthralling new vistas for Bea. Neatly tying black bows in her braids and dressing in her Sunday best, she cruised the neighborhoods looking for funeral crepes displayed on front doors. Sighting one, Bea would approach the house, knock reverently, and announce to whomever appeared that she was a friend of the corpse. Once inside, she played it to the hilt. Putting on her saddest face, she would hover over the body for a correct number of moments, shake hands all over the place as she extended her condolences and then, clucking sympathetically, would make her way out, eyes filled with tears.

"I actually cried real tears!" Bea remembered.

The Canadian National Exposition was an exciting yearly event to which all Canadians flocked, Bea among them. The Fair, inaugurated in 1879, was a yearly tribute to the latest advances in technology and agriculture.

"The thing I always remember about Toronto is the 'Ex.' I used to be absolutely envious over those girls who lounged around giving away free samples. I asked a booth manager if I could please have a job. Apparently, I was not the type to walk around and give away things so I was sent someplace out back to wash dishes. Get *them*!" Bea declined the offer quickly and with great hauteur.

Life dealt little Bea another cruel blow when Lucie announced that she was ready for the choir at Cooke's. From then on it was rehearsals in the evenings and grueling hours in church. Up in the choir loft, Bea was smothered between adults in the soprano section and had no choice but to sit through the sermons. Happily, she had one weapon against the boredom: her imagination! She began with an imitation of the minister. Finding she could elicit snickers from the other youngsters and a few adults, Bea went on from there. One particularly hot Sunday, she idly reached out and snapped off a branch from a potted palm tree close by and began fanning herself with it. That gesture caused quite a disturbance and earned Bea a severe lecture from her mother when she was fingered as the culprit. One poor young man would dissolve into gales of laughter whenever Bea fixed her gaze upon him and raised a haughty eyebrow or pursed her lips in mock disapproval. Naturally, Beatrice feigned innocence when heads turned in her direction.

The final straw occurred one fateful day when Bea found herself stationed alongside a large and obese woman, who, it was discovered later, suffered from a severe case of flatulence. As the group ripped merrily through the hymn of the day, voices rose to a crescendo and, on cue, came to a sudden halt. Bea's neighbor chose that brief pause to give vent to her emotions with a blast of wind. The choir was frozen with shock until Bea, drawing herself up to her full height, turned directly upon the unfortunate creature and hissed, "Well, really!" in a stage whisper heard in every corner of the loft. The remainder of the hymn was lost in the laughter that followed. As a result of that caper, Bea found herself in very hot water. Lucie removed her from the choir and positioned her at the pump handle of the organ. Furious with her mother for this insult, Bea attacked the handle so vehemently that she broke it off. Muriel was speedily transferred to a nearby piano, and Bea's church career was ended.

When Muriel began studying at the Toronto Conservatory of Music, Lucie felt that perhaps Bea's talents should be fostered in a more professional atmosphere. She enrolled her in the talent studio of a Mr. Harry Rich. Harry W. Rich, who earlier had been a fairly well known comedian, founded the Rich Concert and Entertainment Bureau soon after an accident left him confined to a wheelchair. Mr. Rich booked talent throughout Ontario and farther afield, at the same time training young beginners in elocution, mime, and "dramatic gesture." Although Bea always claimed the only thing she and Harry had in common was a mutual hatred, she admittedly had him to thank for a storehouse of gestures and grimaces which became her trademark. By the end of her course of training, she had, according to Bea, "the best set of gestures in Canada." In reality Bea was Rich's favorite pupil as he instructed her in comedy-character songs that she delivered in the guise of geisha girls, organ grinders, or Irish clog dancers. As each new number was added to the repertoire, Lucie whipped out her needle and ran up a corresponding costume. One of Bea's memorable impersonations entitled "Strawberry Girl" was written by Mr. Rich himself.

"Someday you girls will thank me for this!" became Lucie's war cry as each daughter became more and more immersed in her own career. Toward the end of her life, Lucie Lillie was fond of declaring that while she was carrying Bea, she knew she was expecting something special. Time unfortunately had cast a shroud over her memory, so perhaps she can be forgiven for not remembering that it was Muriel she banked on to immortalize the name of Lillie throughout the planet. Lucie saw only one star on the horizon. A scant few years later, however, Providence, with the help of Bea, would prove Lucie wrong.

Lucie began presenting Wednesday night musicales in her home. Very often she would sing one or two numbers accompanied by Muriel. Vocalists and instrumentalists were among the invited guests each week and Mr. Rich was prevailed upon to attend now and then. John Lillie would make a casual entrance in suspenders, sans jacket, which drove Lucie to distraction, although Muriel always secretly admired him for it. Bea would perform one or two of her "character impersonations," implementing the correct hand and eye movements as Mr. Rich counted the house or checked for reactions. At an opportune moment, Muriel would plunge into a concerto or a sonata, hands skillfully flying over the keys with a professional aplomb which would garner her hefty applause.

As the evening wore on, the girls would be excused and sent to bed while the adults continued. The sisters, who by then were attending the Gladstone Avenue High School, would sit quietly at the top of the stairs observing the festivities or would watch through a heating duct in the floor. This went on until one night when Muriel and Bea decided it would be more comfortable if they removed the grate and allowed their feet to dangle down into the room below. This, of course, did not set well with Lucie, who saw them to bed from then on. Without realizing it, Bea was making a mental record, for future use, not only of the mannerisms of her mother but the attitudes and characteristics of the Lillie guests.

Many of Lucie's visitors were sufficiently impressed with the talents of the three Lillie women to invite them to appear either singularly or together at private parties, church functions, and rallies. When Harry Rich signed them as clients, the Lillie Trio was born. Lucie vocalized her classical or semiclassical arias and Bea performed her character songs in costume. Muriel, who accompanied her mother and sister, concertized on her own as well. They soon found themselves in constant demand, and for Harry it was a bonanza. Not only did he represent the trio but he was able to book Lucie, Beatrice, and Muriel as single acts.

For relaxation Bea and a girlfriend spent hours watching silent films. As they sat in the darkened theatre, which was owned by her friend's father, Bea decided then and there to be a movie star. She went so far as to choose her movie star nom de theatre—Gladys Montell. A young lady who attended the same school as Bea, although earlier than she, did go on to become a famous movie star. Her name was Mary Pickford.

When a local drug store decided to run a contest for the "most popular girl in town," Bea knew certainly that it was she. Whoever made a purchase in the store was entitled to a vote, and Bea set her mind on winning it. "It was a combination wristwatch and handcuff. I developed more sickness than I ever had in my life. It was my first experience in acting and it turned out to be so successful I won the watch. My own family must have paid the rent that month for the drug store."

Bea never mentioned schoolgirl crushes, but she did fall head over heels for a school principal she found very handsome, who managed to blow himself up with an overdose of bicarbonate of soda and fizz water. For most of her education, Bea was constantly in the company of females, and Lucie kept a sharp eye on both of her daughters.

As they gained popularity, the Lillie Trio appeared at local theatres and social clubs. Soon they were traveling to mining camps. One such engagement took them twenty-eight miles in an open bus through a downpour. They arrived at their destination looking like drowned rats but the show went on as scheduled. If Lucie felt any engagement to be less than respectable they simply changed the name of the act to the Francis Trio. At one point they were performing in a traveling revue called *The Belles of New York*. While Lucie and Muriel switched to the name Francis, Bea proudly assumed the name Gladys Montell, her future movie alias.

The Belles of New York enjoyed great success with the miners everywhere. However, when a run of bad luck resulted in a week's layoff, the Lillie luggage was impounded by their boardinghouse in lieu of rent until the rest of the company took up a collection enabling Lucie and the girls to retrieve their belongings and return home. There is no doubt that these experiences served Bea well. When she became a star, touring was not a trial to her. By the time she really took to the road, she was a seasoned professional.

Cobourg, Ontario, was a charming resort town on Lake Ontario, approximately seventy miles northeast of Toronto. The area was built around a harbor and the town was easily accessible to the traveler. Many of the steel giants of Pittsburgh built vacation homes there in which they would leave their wives as they continued on to inspect their mining interests in northern Canada. The wives remained in Cobourg safe from the frozen north and other inconveniences. They would vacation along the lake until their spouses gathered them up for the return trip to Pittsburgh. Eventually, citizens of Buffalo and other border towns found their way to Cobourg for summer holidays. Costly homes sprang up throughout the region, as well as many guest houses and hotels.

One of the notable summer residents was a Colonel Cornell of Buffalo. The Cornells owned a large home and spacious grounds along the lake. Retired, the colonel devoted his time to amateur theatricals and sponsored concerts at the Cobourg Town Hall. Through Harry Rich, the colonel booked the Lillie Trio into Cobourg. It was during their engagement there that Bea met Cornell's granddaughter, also an aspiring actress. Slightly more than a year older than Bea, Katharine Cornell and Beatrice Lillie became lifelong friends.

When the Lillie Trio became an important asset to the company, Harry Rich issued promotional fliers and posters that were widely distributed. One advertisement extolled the Lillie Trio as "high class entertainers" who were available as a trio as well as single acts "with window cards thrown in."

Bea's card was headed, "Miss Beatrice Lillie, character Costume Vocalist and Impersonator." Viewers were treated to three charming photographs of Bea, one formal and two in costume, plus many of the favorable reviews printed in Canadian newspapers. Muriel's virtues and accomplishments were printed on the reverse side, and her personal publicity was headed "Miss Muriel Lillie, Talented Pianist and Accompanist," topped by a lovely photograph of her.

Bea's early notices might have been written by Harry Rich himself, they were so glowing. *The Toronto Globe* reported, "Miss Beatrice Lillie and her several character songs won a popular verdict and recalls. Beatrice is a remarkable clever artist with a sweet, powerful voice." *The Galt Reformer* thought, "Beatrice Lillie proved a great favorite and won much applause for all her numbers. She has a wonderful voice." *The Drayton Advocate* proclaimed happily, "Her very appearance was a signal for applause, and she was repeatedly encored." Beatrice Lillie, now in her middle teens, was attracting attention in her own hometown.

As a result of the Cobourg engagements, Lucie was offered the directorship of a church choir in that city. The money was far better than Cooke's had been paying. Muriel continued at the Toronto Conservatory, and it was decided that Bea was ready to attend college. She was sent to live and study at St. Agnes College in Belleville, Ontario. Lucie was determined that Bea would receive a proper education while she concentrated on Muriel's career. Muriel commuted between Toronto and Cobourg, where Bea visited her mother and sister during her time off from school. John Lillie, left behind, turned the Sherbourne Street home into a boarding house. More and more he was finding himself not included in the lives of his own family.

Bea, now separated from her Toronto friends, made a new one in Cobourg. She lived next door to the Lillies and her name was Alice Grosjean. Alice was Bea's constant companion when school vacations enabled her to return home.

Alice remembered Bea as being very quick with a laugh line. When, on their way to ice-skate one winter's day, a lady stopped to ask if they were on their way to ice-skate, Bea answered sweetly, "No, we're on our way to pick flowers, can't you tell?" Bea and Alice maintained the friendship for many years. When Bea became a star and played Buffalo or Toronto, Alice and her husband often visited her backstage or dined with her.

While Beatrice languished at college, Muriel was fast making a name for herself as a musician. "Miss Lillie is considered one of Toronto's most promising musicians and a great future is ahead for her," *The Sentinel Star* of Cobourg reported. Unfortunately, Toronto's most promising musician, winner of the Earl Grey Medal, became a victim of her own impetuosity and, in effect, cancelled out the great future that was ahead. Lucie, who prided herself on being in control of the world around her, failed to keep a sharp enough eye on her eldest daughter, and on October 22, 1912, in Toronto, Lucie was rocked by the news that her daughter, upon whom she had staked so much, had married Mr. John Dinwoodie Burnett.

Lucie was beside herself with disappointment and frustration and anger. The exact effect of it all on John Lillie is not known but, in any case, he probably was not considered either way. But because of his love for Muriel, he was probably behind her at any cost. When Bea was finally let in on the secret, she rejoiced mainly because Muriel had been able to put one over on her mother. Lucie, never the sort to give up without a struggle, began making plans for Muriel to continue her education in Germany, husband or no husband. There seems to exist no record of Mr. Burnett's protestations, if any.

Soon after, Muriel and her mother sailed for Europe, leaving John on Sherbourne Street and Bea miserable in Belleville. Muriel never lived with her spouse, and he was not heard from again for many years.

Lucie was alarmed by the talk of war emanating from Germany and changed their plans. She and Muriel went to London where Muriel began her studies with the renowned Myra Hess. Bea, finding herself with no family nearby, wrote to her father and revealed her hopes for the future. She realized that all efforts were being made in Muriel's behalf but she felt she wanted to give the theatre a try. Knowing there was little he personally could do to contribute to Bea's dream, John scraped together the fare, took Bea to Montreal when her education was finished and, with a tearful farewell, packed her off to London, after which he returned to Sherbourne Street alone.

TWO

Lucie and Muriel met Bea in Liverpool and Bea moved into their small flat near Chelsea. Muriel was busy with her studies and was supplementing the family income by playing ragtime piano in movie theatres. In 1912, a show called *Hullo Ragtime* introduced Irving Berlin's "Alexander's Ragtime Band," which touched off the ragtime craze throughout most of the world. The song was first performed in London by an American, Ethel Levey, at the Hippodrome.

André Charlot, a young and inventive entrepreneur from Paris, arrived in England about the same time as the Lillies did. Charlot was hired by Sir Osgood Stall, the owner of the Alhambra Theatre, as producer-manager. He proceeded to stage some attractive and noteworthy revues until Stoll, alarmed by the lavishness and expense of Charlot's taste, released him. Leasing the Alhambra for himself, Charlot struck out on his own and quickly became master of what would later be known as the "intimate" revue, a description he personally disliked. The term "intimate" actually referred to the small intimate theatres in which he presented his efforts as opposed to the large musical stages employed by C. B. Cochran or Florenz Ziegfeld. In a Charlot production each performer was expected to excel in all facets of the show.

With an armload of Harry Rich's flattering advertisements, Bea Lillie set about searching for recognition as a character costume vocalist and impersonator or, as Bea phrased it, "a serious singer." Unfortunately, the managers listened to Bea politely and, just as politely, turned her down. Muriel accompanied her sister at the piano but even Muriel's expertise did little to aid Bea in finding employment. Eventually, through an agent, Bea succeeded in securing an evening's work as an "extra turn" at the Camberwell Empire. An extra turn was an act, either amateur or semiprofessional, which was presented to an audience between regularly scheduled acts. Bea was engaged to perform three numbers. Lucie conceived the brilliant idea of under-dressing Bea in a trio of costumes. When Bea ended one number, she was to dash off into the wings during tumultuous applause, quickly whip off the top dress and, almost immediately, reappear in front of an enraptured audience in a totally new get-up.

With her sister supporting her at the keyboard, Beatrice Lillie began her music hall debut with little or no success. The cockney audience was not in the least interested in Harry Rich's gestures or the Irish clog and there was hardly a response from the onlookers, although they were noticeably loud. By her third number, however, Bea was ready for them. Stepping forward, she waited patiently for the noisy crowd to quiet down. Then, with a perfectly straight face, she solemnly announced that she would close, "with your kind permission," by singing a song written by Mr. Irving Berlin. "Upon," she declared with an appropriate catch in the throat, "the death of his beloved wife." The ballad was "When I Lost You" and nobody with a conscience dared breathe as Bea sobbed her way through the number, exhibiting gestures she certainly never learned from Harry Rich. At the end of the song the crowd went mad and she bowed off in a blaze of glory.

A small role in a short-lived production of *The Daring of Diane* at the Pavillion came and went unnoticed. Then, in the summer of 1914, André Charlot was ill with scarlet fever in the London Fever Clinic. One of his aides, a man named Magowan, utilized the time by auditioning new talent to be seen by Charlot later. As luck would have it, Bea managed to be included in one of the auditions. While she had not as yet developed her unique style, Bea had begun to use Rich's gestures for comedy relief and was creating a piquant and saucy image which would precede the brittle and satiric one she perfected in later years. Mr. Magowan was impressed, so much so that he tentatively engaged her. Ebullient over his new discovery, Magowan telephoned Charlot at the clinic.

"The way he raved about her you'd have thought it was he, not I, who had the fever," Charlot was to say later. In truth, Charlot was just the slightest bit put out that his assistant would hire an unknown in his absence. When Bea eventually appeared before André Charlot at his office, she opened with a tearjerker only to discover she was getting laughs from the producer and his staff. Undaunted, she plowed on by burlesquing the lyrics. When she finished, she found Charlot, his eyes brimming with tears of laughter, offering her a contract at fifteen pounds a week for three years. The following day, World War I broke out. Bea would always be known for her uncanny timing. The story of Bea's audition for Charlot has appeared in many forms over the years but that was the one she told most often.

Charlot immediately put Bea into a show called *Not Likely*, which was already running. It starred George Grossmith, an immensely popular dancer, singer, and comic, Phyllis Monkman, Connie Ediss, Eileen Molyneux, sister of the famous couturier, and Teddie Gerard. Bea was so new to the theatre that she was not aware of stage doors and arrived for rehearsal through the front of the building. She sat patiently in the back of the orchestra until she heard her name being called. With her appearance in this show, Bea began a friendship with Phyllis Monkman, the singing and dancing comedienne, which was to continue for a lifetime. At her first costume call, she was fitted into a dress cut very low in the front and with no sleeves. Bea, who by then had developed a bosom of ample proportions, was appalled when she saw herself in a mirror. She was terrified of Lucie's reactions to the gown and burst into tears. She had no choice but to wear it. Bea's tenure with *Not Likely* passed unheralded and she failed to impress the audiences with her number, "I Want a Toy Soldier." For a time, Charlot sent Bea on tour with other productions, allowing her to gain more experience and style.

As the war accelerated, male performers were going off to battle and Charlot found that Bea, with her five-foot-three trim figure and youthful look, was a natural to appear as a male impersonator. With expensive wigs to cover Bea's beautiful and full long hair, she made an attractive soldier boy or boulevardier.

"I suppose I should have been more careful. As it was, male impersonating just simply sneaked up on me," Bea remembered. "Almost before I knew it, I was wearing a tuxedo 'with an air'!" In one case it was an air of naivete. Jack Buchanan jokingly referred to her impersonations by asking on which side she dressed. Bea quickly pointed out the location of her dressing room in the theatre.

Lucie was not amused, however, and nagged at Bea about the possibility of Canadian friends discovering Bea disporting herself in such an outrageous manner. But Charlot knew exactly what he was doing, and the one thing he was firmly doing was keeping Lucie at a distance, a gesture she did not take too lightly. There was little she could do since Bea was under contract, although she was still in control at home.

Throughout her career, Bea was slow to learn lines, mainly because she required an audience reaction to assist her in a spontaneous approach to whatever she was performing. Her mind was continually on bits of business and where to insert them. Consequently, she hated rehearsing. Fortunately Charlot recognized this in Bea early on and he added new material slowly. Because of this, she was barely aware that she was learning new sketches and songs. Charlot built Bea Lillie into a star almost without her realizing it.

"Charlot was a darling," said Phyllis Monkman, "such a brilliant man. He found everybody; Gertie [Lawrence], Jack Buchanan, me, Bea, and everybody!" Charlot was known as the man who built performers into stars; C. B. Cochran then turned them into comets, it was said.

Things at home were not so happy. Muriel was not progressing with her career and Lucie Lillie was becoming increasingly difficult toward Bea. Friends supposed that Mrs. Lillie was jealous of Bea's growing success, either because she had no control over it or because she was surpassing her sister, upon whom Lucie had staked so much. As a result, Bea became almost apologetic concerning her success and often remarked that her mother and sister had far more talent than she ever did. Muriel would always feel that she was responsible for Bea's career and never let her forget it. Bea often brought home female friends to spend the night rather than face her family alone. Muriel, always quick to anger, and Lucie, strict and unbending, made for an uneasy home life. Bea was never able to relax in Muriel's presence, fearing that at any moment she might create a scene. In spite of the arguments and disagreements, however, the three Lillie women remained committed to one another for life.

Early in 1915, Charlot was in need of a comedienne for a new show called *5064 Gerard*. (The title referred to the backstage telephone number. Charlot loved titles which made absolutely no sense and continued to use them until he finally settled for *Charlot's Revue*.) He brought Bea in from the road and put her in the show, which opened in March of 1915. Her co-workers were Gaby DesLys, fresh from Paris and New York, Phyllis Monkman, Robert Hale, and the American singer Lee White, wife of star Clay Smith, her oftentimes stage partner. Another American dancer, Harry Pilcer, completed the roster of principals.

The revue was in two acts and twelve scenes. Phyllis Monkman portrayed a Girl Scout with a chorus of Scouts behind her, Robert Hale did an impersonation of Gaby DesLys, and the final scene, called "The Pearl Necklace," had a chorus dressed in white with one or two members placed strategically in black. The effect was to create the illusion of a huge pearl necklace weaving about the stage.

The ensemble consisted of approximately seventy or seventy-five people and could hardly be described as an "intimate" revue. Phyllis Monkman performed a dance number, "The Temple of the Sun." Charlot instructed Phyllis to unpin her hair and let it hang luxuriantly down her back. She was then costumed in a loose-fitting tunic. One night her partner lifted her high in the air, spun her around, and lightly set her on her feet facing the audience. Also facing the audience was Phyllis's right breast, which had rudely popped out of her tunic. Appalled, Phyllis scooped up the renegade bosom in her hand and, instead of escaping offstage into the wing nearest her or at least tucking it quickly back from whence it came, she chose to hike belligerently across the stage in full view of the crowd to the stage manager in the opposite wing where she waved it at him and screamed, "Well, that's a pretty thing!" as if he had had something to do with it.

Coincidental with the problem of Phyllis's errant bosom, the newspapers had been printing complaints from moralist groups concerning the impropriety of certain "Oriental" and "exotic" style dances which were then a fad on the stage. The lack of proper clothing, and exposed arms, legs, and thighs, were causing uneasiness in these groups. Happily, Phyllis's unfortunate experience escaped their scrutiny.

In a sketch called "At Murray's Club," Bea was cast as Miss Foxtrot, but it was in scene three of the first act that she really shone. Under a man's three-piece dark suit designed by Pope & Bradley, the famous London tailors, Bea sported a white shirt with a striped cravat. With her own hair tucked under a man's wig, and carrying a cigarillo in her right hand, Bea sang Irving Berlin's "I Want to Go Back to Michigan" or, as it was listed on the program, "Back to the Farm." With the Charlot ladies chorus behind her, Bea pulled out all stops and electrified the audience. She finished the number to roaring applause and dashed offstage to her dressing room. It was not until the stage manager rushed into the room and pulled her back to the stage that Bea understood she had stopped the show cold! Bea always felt that British audiences found the song amusing because they could not imagine anyone wishing to go back to a place called Michigan.

Later in the same year, Bea went into a show called *Now's the Time*. Contributing to the set and costume designs was a man named Arthur Weigall. Weigall was, by profession, a respected Egyptologist and student of ancient civilizations. He had written numerous books on both subjects, including one on *The Life and Times of Cleopatra*, which eventually became the basis of a film starring Elizabeth Taylor. Eventually, long hours of research and hard work took their toll and Weigall suffered a breakdown and returned to London.

As an avocation he chose the theatre and set about designing scenery, costumes, and writing sketch material. Weigall was married, the father of two young children. He was fond of his son and daughter and his wife but she had no particular interest in his careers, preferring to remain the perfect housewife and mother. Bea liked

Arthur Weigall and introduced him to her family. He was attracted immediately to Muriel. Weigall found her impetuosity and candor exhilarating, particularly after his wife's submissiveness. Despite her temper, Muriel had an enormous heart. She could be impossible but she was kind and she had an extraordinary depth, which Bea did not have, in literature and other outside interests. Muriel was now a strapping woman, much taller than Bea, almost beautiful but with somewhat heavy jowls. Bea, on the other hand, possessed a silent poise. Weigall and Muriel collaborated on some songs for the show, Muriel supplying the music and he the lyrics. It followed that they would become lovers.

Little remains concerning the fate of *Now's the Time* other than on the opening night in October of 1915 the zeppelin raids on London began. As bombs were dropped by the attacking Germans, the audience remained rigid in their seats while the show progressed, but at intermission all hell broke loose as people scrambled for the public phones in order to ascertain the safety of their families. Phone service being what it was in 1915, segments of the audience flowed up and down the aisles all during the second act hoping to find an available telephone. The zeppelin visits became a nightly occurrence. Bea sang a number in the show called "Where Did That One Go, Herbert?" Often the Germans punctuated the song with bombs at appropriate moments. When they did not, the audience mimicked the explosions.

"When the zeppelins made that first night raid in London, I'm afraid my work was forgotten!" said Bea. "The theatre was in a panic and I was mad about it!"

Now's the Time was advertised as "A musical time piece in two hours and ten chimes." It was a review about travels in a time machine and one critic felt compelled to point out that "The authors had an idea that would have been carried out if the producer, the stage producer, the designer of dances and ensembles, the carpenter, the electrician, the dressmakers and all the rest of them had allowed it." Another reviewer stated, "Miss Beatrice Lillie is clever and individual."

Now that Muriel was occupied much of the time with Arthur Weigall, Bea spent many hours with friends Phyllis Monkman, Fay

Compton, and young comedienne Gladys Gunn (later Gladys Henson). Whether they decided that Bea should deduct four years from her actual age at that time is not known, but Bea nevertheless did, and for most of her life she was thought to be four years younger than she actually was.

"Once Bea and I decided to go to the Derby," Gladys Henson remembered. "Everybody else was going and nobody had asked us so we got into a taxi and went! We were in the paddock and one of the horses winked at her. Bea said, 'That horse winked at me, I must back it.' So I told her to back it as I was very good when it came to betting on the horses. She went to find out what its name was and some man standing there said, 'You must be mad, he's a rank outsider!' Beattie bet on the horse and it won.

"I used to stay with her a lot because she didn't want to go home alone and face Lucie in the morning. Lucie used to hate me. She used to absolutely loathe me. She said to me one day, 'If I had a gun you'd be a dead woman!' Her mother was furiously jealous of Bea. The father was a darling. Bea was like a little girl, you know. She was a child really."

Whether this was the beginning of Bea's lifelong aversion to being alone is not certain but the fact remains she always wanted someone somewhere on the premises night or day.

Compton, sister of writer Compton Mackenzie, was an established actress and the widow of producer Henry Pelissier, who died in 1913. Pelissier had been one of the pioneers in the revue art form in England by refining music hall talent and forming it into a succession of acts and musical numbers for the legitimate stage. He and Fay had a son named Anthony. In 1914, Fay married her leading man Lauri deFrece. Fay Compton was enormously popular with British audiences and she and Bea became close friends.

In February of 1916, Charlot presented *A Season of Variety* at the Alhambra. For the first time in London he was presenting Odette Myrtil, a young French chanteuse and violinist. Bea was engaged to appear in the revue and one day she went into Odette's dressing room and introduced herself.

"Bea wore these beautiful wigs over her own hair, which was very long and thick. She looked just like a little boy. She was most lavish.

She gave me a set of brushes, a mirror, and two big perfume decanters. She bought this for me! What made her buy me a hat from Maison Louie; this beautiful hat that she gave me. I wore it forever."

Odette possessed a sense of humor akin to Bea's, which probably accounted for the gifts. The ladies remained fast friends.

When Mabel Russell left Charlot's *Samples* in 1916, Bea joined up with Ida Renee, Bert Coote, Marie Blanche, and the Terry Twins and remained with *Samples* at the Playhouse ("smoking allowed" the advertisements proclaimed) until joining the next revue, *Some*, at the Theatre Royal the same year. Bea ("By permission of the directors of the Alhambra"), appeared opposite Clay Smith, Lee White, Rebla, Gene Gerrard, Guy LeFevre, "Betty," Gladys Voile, and Billie Carleton. Billie Carleton was an extraordinarily beautiful popular singer who had achieved recognition when C. B. Cochran allowed her to replace Ethel Levey in *Watch Your Step*. Although she lacked talent as an actress, Carleton was loaded with personality and became a great favorite with the servicemen out front. Bursting with energy but unable to deal with sudden popularity, Billie found herself involved with a fast-moving crowd. Before she knew it, she was hooked on opium, not terribly surprising since she had been reared in a family of alcoholics. It was, in fact, one of her steady dates who kept her supplied with the drug until, realizing the danger she was in, she swore off and immersed herself in a regimen of horseback riding, golf, and tennis. *Some* opened in June and Bea sang and talked a number with Clay Smith and Lee White written by Richard Whiting entitled "And They Call It Dixie Land." One day André Charlot arrived at Bea's dressing room with a young lady he introduced as Gertrude Lawrence and announced that henceforth she would be Bea's understudy and appear in the show as well. Smith and White had seen Lawrence once in a show out in the hinterlands and had never forgotten her. Lawrence, newly married to a husband who was out of work, needed a job badly and when Charlot found a spot he hired her.

"I don't engage an artist and then find a place for her. First I have the place and then find the artist to fit it," said Charlot. "I never buy names. What I pay for is personality, charm, talent. Of course many of the artists in my revues have won great distinction, but they had no prominence when they came to me."

For the London run, Lawrence had herself billed as Gertie Lawrence. Bea and Gertie began a long-lasting friendship during *Some*. Gertie had a zany quality that attracted Bea, as well as a "terribly grand streak," as Bea called it. She and Noël Coward forever teased her about this and would not let her get away with it around them.

Anton (Pat) Dolin remembered, "I was at the Vaudeville Theatre and Bea was at the Prince of Wales Theatre and I went 'round to pick her up to take her to the Kit-Kat Club to see Sophie Tucker. Bea was taking off one face, as she would say, and putting on another. Gertie Lawrence came into the dressing room and said, 'You know what I've done? I've just taken a house in Berkley Square!' Bea kept doing her eyes in the mirror as she said, 'Aha, then you're going to have to put it right back!' "

With too much time on their hands backstage at *Some*, it was only natural that Bea and Gertie would find some sort of mischief in which to indulge. Unfortunately, Lee White had to bear the brunt of it. White had a number called "Have You Seen the Ducks Go By?" As she sang, the chorus girls, along with Gertie Lawrence, passed in procession behind an upstage wall revealing only their hats, which were fashioned to resemble ducks in a shooting gallery. It was not long before Gertie began popping her head up from behind the wall and winking at the audience. Bea felt compelled to participate in the fun and joined the line from time to time decked out in a man's hat and phony moustache. The number was ruined for Lee White, of course, and it came as no surprise to anyone that White ceased speaking to them both.

John Lillie arrived from Canada and joined Bea and Lucie in the house Bea had rented in St. John's Wood. Muriel and Arthur were living together by then. Lillie admired Arthur Weigall a great deal but was unhappy that he and Muriel were sharing a home since they were both still married.

"You cannot keep a flat in Haymarket and continue this way when you are not married," cried John. "You've got to get divorced and get married!" However, John spent most of his time with Arthur and

Muriel. Muriel granted him the respect and affection he never received from Lucie.

Suddenly America was in the war on April 2, 1917, and Clay Smith quickly composed a rouser called "America Answers the Call." It was interpolated into the show in place of one of Bea's numbers. Smith belted out the news in front of the curtain with great gusto and a good deal of marching to and fro to the banging of drums from the orchestra pit. It was a definite foot stomper, so much so that one night Bea, caught up in a surge of patriotism and just a smattering of pique, began parading back and forth behind the curtain swinging her arms and gesturing wildly. Gertie, unable to resist, joined in. As a result, the two ladies whipped up a wind which rippled the curtain badly in back of Smith and caused a thumping sound as their arms whacked the material. Smith dashed off the stage, cornered Bea and angrily hissed at her, "Where do you think you are?" "The Ritz," Bea is supposed to have answered gaily. The upshot of the prank was that both women were fired by Mr. Charlot. When everyone cooled off, Bea returned immediately to work because Charlot needed her for the new show she was already rehearsing and Lee White intervened in behalf of Gertie.

Show business stories, through the years, are handed down like folk tales and who did what to whom tends to become blurred. Considering their close friendship and working relationship, is it any wonder that an identical anecdote concerning Bea and Gertie appears, told by the ladies themselves? Bea claims that during *Some* she deliberately called in sick in order to enable Gertie to go on for her. Instead of languishing in her bed, she went to see another show and, as the lights were going down, the empty seat next to her was suddenly filled with André Charlot. Gertie, during the run of her show *Buzz-Buzz* later on, was actually ill but was coaxed into popping out of bed to attend the theatre, where more or less the same situation took place. In her case the results were more dire. Charlot, finally fed up with Lawrence's escapades, fired her, this time permanently.

Now that the war had become a world conflict, Bea and other London performers sang for the servicemen at camps and on ships. Bea did songs by Irving Berlin such as "Michigan," and, like Elsie

Janis, the American "Sweetheart of the Armed Forces," she found a new following in the American servicemen who flocked to the theatre in London.

The production which saved Bea from being fired was called *Cheep* and opened in April of 1917, soon after the American forces began pouring into England. Gertie again understudied Bea. Lee White and Clay Smith joined them in this one also. Charlot, a master showman, kept his name before the public with barely a breather between shows and his stars' popularity was given little chance to wane. *Cheep* received excellent notices and ran long enough for Gertie Lawrence to leave and take *Some* on the road, where she now had herself listed in the program as Gertrude Lawrence, and return later as Bea's replacement in *Cheep*.

Ivor Novello was a young Welshman a year older than Bea. Novello, a composer, wrote a war song called "Keep the Home Fires Burning" which was sung throughout the world during World War I. Producers around London knew him as an eager young man anxious to write for the theatre and few were surprised when later he became one of England's foremost operetta composers. Charlot accepted some of Ivor's material for Bea's new revue entitled *Tabs* in 1918 at the Vaudeville. Bea enjoyed top billing and cavorted with Walter Williams, Ethel Baird, and Odette Myrtil. Arthur Weigall designed the costumes. Muriel Lillie supplied the lyrics for "Sammy," one of Bea's songs.

Odette Myrtil had married Bob Adams, one half of a team called The Two Bobs, performers and songwriters. She was now the mother of a year-old son, Roger. Bea had a number called "When I Said Goodbye to You" which she sang dressed, once again, as a soldier. "Miss Lillie renders the song in a simple, straightforward style without any trimmings, just as if its message were a self-evident truth; and it goes, as it deserves, to loud and prolonged applause" said *The Bystander*. (Later, in 1932, Gertrude Lawrence recorded the song.) Gertie once more was employed as Bea's understudy, but not long after *Tabs* opened, Gertie discovered she was pregnant.

Bea and Odette dressed near each other in the theatre. Doors were left open so that they could gossip and hear what was going on around them while making up. They also picked up where Bea and Gertie left off when Gertie, angering Charlot once more, was replaced by Jessie Matthews. Guy LeFevre, a Canadian-born actor, singer, and composer featured in the show was being kept by an older woman who was very wealthy and harbored a haughty and decidedly jaundiced view of actors. One day the lady arrived backstage after a performance to pick up her beloved and was confronted by a newly hired young call boy. When the lady imperiously informed the lad that she was there for Mr. LeFevre, the eager-to-please child raced to the bottom of the stairs and shrieked, "Mr. LeFevre! Your mother's waiting for you!" Bea and Odette slammed their doors simultaneously and collapsed in tears of laughter.

"I had a song called 'Come Out, Little Boy, I'm Waiting for You,' " recalled Odette. "Once in a while, when she felt like it, Bea would cross right in front of me with one foot on the stage and one in the footlight trough and walk straight across. Mr. Charlot finally said, 'If you kids don't stop kidding, I'm going to cut the song out.' "

Bea sang a number in the show called "My River Girl." "She was on a bicycle dressed like a little Eton boy," said Odette. "She wore funny bicycle clips with her white trousers, a terribly narrow coat and a cap. She walked out in front of this backdrop, the most awful scenery you have ever seen, a great woods, half autumn and half mud! She said, 'Oh, good old Boaters' Loche.' Now, Boaters' Loche is a beautiful spot in England, outside of Maidenhead, where the boats come in and people punt. Here was Bea saying, 'Dear old Boaters' Loche, why I remember when there were crewds and crewds of people!' It was very funny." Funnier still was the program which, under the song "My River Girl," listed Bea as "He" and Alfred Austin as "She," but things straightened out in the sketch "Waiting for a Tram" when Bea found herself listed as "She" and Ralph Lynn as "He"!

During the run of *Tabs* there was a young British airman who saw the show over and over again. His name was Robinson and he had a laugh that drove everyone mad because it was loud and came at the wrong moments.

"My God, there he is again!" Bea would moan as she came off the stage. He would go backstage and say Hello to Bea, wearing his medals, and she could not be angry with him.

"Then one night," said Odette, "there was a zeppelin over London dropping bombs. I thought it was in my garden. I looked out and this goddamn zep was so beautiful with all those searchlights on it. As I looked up I suddenly saw a little light go up in the air and drop right into the middle of that cigar and it broke in half. I saw the whole thing and I thought, 'I wonder who that was.' He was in an aeroplane, his own plane, and he went up there without permission and killed himself. He went up and dove into that zeppelin! He committed suicide. That pilot was the man who made us so angry with his laughter!"

Tabs proved another landmark show for Bea in that she met and began her lifetime affection and admiration for Noël Coward. Bea arranged an audition for him with Charlot after Coward was released from the army. Charlot was not thrilled and ordered Bea never to waste his time with trivial composers who could neither sing nor play the piano very well.

"That was the only mistake Charlot ever made," declared Phyllis Monkman. C. B. Cochran, Charlot's rival, nearly repeated the mistake. He saw *The Young Idea*, one of Noël's first plays, and thought Coward had talent. He invited him to contribute dialogue for a new show he was preparing. Coward asked for permission to submit some of his music. "Don't try to do too much. Your dialogue is grand and you write excellent sketches. Stick to what you know," was Cochran's sage advice. Happily, the Master smiled sweetly and then followed his own road to eventual knighthood!

Gertrude Lawrence, having made peace with Charlot, was back with *Tabs*. Her return, mostly because of money worries, was to mark a significant change in her career. When Gertie was nearly seven months pregnant, Bea and a group of friends went horseback riding in Hyde Park, and, as luck would have it, Bea fell from her horse and suffered a concussion and wound up in the hospital. Lawrence stood in for Bea in spite of her pregnancy and received favorable reviews for her efforts.

"Gertie went on for Bea and Bea was livid because Gertie was so brilliant. She copied the intonations, the tricks; every one of the tricks she had," claimed Odette Myrtil. "It was uncanny. She sang like Lee White, whom she understudied, she danced like Phyllis

Monkman, and in the comedy she was Bea Lillie. Out of these three people she became one."

"She was an enormous success. She had more talent than anybody I had ever seen," said Monkman. "She was a brilliant artist."

Odette's theory was corroborated many years later by Douglas Fairbanks, who said that Gertie could see a Maurice Chevalier film in the afternoon and play her evening performance as Chevalier, she was that suggestible. When Bea reported that although she had no news of the horse's condition, she was ready to appear, Gertie dashed out of the theatre and barely made it to a nursing home before her daughter, Pamela, was born on May 8, 1918.

Bea was preparing a new show when the war ended in November of 1918 and the world was at peace once more. London was jammed with soldiers returning to England or embarking for the United States and Canada.

Bea opened at the Kingsway Theatre on January 27, 1919, in a musical farce called *Oh, Joy* and once again found herself in parentheses, this time: "(By courtesy of André Charlot)." The show had been produced in America in 1917 under the title *Oh, Boy* and starred Tom Powers, who was repeating the role in England. Bea nearly appeared with Noël Coward, but a casting error eliminated him from the production. Produced by George Grossmith (star of *Not Likely*, Bea's first endeavor for Charlot), the cast included Billy Leonard, Hal Gordon, Diana Durand, and Dot Temple. Bea, appearing as Jackie Sampson, a young actress, ended up in the leading man's apartment at one point in men's pajamas, which prompted one of the newspapers to say, "As most people are aware, Miss Beatrice Lillie is a past-mistress in the delicate art of appearing to advantage in male costume and although male 'nighties' sounds a little risky, it can be affirmed that Miss Lillie wears them with such grace and discretion that there is nothing outré about them, in fact, she is the very pink of piquant propriety." Lucie most certainly approved of that!

A quartet of ladies informed the audience that "Love, Honor, and Be Gay Is the Vow the Modern Wife Takes," while Bea and Billy Leonard duetted "Nesting Time." Two months later, in March, Fay Compton scored a big hit in Maugham's *Caesar's Wife* and the two friends, both with productions in the West End, were seen around town together at openings, at parties to which they had been invited, and, according to Bea, parties to which they had not been invited. Beatrice Lillie would remember 1919 as the year she met the man of her dreams.

Larry Ceballos was his name and he was dance director for Charlot's new production, *Bran Pie*, Bea's next endeavor, which opened at the Prince of Wales Theatre. Once more Bea was joined by Odette Myrtil. Odette's husband contributed some of the music, and Arthur Weigall executed scenery and a goodly number of the costumes. Ceballos, son of circus acrobats, had performed with his parents since the age of five and later began a career as dancer and choreographer. Charlot hired him after noting his work in a show called *The Girl from Cook's*.

"Larry had bowlegs like you have never known," Odette recalled, "absolutely cockeyed and unbelievably ugly." As her career gained momentum, Bea was finding it increasingly difficult to make necessary career decisions. She had never been allowed to decide anything for herself as she grew up, and now that she was on her own, more or less, she was not capable of making choices except on the stage. As a consequence, Bea commenced the practice of turning over her problems to others, especially to the men in her life.

"Bea always had to have a doormat," said Phyllis Monkman. "Someone to lean on," added Gladys Henson. Most of Bea's friends were inclined to take her affair with Larry with little concern mainly because Bea always seemed to be in love with somebody. It was not so much love as it was her need to have somebody to depend upon, to advise her. Probably Bea's greatest weakness was her inability to face the trying and often serious business of everyday living. The unpleasant and the mundane were distasteful to her and often she pretended ignorance of situations involving herself, leaving them for others to settle. Larry Ceballos, at that moment in time, fit the bill perfectly.

THREE

The post-war theatre in London was booming once again, and marquees boasted the names of Fay Compton; Alice Delysia, whom C. B. Cochran had discovered in Paris at the beginning of the war and later made the toast of London; Jack Buchanan; Maisie Gay, a rotund comic eleven years Bea's senior and one of London's reigning comediennes; Gertie Millar (later the Countess of Dudley), who had been a star since 1903 on both sides of the Atlantic and had recently scored in Cochran's *Houp-la* singing "I'm the Fool of the Family"; George Robey; Mabel Russell (coaxed out of wartime retirement by Cochran to star in *Half Past Eight* in May of 1916); Gladys Cooper; and Beatrice Lillie. Clay Smith and Lee White returned to the States after the war never to have their feathers ruffled by Bea or Gertie again. After Smith's death, Lee White attempted a comeback in the twenties but the show was bad and by then London had forgotten them. The year 1919 was also the year in which Noël Coward would see his first play produced.

Charlot and other of Bea's contemporaries such as Fay Compton and Odette Myrtil saw to it that she was seen around town in the right places such as the Ivy, which was second home to most of the performing artists in London. In 1916 C. B. Cochran had taken over the St. Martin's Theatre. Across the street was a scenery shop which he sold and which the new owners converted into a restaurant called the Ivy. A few brave souls from the theatre dined there, were happily surprised, and in no time it was *the* place in London's theatrical community and remained so for countless years. The Savoy, Ciro's, and Claridge's, places she could not afford on her own, became her haunts. Simpson's on Strand and Rule's were popular with the theatre crowd, the rich, and with royalty, Rule's in particular reveling in its reputation as the trysting place of Edward VII and Lillie Langtry. Bea was one of the first at Murray's when Gertrude Lawrence appeared in cabaret early on.

Phyllis Monkman, then appearing with Jack Buchanan in *Tails Up* at the Comedy, had been seen around town a great deal with young Robert Peel.

The first Robert Peel was an industrialist who made a considerable fortune in cotton. Born in 1750, he constructed a cotton factory in Tamworth, Staffordshire. In 1790 he purchased half of Tamworth from the Marquis Carteret, who then expired in 1796 leaving behind three sons, ten daughters and, one would imagine, an exhausted widow. Peel eventually sold one half of the property to a family named Wilkes. On his portion he built a spectacular manor house boasting one hundred and twenty rooms. After devoting some years to politics, in the year 1800 Robert Peel was created a Baronet.

His son, Robert (all succeeding sons were named Robert), inherited the title and the estate. Robert Peel, second Baronet, is remembered as the most famous and productive of all. He became renowned as Prime Minister of England during Queen Victoria's reign. Sir Robert founded the Conservative Party, repealed the Irish Corn Laws, and abolished debtors' prison. He is better remembered today for establishing the Metropolitan Police Force, the members of which are, to this day, referred to as Bobbies or Peelers, and for instituting the personal income tax. In honor of his accomplishments a bust of Sir Robert is on view at Westminster Abbey.

During his tenure at Drayton Manor, Sir Robert managed to create a showplace with lakes, gardens, and forests surrounding the Great House. The Prime Minister entertained at one time or another Adelaide, Queen Dowager of George IV, Queen Victoria, who visited in November of 1843 with the Prince Consort and the Duke of Wellington, King Louis Philippe, Alexander, Emperor of Russia, and Grand Duke Constantine, the Duke of Cambridge, and Mr. W. E. Gladstone. Unfortunately, Sir Robert came to an untimely death when he was thrown from a horse in 1850.

The following Sir Robert did little to distinguish himself. He was briefly a member of Parliament but chose to devote himself to gambling and disposing of the family funds as well as a few of the more valuable family paintings. Since the first Baronet had had the wisdom to foresee such an event, he saw to it that a private law was passed whereby a certain amount went to the heir of his choice and whatever was left remained in the Peel treasury for the next heir and so on down the line. When Baronet number four came along, he received his share from the estate and the rest went under the control of the government as a trust.

Although Sir Robert and Lady Emily outwardly lived as to the manner born, six months after their son Robert was born on April 7, 1899, all of the Peel china plate was sold for the benefit of Lady Peel and the infant. Some time later the Earl and Countess of Wilton arrived to reside at the manor, whether as guests or paying tenants is not known. Through it all, the Peels kept up appearances by sponsoring concerts, one in 1906 at the manor in aid of the St. Peter's Parish Church, which had been erected by the first Sir Robert. Then in 1907, the Peels donated a solid brass eagle lectern to St. Peter's and on Boxing Night in 1908, Sir Robert gave a party for all the school and Sunday school children, a total of eighty-nine, together with teachers and members of the church choir. As the eldest child of each family left, he or she received a pair of rabbits. But in May of 1912 the Peel trustees' church contribution of five guineas a year was withdrawn, small wonder in light of Sir Robert's sixth or seventh bankruptcy as a result of the family's penchant for spending.

In spite of their monetary vicissitudes, the senior Peels, with the aid of his share of the Peel fortunes, were able to dress and educate their son on a level with his peers. He attended only the best schools and eventually entered Harrow. The future fifth Baronet, however, was restless and found it difficult to finish anything he began. Therefore he deserted Harrow before his appointed time and joined the army at seventeen. Because of his height he soon was assigned to the Coldstream Guards. This enlistment was terminated shortly thereafter when it was feared he suffered from a slight tubercular problem.

In the meantime, Bobby Peel was discovering the London social and theatrical scenes and enjoying them immensely. At one point he gave serious thought to becoming an actor. He had grown to well over six feet tall, was extremely handsome, and was on his way to becoming a prominent young man-about-town when the elder Peels felt it wise to send him off to Australia for health reasons and to perhaps stimulate his interest in a career with some stability to it. Bobby Peel traveled to Australia but found little stability.

"I met Bobby Peel out in Australia," said Cyril Ritchard. "I was in a show called *Going Up* in Brisbane and I was playing my first juvenile lead. We were going to go to New Zealand with it and a couple of other plays. It was around Christmastime and it was very hot. My father, my brother, and I used to sleep out of doors on our mattresses because of the heat and Bobby slept next to me. He had been sent out by the family. Maude Fain was our leading lady, our star, and at the end of our three-week season I knew she was seeing a lot of Bobby because Bobby was staying at the same places we were. He was always around. When we were going to Sydney, we were steaming up the harbor and somebody came to me and said, 'Have you seen Maude Fain?' I said no. She wasn't on board. She had gone to an island to have a child with Bobby. He must have been out there sometime before this and she had met him in Sydney obviously. So she didn't come to New Zealand and she had the child and brought it to England."

Maude Fain was originally from America and had gone out to Australia where she became a well-known stage and early film actress. She was older than Bobby Peel. Fain later returned to Australia and married a serviceman. Bobby Peel then turned his attention to Phyllis Monkman.

"He was a sweet boy," said Phyllis, "and he used to come about with us. He hadn't got a penny in the world in those days. Bobby Peel was in love with me and I was never in love with Bobby Peel. He was as weak as water. Very, very good-looking. I was playing at the Comedy with Jack Buchanan and I'm going very late one night and the stage-door keeper said, 'There's Sir Robert Peel to see you.' I said, 'I can't see anybody, I'm very, very late! So I sent my dresser out and said, 'Go see what it is.' She told Sir Robert I was making up and was very, very late. And he came in, of course, with a solicitor! I'm not a fool. I said, 'How do you do, Sir Robert, and I think I know what you've come for. You think I want to marry your son. Well, I don't! I'm afraid my heart rules my head and I'm not in love with Bobby. He's a sweet boy but he's as weak as water and he's going about with the wrong people and you ought to stop him.' Then Jack Buchanan and I went over to the Casino de Paris in France."

After a performance one night, Bea joined Fay at Simpson's on Strand for supper. During the meal she was introduced to Mr. Robert Peel, whom she thanked effusively for flowers she mistakenly imagined he had sent her. Peel allowed her to pour out her gratitude and then informed her he had never sent her any flowers. Flowers or not, it was to be an eventful night for Bea. Mr. Peel began to call. Fay and most of Bea's friends were delighted, and Lucie Lillie was beside herself. What Mr. Ceballos felt is not known, and, egged on by Lucie and Fay and others, Bea began to appear about town with Robert Peel. They were an incongruous pair at best with Bea measuring in at five feet three inches and Bobby a mere six four.

Peel was living far beyond his means on an allowance from the Peel trust and was selling automobiles to supplement his income. He was extravagant, flamboyant, and heir to acres and acres of land and a well-respected title. Money or no money, Peel was welcomed everywhere and when he had extra cash in his pocket, he took Bea with him. Possibly the assurance and equanimity Bobby Peel displayed in the face of the attention shown him led Bea to perceive it as strength. She felt she had found a man she could lean upon and trust. Actually Robert Peel was in love with the theatrical scene. Phyllis provided him with the entrée but she was out of his life. Who better than Beatrice Lillie, attractive, amusing, and a vital part of the London stage? Peel had entertained thoughts of becoming an actor once and he enjoyed the easygoing life associated with the profession.

Then one day Bea wandered into Odette's dressing room, this time in a serious frame of mind. "You know, I think I should marry

Bobby Peel. He's an important man, a big name, and I should seriously do something about my life."

The engagement was announced in October and the press had a great time with "Baronet to Wed Actress" or the other way around depending upon which paper one read. Bobby Peel was mistakenly hailed as an heir to millions. There was a certain amount coming to him as eldest son thanks to the foresight of the first Sir Robert, but, unfortunately, Peel had a habit of spending it before he received it.

Phyllis Monkman arrived back from Paris in time to be invited to the engagement party at 12A Kensington Gore in a house formerly owned by the actress Gaby DesLys. Phyllis, claiming it did not matter a whit to her, attended.

"When I went to Paris, Bobby Peel was in love with me saying, 'Please marry me,' and all that nonsense. At the party Bobby said, 'I've always been in love with you, can I talk to you?' " Phyllis refused.

Things were not much better in Bea's corner where Phyllis discovered her surrounded by friends and crying her eyes out over her love for Larry Ceballos.

"Larry Ceballos was still in her life at the time," said Gladys Henson, "and at the engagement party she was crying buckets over Larry Ceballos! At her engagement party to Bobby Peel! Bea had one great fault. She could never make up her mind what she wanted to do. It was the same with getting married, whether to marry Bobby Peel or not. In the end she did because she made the appointment."

On Peace Day, 1919, there was a great victory ball held at Albert Hall. Fay Compton took a box and invited Bea, Noël Coward, Billie Carleton and her escort, and others. The party went on until the early hours with everyone imbibing heavily. The following day, Bea marched into the Savoy Hotel, approached the front desk and asked for Billie Carleton. When told that Billie Carleton was dead, Bea, still celebrating the night before, demanded to be taken to the body. She was taken to Miss Carleton's room, where she had in fact died of an overdose of cocaine.

Larry Ceballos eventually found his way to Hollywood via New York and became a very successful dance director for Warner Brothers. He lived in California until his death at the age of ninety. Bea never mentioned him again. She, on the other hand, did keep her appointment at Tamworth where she journeyed in January of 1920 with Lucie, John, and Muriel for her marriage to Robert Peel on the tenth. Elsewhere the wedding had been described as an affair of great elegance, but in actuality, it was something less than that, albeit a lot of fun.

Odette, who attended, reminisced affectionately. "It was the most ridiculous wedding that I have ever seen. There were signs on the walls outside, Lot 75, Lot 37. They had obviously been selling land at auction. We arrived on this special train, all the actors in the world, all these hams. The town had great banners, WELCOME LADY PEEL, all over town, and when we got to the house there was no place to sit down because the caterer hadn't opened the chairs, which had been rented from the local undertaker. They were leaning against the wall in the dining room. The only furniture in the house was a bed and a couple of chairs and a place for Bea to make up in this bedroom, so I, Gladys Henson, and Fay Compton were in the bedroom kidding with her. Bea was putting on her veil crooked and backwards, fooling around. We were drinking champagne already and off we went to this church, this beautiful little church, with everybody singing hymns and little choir boys in clean white surplices and suddenly to see Bea coming down the aisle, I mean like the Virgin Mary."

Fay's son Anthony was ring bearer, Muriel was a bridesmaid, and John Lillie gave his daughter away in the church of St. Paul, Drayton Bassett. Phyllis Monkman, for reasons known only to herself, did not attend and Sir Robert and Lady Peel did not put in an appearance. Perhaps Sir Robert felt another visit similar to the one he paid to Phyllis would be redundant or too late or perhaps his lawyer was out of town. In any case, Lady Peel remained where she was in Switzerland. The true reason for their absence may have lain in the fact that the elder Peels hoped for a more lucrative marriage for their only son. An up-and-coming international star did not fit the bill, but then they had no way of knowing what lay ahead for their new daughter-in-law.

Bobby's parents did, however, send along some jewelry for Bea. A rope of perfectly matched natural pearls and a diamond and emerald necklace were among the baubles. Bea scrupulously hung on to the jewels through thick and thin but the pearls did manage to disappear toward the end of her career.

Back at the manor house the celebration continued well into the night, at least until it was dark enough to set off the tons of fireworks gathered together for the occasion. Villagers, press, and friends mingled with the wedding gifts and champagne. The food was sumptuous and plentiful. Just who sprang for the feast was never made public. Perhaps Alfred Hughes, the caterer, saw a good thing and did it for the notoriety, since his company received almost as much attention in the newspapers as the happy couple did.

It was a joyful randan for everyone concerned. Finally Charlot gathered together all of his group capable of maneuvering on their own and they departed on the special train along with the press. The villagers got home as best they could. According to Odette, the younger Peels returned to London where Bea spent the night with Larry Ceballos and Bobby slept at his club. According to other sources, Bea and Bobby spent the night in the one furnished room at Drayton Manor.

There was no doubt that Bea waltzed into the Roaring Twenties on cloud eight-and-a-half! As she approached her twenty-sixth birthday, Bea had fame, a handsome stalwart husband, a title beckoning in the future, a huge estate, sans furniture—and practically no money! Obviously she was leaving it up to her spouse to correct the last two deficiencies. The press followed close upon their heels everywhere they went and the names "Mr. and Mrs. Robert Peel" appeared daily in the gossip columns and on invitations from every prominent hostess in town. Mrs. Robert Peel announced firmly to reporters that she was intent upon retiring from the stage to play the role of wife and mother. Later she denied ever saying that. There was talk of restoring Drayton Manor to its original grandeur. Skeptics paid little heed to the press releases, however, realizing that Bobby Peel did not possess the financial resources for any improvements on the Peel homestead, while Bea, with her own family to support, had never been allowed the luxury of banking her weekly salary.

The newlyweds chose Monte-Carlo for a honeymoon, an idyllic location, especially for Bobby Peel, who, Bea was to discover, was addicted to gambling. Aside from the fact she could not afford to indulge in the sport, Bea found serious betting a bore. Consequently, for a great part of their stay, Bea was left to her own resources. Fortunately there were acquaintances visiting Monaco who saw to it she was kept busy while Bobby lolled away the hours at the tables. When her husband neglected to return to their room at all one night, Bea was so incensed she left the hotel early and spent the entire day with friends. She imagined Bobby frantic with worry and crying his eyes out over her absence or perhaps begging the police to drag the Mediterranean for her body. As evening approached, however, her anger turned to pity and she returned to the hotel, her heart brimming with forgiveness. Bobby Peel was sound asleep. He did not even realize she was missing.

Bea was becoming concerned over the state of their finances when Bobby burst into the room one night shouting that he had broken the bank at Monte-Carlo. Immediately, Bea extracted his promise that they would flee the country at daybreak, cash in hand. Peel contacted the concierge and made reservations on the morning train to Paris. By an odd coincidence, which Bea always suspected was arranged by the casino, Monte-Carlo was in the middle of a railroad strike at daybreak. There was no visible means of egress from Monaco. While Bea fretted over their predicament, Bobby managed to slip once more into the casino and lost every penny they had. The happy couple borrowed cash and an automobile and returned home, in silence.

Bea learned early on that her marriage had not been created in paradise. Bobby was wont to live beyond their means and his income from the Peel trust was not adequate to support them and his extravagant habits. But just to prove to Bea he was seriously thinking of their future, they retired temporarily to Drayton Manor while Bobby occupied himself with writing a motion picture script. He had high hopes that an American film company would snatch it up. Shortly before Bea's birthday in May, he booked passage for them on the *Finland* to New York where he planned to hawk his scenario to the highest bidder. It turned out to be a gay and social crossing for the Peels, who were popular and in great demand at dinners and parties. Bea was able to put aside her money worries for a time and Bobby obliged everyone by climbing the smokestack, which prompted Bea to say to reporters who greeted them upon their arrival, "I'm glad we are in America and that there is Prohibition here!"

In New York it was Bea who attracted the interest and not Bobby's script. Representatives from Ziegfeld discussed the possibility of Bea's appearing in an edition of the *Follies*. Charles Dillingham and others expressed their interest but, as tempting as it sounded, Bea was forced to turn them all down for one terribly good reason. She was pregnant and wished to return home. With Bea on one arm and his scenario under the other, Robert Peel returned to London.

The lack of proper facilities and medical attention near Drayton Manor induced Bea to lease a house in London on Marlborough Place, not far from her parents. This added a great deal to the Peels' financial burdens especially since Bea had no income at the time. In the end, it was Ivor Novello who came to Bea's rescue and footed the bills for the birth of Robert Peel, the sixth and future Baronet, in December of 1920.

"Bea's house was across from my flat and I went over to see her," recalled Phyllis Monkman. "The thing with Bobby Peel didn't matter to me. I was the first person to hold the little boy in my arms."

Lucie was there from the start and quickly became Bobbie's unofficial nurse, guardian, and confidante for the rest of his life. Through a friend of Odette Myrtil's, Bobby secured a position as manager of the Court Theatre. There were trips to Drayton Manor with young Bobbie where they were photographed by the lake or with their dogs. Even there little Bobbie was with a nurse or Lucie most of the time.

"She didn't take care of Bobbie when he was a little kid, the mother took care of him," said Odette. "How we used to laugh at that mother who sang. That is where Bea got the idea of singing the way she did. She used to copy her mother to make us laugh. When her mother started to sing, Bea would look one way and I'd look the other and we just wouldn't dare look at each other. I could see Bea's pearls shaking from the laughter."

Bea would continue to depend upon her friends to amuse her. "You had to give of your time entirely to Bea," said Odette. "She wasn't really interested in you. She was fine when she wanted you around but she would never make an effort to ask you to be with her."

Bea did not waste time learning how to cook, or sew, or garden and had no interest in anything connected with housekeeping. But the overwhelming and constant problem in Bea's married life was money and, when theatrical offers began coming in once more, she considered them seriously. Maisie Gay was leaving *Up in Mabel's Room* and when Bea was offered the role by the producer, Sir Charles Hawtrey, she grabbed it though the show had been a failure from the start.

"I was bored by society parties and balls," she said, rather grandly, to the newspapers, "and every night at eight o'clock I became fidgety and nervous. Something important seemed to be missing from my life so I went back on the stage determined never to leave it again."

Actually, marriage and motherhood achieved, it was money and security that were important and missing from her life. Her family was still hanging over her head and there was little income for all of them. Secondly, Bea's boredom stemmed from her complete lack of interest in the world outside.

"She had no interests other than the theatre. Her work and only her work," Phyllis Monkman believed. Bea seldom read anything other than the columns in the newspapers. She hated lectures, formal dinners, and museums. Bea was entirely guileless, however, and possessed an almost innocent outlook toward the world which many interpreted as selfishness or lack of interest. This trait enabled her to turn her problems over to others and to concentrate on that which made her happy. John Gielgud felt that Bea's childlike view of the world contributed to her genius. She also found it difficult to relate to strangers or those outside the perimeter of the theatre, although, because of her upbringing, she was gracious and well mannered with nearly everyone who approached her. She usually ended these encounters with a Lillie bon mot and left her admirer laughing. At the height of Bea's fame, a salesgirl in Bloomingdale's basement shrieked, "Miss Lillie, everyone in the store knows you're in the basement!" "Good," remarked Bea. "Maybe I'll do my next show down here!" When Bea attended a gathering at the English

Speaking Union in St. Louis, a long-legged English maid galloped up to her as she entered and eagerly offered to take her mink coat. "Certainly not," gasped Her Ladyship, gathering the wrap around her, "nobody's seen it yet!"

As *Up in Mabel's Room* was grinding to a halt, André Charlot was putting together a revue to be called *A to Z* which would star Bea, Jack Buchanan, and the Trix Sisters, Americans who sang close harmony at the piano and were extremely popular in England at the time. In addition to their vocal histrionics, the ladies were known in the trade for their frequent tempestuous battles, but their combined talents bound them together in spite of the tiffs.

A to Z opened on October 11, 1921, to great reviews but without Bea. Unfortunately, at the last minute Bea had become ill and was hospitalized. Charlot, despite his vow never to employ Gertrude Lawrence again, relented when he recalled her success the first time she substituted for Bea and he called her in.

"Charlot proves that he knows the revue business from A to Z," echoed the press the following day.

A to Z hopped through the alphabet in twenty-six scenes. Jack Buchanan was responsible for staging the musical numbers as well as appearing with Gertie in songs and sketches, including one called "Limehouse Night" by Thomas Burke, a sort of Chinese "Slaughter on Tenth Avenue" which Lawrence and Buchanan dramatized in verse and movement. Ivor Novello composed much of the music including "And Her Mother Came Too," which became a standard of Buchanan's. *A to Z* was such a resounding hit that as featured performers left the show and were replaced by others, new material was added and the show became *The New Edition of A to Z*. Thus, Teddie Gerard, back from her New York successes, went into a new edition on January 23, 1922, and Maisie Gay joined the show when the Trix Sisters left the following May.

Bea, meanwhile, was back in circulation once more, attending the theatre and various parties around town with and without Bobby and often with Fay Compton or Gladys Henson. Charlot, Coward, and Ivor Novello supplied Bea with the social life she enjoyed most, the theatre with all its make-believe and excitement, a place where she felt at home and in control. Novello had a flat atop the Strand

Theatre and his late-night soirees became de rigueur for anybody who was anybody in theatre or society. They were a name-dropper's paradise. Actually, Ivor was not particularly interested in party giving, the parties just seemed to find him.

In order to reach these jamborees, guests were forced to take their lives in their hands by ascending slowly in a dilapidated elevator that invariably scared hell out of newcomers. Many of the more hardy never surmounted their terror. Three or four guests at most squeezed into the upright coffinlike box, one of them pulled a rope, and with an ear-splitting screech off it went. The visitors would huddle together in horror as the elevator swayed and bumped its way to the top where it usually hit the roof with a bang and then sank slowly back down to the ground floor. Then the process would begin once more.

In spite of this obstacle course, company flocked to Ivor's and risked their lives in the lift to reach his apartment at 11 Aldwych. Across one end of a long living room was a raised platform with two pianos, usually with someone or perhaps some two playing. Musicians played, singers sang, and actors acted at the drop of a hat. Nobody got away without contributing something. The standard price of admission to any of the gatherings was a new joke or a heretofore unknown bit of gossip.

Frequent visitors to the rooftop galas were Their Highnesses the Prince of Wales, later Edward VIII, and his brothers, the Duke of Kent and Prince Albert, the future George VI. Bea broke up the proceedings when all three arrived together one night by inquiring if it would not be more prudent if they traveled separately in that deathtrap of an elevator. The Prince of Wales was smitten with Gertrude Lawrence, and Prince Albert had his eye on Phyllis Monkman. Perhaps Ivor's attracted them when, it was reported, Queen Mary complained about the late-night merrymaking in the Prince of Wales' quarters at Buckingham Palace.

One day, Michael Anthony, a handsome young actor, escorted Bea and Gladys Henson to a reception for the Prince of Wales. When they arrived, Bea excused herself and ducked into the ladies' room to freshen up. When she returned, her friends were nowhere to be seen. She searched the room for Gladys and finally thought she spotted Anthony with his back to her talking to a group of friends. Bea quickly walked up behind him and whacked him on the back demanding, "Where's Gladys?"

"Gladys who?" asked a surprised Prince of Wales as he spun around.

"Gladys . . . you know Glad . . . Oh, Christ!" groaned Bea as she sank into a curtsy.

When Gertrude Lawrence left *A to Z,* Bea finally joined the cast. At one point a critic who re-reviewed the show stated, "There are other fresh features, including a Limehouse scene in which, at the end of the dance, Miss Teddie Gerard, looking properly scared, stabs a pursuing Chink [sic]." The "Limehouse scene" he referred to was "Limehouse Blues," which Gerard introduced. Continuing his "musical chairs" policy, when Maisie Gay departed, Sophie Tucker, who was starring in cabaret in London, went into the show.

"For a minute," according to Bea.

Dorothy Dickson, the American actress, arrived in London in 1920 to appear in *London, Paris, and New York.* She was such a hit that she stayed on to appear in *Sally* and *Sunny* and became the Marilyn Miller of London. Dickson remained in England for the rest of her life. Dorothy and Bea eventually became very close friends.

"I first saw Bea in *A to Z.* Gertie Lawrence was still romping about the stage a lot. She did broad and slapstick comedy. She hadn't yet become that chic person she did marvelously later on. She was kind of rough and tumble—knockabout. Bea was this absolutely still person, and getting laughs. I'd think, 'What is she doing to get these laughs?' She'd raise her eyebrows and there'd be a big laugh. I'd never seen anybody who could get those things so easily. She had an overwhelming presence."

Bea's situation financially was not much better even though she had returned to work. Bobby Peel, unfortunately, while Harrow educated, had not been prepared to be anything more than a country gentleman.

"She lived in St. John's Wood and we lived in Maida Vale," said Odette Myrtil. "Roger [her son] was a little bit older than Bobbie and I used to give her all his clothes. They didn't have any money. André Charlot paid low salaries. I had a husband who was earning a living and we were well off. Bea was taking care of her mother, Muriel, and all that gang. Bobby was making his salary as a manager but they were very poor. We used to have parties. Gertie Lawrence had Pamela, we had Roger, and Bea had Bobbie. We were always together. He came to our house so I sent Roger over to his house."

Gertrude Lawrence's daughter Pamela remembers Bobbie Peel as a very shy boy at the parties. "Bobbie Peel I remember only from a rather horrid occasion when my mother gave a huge fancy dress birthday party at the then highly fashionable Kit Kat Club in London. Bobbie was a guest and I was sent back home for teasing him very loudly in front of all the other children for being shy. In those days he lived with his grandmother."

Bobby's spending and the burden of Bea's family put a strain on the marriage in spite of Bea's penchant for ignoring the more unpleasant things in life.

Odette recalled, "One time there was a terrible argument in the dressing room and when Bea got home, she threw all of her jewelry in the garbage can outside of the house. The next morning, of course, having awakened and sobered up, they ran like hell and got it all out." The fact that she would repeat the story to Odette is an indication of Bea's ability to laugh at herself and ridiculous situations.

"She would do the silliest things. We were in a cab with Bobby. She, next to Bobby, started a row. As we got to my house, she was coming in, she wanted to pay the taxi but he put an awful lot of money on her lap that he wanted her to pay the cab with. She got up and left and all this money was floating about the cab. I didn't pick it up, it wasn't my money!"

The Prince of Wales came to see Bea perform in one of the theatres Bobby was managing. He asked to be taken to Bea's dressing room afterwards. The Prince had no idea at the time who Bobby was as Peel led him backstage. On the way, it was necessary to pass through a very low fire door. The Prince and Bobby ducked their heads as they went through. The Prince was telling Peel how wonderful Beatrice Lillie was on stage and when Bobby announced that he was her husband, the Prince stopped so suddenly that Bobby straightened up and nearly knocked himself out against the cement door frame.

The Nine O'Clock Revue in 1922, with material written by Muriel Lillie and Arthur Weigall, was Bea's next show and proved to be a hit. The show ran for nearly a year, with Bea appearing in one number looking for all the world like an angry suffragette as she sang "The Girls of the Old Brigade" and a number called "Susannah's Squeaking Shoes," written by Muriel and Arthur. Muriel protested when Bea spoke the words instead of singing them. But Bea did not listen because America was beckoning.

FOUR

In 1923 Arch Selwyn, half of the Selwyn Brothers team of American producers and theatre owners, contacted André Charlot regarding the possibility of presenting a Charlot Revue in New York. Charlot decided it was time to take the plunge and, contracting his three biggest stars, Bea, Gertrude Lawrence, and Jack Buchanan, he agreed to present *André Charlot's London Revue of 1924* in New York on or about the following New Year's Eve. The news media on both sides of the Atlantic picked up the story and the tidings caused a stir in theatrical circles. In New York Ziegfeld's *Follies*, Carroll's *Vanities*, and White's *Scandals* were the Broadway fare theatregoers were flocking to see. Charlot made a special voyage to New York to discuss the production with the producers and the press.

One London paper wished Charlot luck, stating that, "In this exchange of shows between New York and London, America seems to win." Then in May *The Daily Graphic* called upon Charlot's stars to "form themselves into a championship team to show established revues in New York that the English have revue abilities of their own!"

Selwyn ruffled Mr. Charlot's self-confidence slightly but only momentarily by suggesting that he Americanize some of the offering, a battle that Charlot fought to the death, to his credit, on the boat over, through the Atlantic City tryout, and into New York. Instead, Charlot began picking and choosing material from *A to Z* and past productions for the 1924 New York edition.

Julia Chandler, the Selwyns' publicity agent, arrived in England in July in order to meet and then acquaint American audiences with the English performers. After seeing Bea in *The Nine O'Clock Revue*, she referred to Bea as "the Charlie Chaplin of London" and, in a release which was printed in *The New York World* the following September, she wrote, "Under the strata of her cockney comics one senses that same dramatic instinct of which Chaplin makes one feel so singularly conscious even in his most grotesque moments. Threading my sense of amusement was always the consciousness that she could turn my laughter into tears with just the twist of an intonation. And that is her charm."

On August 12, André and Mrs. Charlot arranged a party for Miss Chandler to which they invited Bea, Gertrude Lawrence, and Gertie's friend, Philip Astley. They took their guests boating on the Thames, had tea in Maidenhead, and a sit-down dinner at the Charlot home in St. John's Wood. Miss Chandler complained that offstage Bea's reserve was impossible to penetrate. She asked Charlot if Bea was always so inarticulate. He replied, "Away from the theatre only. I have seen her entertain the elite of London in her dressing room without a shadow of shyness, but out of her professional atmosphere, she is invariably reticent."

Bea was hardly restrained when Hannan Swaffer, a particularly irascible critic of the time and one of Noël Coward's pet hates, suggested that American audiences would probably not understand or appreciate Bea's humor. She was threatening not to go to New York because of Swaffer's remarks and it was only because of her faith in Charlot's talent and intelligence that she finally agreed to stand by her initial decision to appear in the States.

Selwyn dispatched another of his publicity men to London to stir up some additional newsworthy gimmicks to stimulate interest in the forthcoming *Charlot's Revue*. The gentleman came up with a "Most Beautiful Blonde Barmaid in Britain" contest in which the winner would travel to America with the show as a chorus girl. He rigged the contest by choosing a young lady whom he found appealing, a bar mistress at Rule's restaurant named Bobbie Storey. The winner's name was cabled to the press in America and Storey was hired.

While *André Charlot's Revue of 1924* was still in rehearsal, *The Nine O'Clock Revue* opened in New York and was not a hit, again fortifying the popular verdict that America had the edge on revue theatre. One paper did suggest that perhaps if the show had presented bigger stars it might have lasted.

When the show was finally rehearsed and ready for New York, Charlot booked it into the Hippodrome in Golders' Green (a suburb of the city which a New York paper referred to as the Yonkers of London) for a week. A local reporter wrote that the Prince of Wales laughed as heartily as anyone else at Gertrude Lawrence's comedy. With the Prince's laughter ringing in their ears, Bea and the entire company of *André Charlot's Revue of 1924* set sail just before Christmas of 1923 on the *Aquitania* bound for New York. Bea left her son in the company of her mother and her husband to his own devices.

According to Bea, the trip over was a round of holiday dinners and parties. Many of the passengers had seen Charlot's revues in London and Bea and Gertie were well known to a host of travelers and therefore in great demand. Lawrence discovered her audience among the more social element aboard, Max Aitken, later Lord Beaverbrook, the newspaper tycoon for one. Max Aitken led the festivities for most of the voyage and is generally credited with naming Lillie, Lawrence, and Buchanan "The Big Three," a nickname which remained with them for the run in New York. Bea also met for the first time Alastair (Allie) McIntosh, prominent man-about-town and former army captain. McIntosh had served in France during the war and one night, on a bender with the boys, he and his companions became rip-roaring drunk and staggered blissfully to their respective tents and passed out. Unfortunately, a soldier in their battalion had just died and was scheduled to be buried with full honors the following morning. Since the top brass were out on a reconnaissance mission, the job of officiating fell to a badly hung over McIntosh. Weaving precariously, he managed to dash cold water on his face and muster up what passed for military deportment. He remained valiantly on his feet next to the grave during the ceremony and nearly sobbed with relief while taps sounded, ending his ordeal. When the gun salute exploded a few feet behind him, Allie, who had completely forgotten that part of the ceremony, was not prepared and leapt screaming into the grave face-down on the coffin. Two enlisted men came to his rescue and dragged him out, whereupon he managed a feeble salute and stumbled back to his cot and collapsed.

"He married Constance Talmadge, you know," said Bea, "and he loathed Hollywood. There was one famous agent he absolutely hated. Somehow he got hold of that photograph from the Smithsonian of the man with the elephantiasis of the testicles, the man who had to carry them in a wheelbarrow! And he had that agent's face superimposed on the poor man's picture. Then he rented a plane and threw hundreds of those photos down on top of Beverly Hills. He was very naughty. When he finally left, he rented another plane and stood in the open doorway and peed down on everybody." Her admiration for McIntosh was boundless.

As Christmas Eve approached spirits were high and the excitement of the holidays pervaded the entire ship. Then the New York skyline came into view and Bea felt her first twinge of stage fright and loneliness. For the first time she realized she was on her own with no husband to watch over her. Reporters came aboard immediately and dashed past everybody to photograph and interview Bobbie Storey. As they waded through customs a reporter did ask Bea what she felt landing in America. Bea managed to mumble "homesick" and let it go at that. In a subsequent interview she did admit that on her arrival she felt as if she had been shot through the middle.

Mingling with high society as they were, the subject of the correct place to stay in New York arose. McIntosh suggested any number of the better hotels but felt the Ambassador was the only place for stars of their magnitude. He arranged for the ladies to bunk at the home of socialite Schuyler Parsons the night of their arrival and promised to contact the hotel which was owned by his friend William Rhinelander Stewart.

As lovely and elegant as it was, the Ambassador Hotel was way above their means and Bea, Lawrence, and Buchanan, pooling their money for a taxi, quickly checked out and moved to the Algonquin.

Even though the rooms were tiny, they felt more at ease in the smaller hotel and they soon became friends with the famous Round Table group, the writers, critics, and wits of the day such as Robert Benchley, Heywood Broun, Marc Connelly, and a brash young newspaper man from Chicago, Charles MacArthur, who would play a large part in Bea's life in spite of the rumor that Dorothy Parker was mad for him.

André Charlot's Revue of 1924 with Beatrice Lillie, Gertrude Lawrence, and Jack Buchanan had its initial performance January 2, 1924, in Atlantic City where it played for a week. Selwyn continued to complain that it was too English and not very good. He felt Bea was not giving her all at rehearsals and was worried about "March with Me," which he wanted to remove from the show. Seeing the revue in an American setting, Selwyn was not so sure he had made the right choice. Charlot, ruled by his instincts, ignored Selwyn and the production moved into the Times Square Theatre exactly the way Mr. Charlot wished, although an odd footnote in the program made note of the fact that a sketch called "Incredible Happenings" had been produced by Charlot in London. "Since then it has been staged by the American producers without the permission of Mr. Charlot," the New York audiences were informed. Mr. Selwyn's appraisal of the show combined with Hannan Swaffer's earlier comments did little to raise Bea's spirits, especially after another know-it-all commented that even though Atlantic City had accepted them, she was not to take it to heart since they were an easier audience than New York.

Opening night of *Charlot's Revue*, January 9, 1924, is now legend. Bea appeared in ten scenes, beginning with "How D'you Do?" sung by the entire cast followed by songs such as Novello's "There Are Times," Coward's "There's Life in the Old Girl Yet," "The Bolshies Quartette," and others, until the finale and the song "Night May Have Its Sadness." Mr. Selwyn knew nothing of Bea's inability to rehearse anything full-out so obviously could not have been prepared for what occurred during the opening night performance of "March with Me" with Bea, dressed as Britannia and leading a battalion of similarly garbed Girl Scouts, crashing into her followers while attempting to retain her dignity and her helmet, shield, and spear. How could he have anticipated a hysterical audience on its feet applauding and screaming for more of the number he insisted be cut from the production?

American audiences, used to feathers and sequins and long-stemmed show girls, were seeing artistes who doubled, tripled, and quadrupled in sketches, songs, and dance. Gertrude Lawrence, Robert Hobbs, and Fred Leslie in "Limehouse Blues" brought down the house and Jack Buchanan found himself a new matinee idol. Herbert Mundin was suddenly a star and Constance Carpenter and Jessie Matthews, while performing in the chorus, later went on to better things. Dorothy Blanchard did not do too badly either. She became Mrs. Oscar Hammerstein II.

The crowds backstage and outside on the street left no doubt in Bea's mind as to the success of the evening. Hundreds of people gathered in front of the theatre, nearly bringing traffic to a halt on Forty-second Street.

The New York Tribune declared, "At the finish they had reason to be the happiest band of visiting Britishers since Bunker Hill."

"Miss Lillie is probably the most winsome comedienne who has come to us from across the waters in a long time," cried someone else.

Another writer compared American and English revue stars by stating, "in *Charlot's Revue* the stars do a great deal more and appear so often you feel that you know them very well at the end of the performance."

Variety headlined its review "André Charlot's Revue Clicks."

And in Bea's behalf were such statements as "Beatrice Lillie, really very young and pretty, sacrifices her looks to burlesque several numbers and she is the hit of the show." "She is a dream of an artist," applauded one daily paper. *The New York Times* raved, "No amount of advance description can take the edge off the enjoyment that is to be had from seeing and hearing Miss Lillie sing 'March with Me.' There is no one in New York comparable to Beatrice Lillie."

Overnight, the Big Three were Broadway stars and it wasn't long before Bea was being imitated by cabaret performers in London and New York. In *The Grand Street Follies* a comic was impersonating Bea on stage shortly after *Charlot's Revue* opened. Also in *The Grand Street Follies* was Paula Treuman, who later understudied Bea in *The Show Is On*. The Round Table crowd introduced them around town but Bea had eyes for no one but MacArthur. Charles MacArthur had been having an off-and-on affair with Dorothy Parker. He was married but separated from his wife, who remained in Illinois when he made the move to New York. MacArthur was a former Windy City newspaper reporter, devilishly handsome with curly hair, greenish eyes, and a wicked sense of humor which attracted Bea immediately. She and Charlie began spending a great deal of time together.

Gertrude Lawrence felt the hotel was cramping their style and she persuaded Bea to share an apartment with her.

"We got them that house up on Fifty-fourth Street," recalled Marc Connelly. "We used it as a headquarters more or less. At night Bea would be surrounded by all her friends from the theatre and Gertie would have bank vice presidents all around her. Every now and then the girls would have a big sale. They would sell dresses they were finished with to the kids in the chorus."

The house on Fifty-fourth Street was actually a duplex apartment in a small building near Sixth Avenue. It was only a matter of time before, like Ivor Novello's in London, it became *the* place to be invited. Every important name on Broadway showed up at one time or another. George Gershwin, Oscar Hammerstein, Schwartz and Dietz, producers, actors, and directors rubbed elbows with Park Avenue, Palm Beach, and Southampton, and, upon one occasion at least, with the Prince of Wales.

"They gave these enormous parties every night," said Odette Myrtil, "and Bea would be sitting in the corner getting blind and Gertie would be like Lady Astor greeting all the people, 'Do come in!' and being so charming. Bea would be kidding around and paying no attention except finally one day she said, 'You know, I think I'm a little upset about the whole thing because I'm paying half of this and I'm getting absolutely no glamour whatsoever.'"

Bea's concern about expenses is to be understood. The move to Fifty-fourth Street was intended to cut down on their overhead and Charlot's salaries were not exactly on a par with Ziegfeld's. In April the company participated in Equity's annual show and Bea sang "March with Me" and from then on it was a round of benefit appearances as far away as the Hamptons. In May, Lady Emily Peel, Bea's mother-in-law, died in Florence but it was hardly a blow to Bea, who had never met her. During the summer, Bea and Gertie were invited to Southampton on weekends for swimming and parties.

At one point Lucie arrived with Bea's son. Whenever he was taken to see the show, Bobbie would lie down on the floor of the box each time the audience laughed at his mother. His being there made Bea very nervous. During rehearsals he enjoyed exploring the theatre.

"He was a darling little boy," remembered Marc Connelly. "I had a house for the summer at Sand's Point and Howard Dietz and Bobbie Peel were playing with a boomerang or something when Bobbie came in and said, 'I'm terribly sorry, we have broken a window,' and Howard Dietz said, '*We* did? I did!' Bobbie was sharing the blame."

Not long after the show opened Cyril Ritchard arrived in New York and almost immediately went to see *Charlot's Revue* with an eye toward replacing Jack Buchanan. Buchanan had notified the management that he had previous engagements in London and would not continue with the show after the first three months. It was Bea's first introduction to Ritchard.

"Bea was the answer to everything I dreamt about comedy when I first came to America," Ritchard said. "It was the understatement. She treated 'March with Me' as if it were a ballad."

When Gertie was introduced, she studied Ritchard for a moment and then turned to Bea.

"Don't you think he looks like Bobby?" she gushed.

"No," snapped Bea and ended the discussion.

Buchanan left and was replaced by Nelson Keys, not Ritchard. Bobby, meanwhile, decided to try his luck once more down under, this time at sheep herding, and was making plans to return to Australia.

The Selwyns decided to extend the run of the show and moved *Charlot's Revue* to the Selwyn next door. In August the entire company journeyed to Southampton and performed a benefit for the Southampton Hospital as a way of saying good-bye. On closing night of *Charlot's Revue of 1924* the audience proved as jubilant as the opening crowd, which is not surprising since most of them had been there on January 9. There was cheering at the end of the show and tears when performers and audience joined hands for "Auld Lang Syne." Flowers were everywhere and most of the audience waited in the streets to wish them all farewell. It had been a glorious nine months for the company. Bobbie Storey, the Most Beautiful Blonde Barmaid in England, unable to cope with the notoriety and excitement, later did herself in by turning on the gas jets in her hotel room.

Bea and Gertie packed their belongings and set forth on tour. In Boston, Gertie became ill and was diagnosed as having pleurisy and perhaps pneumonia. She held out until Toronto and then had to leave the show. Bea carried on, the only one of the original Big Three. She toured through the holidays and early in 1925 arrived in Chicago where she found Charlie MacArthur under her bed one night. How he finagled a key from the desk Bea never knew but she came home one evening, bathed, and prepared for sleep with Charlie hidden under the bed the whole time. She was more amazed at his patience than angry with his antics.

A telephone call on February 13, 1925, changed Bea's life once again. Sir Robert Peel, her father-in-law, was dead and she was now Lady Peel. The newspapers called and when they asked her how it might influence her career she could only answer that she would probably have to work more. Bobby Peel was on a ship returning to England when he received the news. The show ran two more weeks in Chicago and plans were made to transport the company back to New York and straight to England. Bea managed a day or two in New York and received congratulations from her friends and then headed home.

There were reporters on board the ship and Bea said later, "I was playing it terribly grand, very Lady Peel all over the place, when one of the actors came up the gangplank. He was absolutely stinking. One of the reporters asked me something or other and I turned to answer him when this actor suddenly slapped me on the back and yelled, 'Hello, old cock!' and I went head over heels down some steps right in front of everyone! I was livid. He spoiled my whole act!''

Gertrude Lawrence was sufficiently recovered from her illness to join the company on the *Olympic* when it stopped at Cherbourg, and standing next to Bea, she waved madly at the crowd in Southampton who came to welcome them home. Bobby, and Lucie with little Bobbie, were waiting to take Bea to Drayton Manor to begin her life as Lady Peel.

Charlot immediately gathered the cast together and presented a special midnight matinee of *Charlot's Revue as Seen in America*. Actors from all over London rushed from their final curtains to the Prince of Wales Theatre to see the performance. Noël Coward, Tallulah Bankhead, Fay Compton, Maisie Gay, and Phyllis Monkman were among the celebrities who crowded into the theatre.

Referring to Bea and Gertie, one newspaper reported, "The welcome they received on the first night proves how popular, and deservedly popular, they are."

"In Noël Coward's 'There's Life in the Old Girl Yet,' Miss Lillie proves her unique capabilities as a fun-maker," wrote another. The performance sold out and the demand for seats was so pressing that Charlot ran it for two nights.

Work began immediately on *Charlot's Revue of 1926* and Charlot presented a new edition of *Charlot's Revue* each month from then on, adding and deleting material as he shaped a new American production. Bea appeared in the August edition and sang "Snoops the Lawyer" which became a standard of hers.

Arthur Weigall divorced his wife, and Muriel, after establishing contact with her husband in Canada, sued for divorce also. Mr. Burnett obligingly allowed Muriel to claim infidelity on his part and graciously sent her a cable listing the names of his bogus lady loves.

As Lord and Lady Peel, Bea and Bobby were again very much in the news, although Bea remained the major breadwinner. Because of her heavy rehearsal schedule, there was little opportunity for her to spend time with her son, now in his fifth year. Little Bobbie was with Lucie most of the time. Lucie brought Bobbie to a matinee one day to see his mother. He sat solemnly through the performance and in Bea's dressing room later he could only mumble sadly, "They laughed at you. You mustn't try so hard to be funny." Bea did not know whether to laugh or cry. Buchanan rejoined the company and in November *Charlot's Revue of 1926* set forth once again for America. This time Bea was accompanied by Bobby Peel. Author Michael Arlen was aboard also heading for New York where the American production of his play *The Green Hat* starring Katharine Cornell recently opened. Winter storms in the North Atlantic delayed the *Coronia*, and the Baltimore opening had to be postponed. A special train was ordered by the producers to rush the company south as soon as they disembarked. When the ship finally tied up at the pier in New York a Bagpipe Society Band appeared at the gangplank to serenade the arriving Sir Robert and Lady Peel. Unfortunately, the press agent who dreamed up the welcome mistakenly thought Bobby Peel was Scottish. Buchanan quickly informed everybody of his Highland background and the band played on without losing face.

Charlot's Revue of 1926 boasted material by Noël Coward (who had just opened in New York in his play *The Vortex* to rave reviews), Ivor Novello, Muriel Lillie, and Arthur Weigall. There were no doubts or insecurities this trip, as New York went all out to welcome Charlot's Big Three back. Percy Hammond wrote in *The Herald Tribune* on November 11, the day after the show opened, that "the sidewalk bordering the theatre was thronged with hysterical persons pleading to be let in. A velvet carpet had been put down and squads of police saw that no disorder occurred." Ticket envelopes contained directions on how to approach the theatre entrance by automobile from various directions. The curtain was advertised at 8:45 and balcony seats went for $4.00. Mr. Hammond had attended a rehearsal and upon leaving the theatre early to write his review was offered cash for the ticket stub by a bystander.

Alexander Woollcott called it a reunion not a performance. "*The Charlot Revue of 1926* began coming back to town last evening," he wrote, "and at midnight it was still on its way. All New York tried to get into the Selwyn Theatre to celebrate the return. At its first New York performance, I suspect that Mr. Ziegfeld and Mr. Berlin fairly laughed themselves into a coma at the innocence of this

London manager for thinking that any revue so airy and unpretentious would not be trampled underfoot in New York."

Bea and Gertie appeared in the sketch "Fallen Babies," an outrageous satire on Noël Coward's London success, *Fallen Angels*. Attired in baby bonnets, the two ladies sat side by side in baby carriages (from Macy's) discussing what babies were coming to as they drank from a policeman's liquor bottle left by the nurse in one of their carriages. Bea received cheers for a repeat of "March with Me" and sang "Susannah's Squeaking Shoes" by Muriel and Arthur. Ivor Novello contributed "There Are Times," a "chin up" type of song, which Bea sang and later recorded. Bea warbled a little number by Noël Coward entitled "A Little Slut of Six," and in "After Dinner Music" depicted a diva entertaining at the piano who sang only Noël Coward selections.

Audiences received their initial look at the "new" Bea Lillie in 1926. On her previous visit, she accepted an invitation to visit on a yacht in Southampton where she became friends with actress Hope Williams. Williams' cropped blond hair became a topic of conversation and the actress told Bea that she had the perfect face and head for such a cut. After some persuasion from other friends, Bea allowed Hope to cut her hair and shape it into a boyish bob. The effect was stunning but Bea was afraid of Charlot's reaction and for a time she pinned braids over her ears and appeared in public as she always had. When a friend touched one of the braids and it fell off Bea's head, she never put it back on again and her cropped head became her trademark along with her famous pillbox hats. Just before *Charlot's Revue of 1926* opened, an enterprising department store in New York announced their new Eton Crop "as worn by Miss Beatrice Lillie in *Charlot's Revue of 1926*." Bea would run a brush through her hair, tie a black ribbon around her head, affix one of her hats with combs inside to the ribbon, and in minutes she would be ready to pick up and go. Bergdorf's supplied hats for Bea over the years and though she constantly complained about the prices, she continued to order them.

People came from all over the country to see the 1926 edition but it was never the hit that the first one was. Soon after it opened in New York, Charlot booked Bea, Jack Buchanan, and Gertie Lawrence into a club to which he had lent his name called Charlot's Rendez-vous and they performed in cabaret till after New Year's to audiences made up of the bluebloods of society and theatre, from Ethel Barrymore to Harpo Marx. Bea's husband, meanwhile, had returned to England still searching for an elusive career.

FIVE

In February, the Selwyns sent the show on a tour that took the company all the way to Los Angeles. All Hollywood turned out to greet and entertain the company and Bea met Charlie Chaplin, then married to Lita Grey, Buster Keaton, John Gilbert, and Valentino among others. Though the show was a hit in Los Angeles, there was not the vast audience to draw on that New York offered. Consequently, Charlot decided to cancel a long tour of the States and instead closed the show in Hollywood. Bea was invited to San Simeon, the home of William Randolph Hearst and Marion Davies, as well as to countless parties in Los Angeles and was approached by studio officials interested in her for films. She finally did agree to make her first silent later on that year. On closing night at the El Capitan, Bea arrived on stage at one point near the end of the show and, to her horror, noticed that a great many of her friends had apparently left the theatre. Then, during the finale, she was thunderstruck to discover them all on stage with the cast. Valentino, Chaplin, Fairbanks, John Gilbert, and others joined hands with the audience and company to sing a tearful "Auld Lang Syne" as the curtain fell.

"I'd been invited out to Hollywood to do some work and said I'd do a picture for Bea. We went out and got a house," recalled Marc

Connelly. Once again Lucie brought Bobbie over to visit and they joined Bea in Hollywood. "He'd go around saying, 'Yes, Milady,' 'No, Milady,' imitating everyone. The only time I ever remember Bea being serious was coming downstairs one night after we put Bobbie to bed and she said, 'Thank God he won't have to go through any war.' Once when Bea reproved him with, 'That's not funny!' he began saying, 'Well, is *that* funny?' when he did do something."

The name of the film was *Exit Smiling.* Jack Pickford, brother of Mary, played opposite Bea in a tale about a troupe of traveling players and a girl who falls for the juvenile. She saves him from problems when he plays his hometown. In the end he deserts Bea for the girl who lives down the street. The picture began shooting in August of 1926. Director Sam Taylor bragged that his sets were the smallest picture sets ever built. The whole set was only a few feet square. Bea did not enjoy performing for a camera. She missed the audience reaction she was used to and had no way of knowing if what she was doing was funny. The technicians were too busy with their own work to pay attention to what was happening in front of the camera.

"There was a funny line in it written by a man named Whalen, the title writer," said Connelly. "There was an actress who he said had 'created the role of Nothing in *Much Ado About Nothing.* It was credited to me unjustly.' Tim Whalen was his name."

Bea had reason to know that name. His wife sued Bea for alienation of affections and asked for $100,000. The suit was later dropped and never mentioned again. In the meantime Bea enjoyed her stay in Hollywood. She alleged she had an affair with screen idol John Gilbert, all the while imagining she was in competition with Greta Garbo. Then she gave a party and invited Rudolph Valentino. Mr. Valentino eventually departed only to return later claiming he had left his watch there by mistake. Bea topped the Gilbert story by insisting she and Mr. Valentino made love in a porch swing.

By the time Bea finished the film she was committed to a show originally called *Lucky* but later was changed to *Oh, Please!* Produced by Charles Dillingham, the story concerned a man and wife whose passion was purity. It was nearly a bedroom farce but missed on every score according to most of the critics. *Oh, Please!* opened at the Fulton

Theatre in December of 1926. It boasted a libretto by Anne Caldwell and Otto Harbach with music supplied by Vincent Youmens. Bea, Charles Winninger, Helen Broderick, Nick Long, Jr., and Charles Purcell did their best against uneven odds.

"If we never had Beatrice Lillie we might better never have been born," cried Robert Benchley. "If for no other reason Miss Lillie should go down in history as the only human being who ever made an Anne Caldwell book funny." Although *The New Republic* felt Bea was better suited to a revue it added, "In *Oh, Please!* Miss Lillie is as astonishing as ever. Her comic gift is one of the best in the world. Our delight in her is endless."

Alexander Woollcott felt compelled to say, "The evening is Miss Lillie's though I could not blame her if she did not particularly want it." "She proves herself a whole show needing only a stage and her eyebrows to make *Oh, Please!* hide behind its scenery," and "The clowningest lady clown in captivity," rounded out the compliments.

Financier Otto Kahn's personal comment was, "It's a monologue by Beatrice Lillie with incidental music." Robert Benchley voiced his opinion of the incidental music by stating, "As for the score, it is pleasant, but Mr. Youmans, like Mr. Gershwin in *Oh, Kay!*, seems to have been taking it easy this season."

Bea was pleased with her reviews. "In London, you know, a dramatic critic wouldn't smile if he died," she said.

Bea managed to insert "The Girls of the Old Brigade" from her *Nine O'Clock Revue*, which livened up the show and later still, at an actors' benefit performance, she slipped in "March with Me" and it stopped the show once more.

In the meantime, Bea continued her romance with Charles Mac-Arthur. It was through Charlie that Bea met Neysa McMein, the American artist, who was a great favorite of the Round Table group. She later painted a formal portrait of Bea which adorned Bea's living room wall in New York. McMein, who moved with facility through social and theatrical coteries, was gifted with sensitivity and humor, which made her a natural for the group at the Algonquin. Her country home as well as her New York studio on West Fifty-seventh Street were constantly bristling with throngs of theatrical and literary lights such as Lynn Fontanne, Alfred Lunt, Harpo Marx, Ring Lardner,

Katharine Cornell, and Robert Benchley. Neysa's guests milled about sipping cocktails while she, on a dais wearing a beret, painted on as if she were alone in her artist's smock, a spare paint brush gripped in her teeth. Bea admired McMein's informality and earthy approach to living.

Once Neysa went to a fancy dress party masquerading as a cave woman, her hair flying about her face wildly and wearing animal skins and fuzzy slippers. She carried a huge meat cleaver as a prop. She arrived at her destination, announced her name to a startled butler as she swept in, and was ushered into a formal drawing room where six amazed strangers, all in strict formal attire, stared at her as if she were a madwoman.

"I think there's been a horrible mistake," she declared and then proceeded to join them for drinks. The fact that she had burst in at the wrong address did not faze her in the least and Neysa and her hosts quickly became good friends.

Worried about the possibility of a short run with *Oh, Please!* Bea decided one day to call London from her dressing room phone in an attempt to stir up some interest in a summer show there. She was told to remain where she was as the reports indicated that her business was good. Later Bea found out that her company manager had the phone operator connect her with her New York box office and the treasurer on duty was her "London" contact. She cabled her availability after discovering the trickery.

A year or so before, Bea met and became friends with comedienne Fanny Brice, the great Ziegfeld star. Brice went to see Bea in *Charlot's Revue* and she was nervous appearing before America's favorite comic. As it turned out, she had little to worry about. Bea and Fanny Brice became close friends and remained so until Fanny's death.

"Fanny had a great influence upon Bea," recalled Odette Myrtil. "They would call each other up from all over the place, sometimes in the middle of the night, and launch into a joke or a story without even saying hello first."

An item appeared in the newspapers that Fanny was asking advice from Bea regarding her divorce from Billy Rose to which Bea responded, "How could I advise her about a divorce never having had one myself?"

She and Fanny were regulars at Reuben's restaurant and later at Dinty Moore's on West Forty-sixth Street. For years, after Brice died, when Bea was in Moore's, she would ask for the waiter who served Fanny and herself.

Her brilliant comedy aside, it was Brice's earthy humor and great common sense that attracted Bea. Bea often told wonderful stories about her friend and respected her opinions probably more than anyone else's. When Fanny traveled, she hid her jewelry under the mattress in her hotel room until she was robbed one day. The thief was captured but Bea always laughed over Brice's admiration for the crook because he was clever enough to think of looking under the mattress.

At home, Bobby Peel now had control of a dance hall in Birming-ham and had formed his own band in which he played the saxo-phone. Peel had some success with the orchestra for a while, and business with the catering company and the adjoining dance hall improved when he took over due to the publicity his name attracted.

Oh, Please! managed approximately seventy-five performances before it closed in New York in February of 1927. Bea enjoyed a quick trip to Palm Beach to see Ziegfeld's *Palm Beach Night* revue and then was back in New York in time to appear at the Dollars and Sense Ball for cancer research. One night, with Len Hanna, the Cleveland socialite, as her escort she dropped into Texas Guinan's club on West Fifty-fourth Street. At a nearby table she spotted actress Lenore Ulric with Henry Hull, the actor. As Texas Guinan was busy belting out "The Prisoner's Song" the police arrived and the place was raided. Happily, the guests were not detained and Bea rather en-joyed it all.

Exit Smiling finally premiered in New York in January of 1927 at the Lexington Theatre but the reviews were not favorable. One screen magazine was quick to point out that Bea was rumored to be the Prince of Wales' favorite comedian back in her own hometown. Bea fared better with another reviewer who raved, "She promises to be the feminine Chaplin of the screen. Her humor is whimsical, pathetic, and simple all in one, and the story all the way through is seen through roars of laughter—with a lump in the throat."

Oh, Please! made it to Chicago and then Bea went on a vaudeville tour after agreeing to appear the following year in a new musical called *The Little Darling* with music by Rodgers and Hart. Before the show closed, however, Bobby announced that he would be standing for Parliament the following year on the side of Labor from the Tamworth–South Staffordshire district where his grandfather served when he entered politics. Then Bobby traveled to America to visit Bea in Chicago after calling her on the transatlantic phone at great expense to inform her of his arrival time. Bea slept through the appointed hour and woke up to find him standing beside her bed. To square the oversight, she burst into a description of the new saxophone she had bought him. Later, when he was not looking, she dashed out and purchased one.

Bea's Orpheum circuit tour took her as far west as San Francisco, down the coast, and back through Ohio and on to Washington, D.C. In Ohio they posted her stage name and underneath it, in smaller print, "Lady Peel." In "After Dinner Music," which Coward had written for her in the 1926 *Charlot Revue*, she was again the grand prima donna but this time began the number by addressing the audience.

"Ladies and Gentlemen, I am sure you will appreciate what a comedown this is for me. Me what's always 'ad me own 'orses!" The audience took her at her word and the act fell straight on its face. Many women began to sniff and at the end of her monologue Bea swore an attempt was made to take up a collection. In Washington Bea was entertained by Mrs. Evelyn Walsh McLean, once the owner of the famous Hope Diamond. On the whole the tour was lucrative and successful for Bea, proving she drew audiences from every walk of life.

With very little free time to spare, Bea managed a two-month trip home. Bobbie had been staying with Lucie, whom he now referred to as Mumsie, a name which remained with her from then on. Lucie forbade him to address her as Grandma or Grandmother. John Lillie finally convinced Muriel and Arthur that they ought to marry and, to make him happy, they became engaged.

Bea sailed back to the United States on the *Barangaria* and moved into the Dorset Hotel. During her tours with *Oh, Please!* and the vaudeville circuit, Bea learned of Charles MacArthur's interest in actress Helen Hayes and of Miss Hayes' unabashed affection for him. Hayes, of course, had known all along of Charlie's liaison with Bea but she persisted in her pursuit even though she had been warned she did not stand a chance. When Bea arrived back in New York, she called Neysa McMein and asked her to arrange a meeting with Helen Hayes. Helen arrived in a nervous dither, but Bea was quick to realize it was over and put her at ease by informing her that Charlie was all Helen's. She gave the silk robe she had bought for Charlie to somebody else.

Many of Charlie's friends felt that he was ready for a serious and sober relationship with a less forceful and extroverted woman than Dorothy Parker or Bea. Many years later when I asked Bea why Charles MacArthur had married Helen Hayes, she smiled and answered, "Probably because he was in love with her." In any case Bea, Helen, and Charlie remained extremely close.

While Bea was in rehearsal for her new show, the title of which had been changed from *The Little Darling* to *She's My Baby*, Gertrude Lawrence obtained a divorce from her first husband. One newspaper hastened to reassure Gertie's fans that "Miss Lawrence's friends are certain that she will marry again."

She's My Baby was written by Guy Bolton, Bert Kalmer, and Harry Ruby with the aforementioned Rodgers and Hart, who were represented on Broadway at the time by *A Connecticut Yankee* in which Constance Carpenter, former chorine of Bea's Charlot *Revues*, was singing "My Heart Stood Still" to great acclaim. Billed as a farce, *She's My Baby* presented, along with Bea, Clifton Webb, Irene Dunne, Jack Whiting, Nick Long, Jr., William Frawley, and a chorus that included Geraldine Fitzgerald and George Vigouroux. George would appear once again in Bea's life many years later.

The show opened January 3, 1928, after its initial tryout in Washington, D.C. The Washington critics were not impressed with the production. In New York, *She's My Baby* was not popular with the reviewers either. Bea sang "A Baby's Best Friend (Is Its Mother)" and spouted lines such as "I'm a sort of Rotarian myself—I only eat meat once in a while!" Clifton Webb and Irene Dunne were well received while the Tiller line of girls from London danced heartily to a lukewarm reception.

Alexander Woollcott called it "a farce that is so stale it is musty. The whole enterprise leans so heavily on the comic from Canada that she will be black and blue by the end of the week." Continuing on Bea's side he wrote, "When the unflagging Beatrice Lillie trotted solemnly onto the stage of the Globe Theatre last night she was greeted by the fondest and most cordial welcome I had heard a first-night audience give way to in more than a year."

During the relatively short run of *She's My Baby* Bea accomplished a great deal professionally. She and the producers decided to present a special invited matinee for, as the publicity stated, all of her friends as a token of appreciation for kindnesses bestowed upon her in Hollywood. No tickets were sold for the performance and among the many Broadway and Hollywood names who attended were Lionel Barrymore, Al Jolson, George Jessel, Ed Wynn, Harry Lauder, Pauline Lord, and Franklyn Farnum. Marilyn Miller and others requested "March with Me" and Bea added it to the show for the matinee and the remainder of the run. After the performance Bea and Clifton Webb posed for pictures with Charlie MacArthur and Helen Hayes, Katharine Cornell, Judith Anderson, and Cathleen Nesbitt.

Old Gold paid her a healthy sum to advertise their cigarettes, which she did in a glamour ad and then one night she partied after the show with Whalen Echols, Harold Ross, publisher of *The New Yorker*, and Mrs. Ross. As their taxi drove down Ninth Avenue at two in the morning, it was struck broadside by a roadster as they turned onto Forty-sixth Street. Bea was thrown to the floor and received a broken rib as the offending car sped off. Ross took her back to the Dorset where a doctor attended to her. Shortly thereafter, Bea agreed to join other Broadway stars for the Forty-fifth Annual Benefit of the Actors' Fund, which took place at the Jolson Theatre. Boxes went for as high as one hundred dollars and the entire venture raised a grand total of fifteen thousand dollars!

Since every comedian is accused of wanting to play Shakespeare, Bea accepted an invitation to perform at a Shakespeare Memorial

Performance Benefit for the Shakespeare Foundation. She was asked to play Audrey in *As You Like It* for a Shakespearean symposium put together by Lawrence Ayre. Surrounded by Eva Le Gallienne, Leslie Howard, Peggy Wood, Judith Anderson, and Katharine Cornell, Bea held her own until she said the line "I am not a slut!" as only Bea could, whereupon the audience screamed with laughter and she stopped the show.

She's My Baby struggled through nine weeks and when it closed Bea went home. Once again Bea and Bobby were quoted as planning to restore Drayton Manor but it was all fodder for the interviewers. There was no marriage per se to justify such expenditures and far from enough cash to achieve it. Bea was not in love with Bobby Peel, she never had been; he was simply there and Bea was used to having him around. Probably the most that could be said concerning their feelings was they were fond of one another. There was no hint of divorce simply because there was no need for one. Bea had her career to occupy her time, Mumsie was raising Bobbie, and Peel was concerned with his various projects, none of which seemed to get off the ground, and eventually he proceeded to drop his plans to run for Parliament.

During her stay in London, Bea made her first appearance on the stage of England's mecca of vaudeville, the Palladium. She performed one of Noël's sketches and sang a selection of her numbers. Ivor Novello had just fared badly as a vaudeville performer at the same theatre. "Bea Lillie dies at the Palladium" reported *Variety*, the theatrical newspaper. The London audiences simply did not grasp Bea's humor, especially on a vaudeville stage. Bea always felt American audiences were more sophisticated and quicker in picking up her nuances and impressions. To prove it, she once appeared in London and sang a number which had been very successful in New York. When the audience did not respond, she dressed up in a funny costume and they loved it.

"I don't know why it is," she exclaimed, "but most Englishmen are from Missouri. They have to have their humor laid out on a table."

In New York, Charles MacArthur became the proud co-author of a new hit play called *The Front Page*, which opened, ironically, at the

Times Square Theatre where Bea experienced her initial success with Charlot. Helen Hayes, who was appearing to great acclaim in *Coquette*, was given the night off to attend the opening. Three days later, on August 17, 1928, Charlie and Helen were married.

C. B. Cochran, affiliated for a second time with Noël Coward, was the producer of a smash hit revue called *This Year of Grace*, which Coward had written. It starred Maisie Gay and Jessie Matthews, another former Charlot chorine, Douglas Byng, and Sonnie Hale. Coward wrote "A Room with a View" and "Dance, Little Lady" for this show and Cochran signed Bea as his New York star. Bea was not completely satisfied with the material but Noël promised her new songs and she agreed to go. Then Cochran persuaded Noël to appear opposite Bea, but rehearsals were delayed for two weeks while Coward recovered from an operation for hemorrhoids.

The show rehearsed in London, which allowed Bea to be present at the wedding of her sister and Arthur Weigall. John Lillie, after assisting in this task, packed his belongings and quietly moved away to Ireland.

Noël Coward interpolated two new songs for Bea in the American version of *This Year of Grace*. She was given "World Weary," which became a Coward standard, and "I Can't Think," a take-off of Gertrude Lawrence singing a torch song. Once again, Bea said good-bye to her husband and son and departed for New York. There was a week's tryout in Baltimore during which nerves were stretched to the breaking point despite the assurances of the Lunts, who were appearing in Baltimore at the time, that the show was wonderful. Bea and Noël, as much as they respected and loved one another, were constantly battling. Noël insisted Bea was not singing his lyrics as he had written them, and Bea protested loudly that her material was not up to par. She also demanded that other parts be given her to perform but Coward and Cochran stubbornly refused to accede to her demands. By the time the show arrived in New York, practically nobody was speaking to anyone backstage or out front. Bea's jitters stemmed from the fact that her material had been written for Maisie Gay, who played it brilliantly, and she knew there would be comparisons. Also, Bobby was not there to fall back on. She was fighting her battles alone, which only served to darken the picture. As the final dress rehearsal approached Cochran and Bea were shouting at each other. During a technical rehearsal everything that could go wrong with scenery and lights did so, and Coward, unable to take the strain any longer, went for a long walk, leaving the rehearsal in Mr. Cochran's hands. Bea threatened to walk out and Cochran promised to report her to Actors' Equity, which changed her mind instantly.

Dress rehearsal was a shambles. Bobby Peel arrived for the opening and took Bea home to rest. He called Cochran the following day and said, "I've just spent a terrible night with your leading lady!"

"I'm glad you had to sleep with her, not I," C. B. growled.

This Year of Grace was a howling success. It opened on November 7, 1928, and E.V. Osborn reported the following day, "Everybody was on his feet, everybody was cheering and the stage curtain was bobbing up and down!"

Noël attempted a curtain speech and Bea managed to mumble a thank you to the audience. When the final curtain fell amidst the applause and shouting, she and Noël fell tearfully into each other's arms and the battle was ended. Then Bea and Cochran patched up their differences and the company went off to celebrate and read the early reviews.

Robert Benchley waxed poetic with, "Unless someone in America is able to do something that approximates Mr. Coward's feat, we shall always feel that it was a mistake to break away from England back there in 1775."

They all loved Bea. "It is more devastating to see one corner of her mouth twitch than to see some comedians fall down stairs. When she smiled she was almost as irresistible as when she did not smile." "*This Year of Grace* is not as good as Miss Lillie and no show, I should imagine, ever was." "Miss Lillie's comedy, whether it be subtle or broad, springs from an alert intelligence which plays around ideas as flames lick around a fresh log." Robert Garland headlined his review "Lillie Scores Again." One paper declared, "Mr. Coward did almost everything connected with the show save invent Miss Lillie," and another said, "Mr. Coward and Miss Lillie are at their enchanting best." She was called gifted beyond measure. George Jean Nathan hated everything about the show while another writer felt the first act in London was better than it was in New York but the second act in New York was superior to the second in England. Somebody else felt that "Dance, Little Lady," in which Florence Desmond danced until she dropped, should serve as a warning to all the Blackbottomers (the Black Bottom was the dance craze at the time).

The following night, Gertrude Lawrence opened at the Alvin Theatre in *Treasure Girl*, which did not amuse the critics. Robert Benchley referred to it as a "wet albatross" and it only ran two months in spite of a score by George and Ira Gershwin.

There was no doubt the magic couple that season was Noël Coward and Beatrice Lillie. They were invited everywhere and were usually asked to perform numbers they did in the show. Noël and Bea obliged only at benefits and his music was always played as they entered various nightclubs around town. Noël Coward extended his contract from three to six months during which time he put the finishing touches on his new operetta *Bittersweet*.

Alexander Woollcott began Sunday breakfast get-togethers at his apartment, rituals to which Bea found her way occasionally. The world showed up at his door: actors, composers, and writers, including most of the Algonquin Round Table. Charlie MacArthur and his co-author, Ben Hecht, flushed with success, usually attended. Both men, because of their irreverent exposé of the newspaper profession in *The Front Page*, were referred to as the Katzenjammer Kids. George Kaufman and his wife Beatrice, Thornton Wilder, the Barrymores, and the Lunts all mingled with a variety of guests from many professions.

Bea took to the endorsements once more and appeared in an ad for Lux Toilet Soap. The advertisement displayed a rather elegant photograph of Bea and a cartoon of a lady on a telephone:

> MY DEAR, I'm so exCITED I could eat PARSNIPS and never KNOW! Because JEROME after acting like NOTHING HUMAN for weeks, took me to see Beatrice LILLIE last night. And she looks GOrgeous in EVEning clothes because she has beautiful skin, and she uses Lux TOILET soap, which is the REASON, I mean it really IS, because I use it—MYSELF

When the show closed, Bea headed west again and appeared in a film for Warner Brothers called *Show of Shows*, Warner's contribution to the stream of all-star musical extravaganzas which were being ground out by every studio in Hollywood. Bea shared the film with Myrna Loy, Louise Fazenda, Frank Fay, John Barrymore, Richard Barthelmess, and Loretta Young, among others. The film used approximately five hundred chorus girls and consisted of song and dance numbers with sketches performed by the stars belting out wisecracks and snappy chatter. Barrymore interpolated a scene written by a playwright named Shakespeare.

On her way back to England, Bea appeared at the Palace Theatre in New York where she fared far better with the audiences there than she had at the Palladium earlier. She did three a day in October and again during the week of November 23, 1929. Billed as "Beatrice Lillie, the Great International Stellar Comedienne," Bea followed "Buster Shaver and His Tiny Town Revue." She was next to closing and did her "References" sketch in which a discharged maid is interviewed by a prospective employer who mistakes her for the lady of the house. She concluded with "songs from her repertoire." The pianist, Sam Walsh, played for her.

Bea was able to spend the holidays with Bobbie and her family for a change. She and Peel were leading separate lives although it was not generally known. Bobby was interested in a divorcee and spent his time with her. Lucie, now called Mumsie by everyone close to her, was raising Bobbie. John Lillie, all but forgotten, resided quietly in Ireland where Bea sent him checks regularly. Once, when Odette Myrtil played in Ireland close to where Lillie lived, she invited him to a performance. Each time Odette appeared on the stage, John would nod and wave wildly to her.

Bea joined up with Charlot once more in a revue called *Charlot's Masquerade* in which she worked with Henry Kendall, Constance Carpenter, Florence Desmond, Anton Dolin, and others. Anton Dolin (his Christian name was Patrick) would go on to become an international ballet star and choreographer and remain one of Bea's staunchest friends. *Charlot's Masquerade* was not a hit, unfortunately, and ran less than one hundred performances.

"I was so upset, I almost committed Harry Kendall," became one of Bea's favorite expressions.

Bea was off to New York and then on to California and a new film.

During a farewell get-together with Tallulah Bankhead, currently the toast of London, Tallulah decided it would be great fun if everybody leaped into automobiles and drove to Southampton to see Bea off. Everybody included Leslie Howard, Audrey Carton, Tallulah, and special guest star Aimee Semple McPherson, the American evangelist who was currently holding meetings at Albert Hall. Everyone squeezed into one vehicle but halfway there the car broke down in the fog and they all got out and pushed it along the road while singing at the top of their lungs. Bea made the ship and Tallulah and Aimee made the papers, who attempted to make more out of it than it actually was.

The MacArthurs were now living at 25 East End Avenue, a new building looking out upon the East River. There was a spacious six rooms with four baths across the hall from them which they insisted Bea investigate. Bea was spending more and more time in the United States and felt a permanent home was far more expedient than checking in and out of hotels. She loved the flat and purchased it in March of 1930 for $21,000. Immediately the dining room overlooking the East River became Bea's bedroom, the butler's pantry her bath, and a study overlooking East End Avenue was transformed into a dining room. The arrangement left Bea with two guest bedrooms.

Opera star Grace Moore offered Bea a ride to the coast in her private railroad car. Moore was on her way west to film "A Woman's Morals," the story of Jenny Lind. Bea and Moore set off for California via Dallas, where the car was left on a siding to allow Grace to fulfill a concert engagement. Not relishing the idea of spending the evening alone in a deserted railroad yard, Bea phoned the concert hall, informed them who she was, and secured a seat for Moore's appearance. Grace warbled her way through *La Bohème* and other concert favorites as Bea sat front row center engrossed in the evening newspaper.

In Hollywood she made *Are You There?* with John Garrick, Olga Baclanova, and her old friend George Grossmith. It was Bea's first full-length talking film. In it she played a lady private detective out to expose a gold digger who is after a Duke. Four songs were dropped from the film and it never went into general release. The experience convinced Bea that filmmaking was far more taxing than a stage performance. She was still not happy with the silence that greeted her comedy on the sets, and she hated not knowing if she was funny. The early morning studio calls were not much to her liking, either.

Bea returned to the Palace in New York once more in February of 1931, appearing on the bill with Doc Rockwell and Gus Van. Following Noble Sissle and his orchestra, Bea again appeared next to closing.

Dwight Deere Wiman offered Bea *The Third Little Show*. Wiman and his associate Tom Weatherly had produced *The First Little Show*, which was a tremendous success with Clifton Webb and Libby Holman and marked the first collaboration between Howard Dietz and Arthur Schwartz. One of the high spots was Libby Holman's "Moanin' Low." A second edition of the show was produced with little success. Now with Bea, Ernest Truex, Walter O'Keefe, and Constance Cummings brightening up the marquee, Wiman pronounced it "The Aristocrat of All Revues" and hoped for the best when it opened on June 1, 1931. Charlot graduate Constance Carpenter appeared in the show, along with Edward Arnold and dancer Carl Randall. Noël, S.J. Perelman, and Marc Connelly contributed sketches and Herman Hupfeld supplied a song which was sung by Walter O'Keefe and became a hit tune, "When Yuba Plays the Rumba on His Tuba." Bea carried most of the show and introduced "Mad Dogs and Englishmen" by Noël Coward, a number set in the tropics which deplored his countrymen's habit of "going out in the midday sun." She did a satire on Ruth Draper, the monologuist, called "On the Western Plains," in which she requested the audience to "imagine far too much."

It was in *The Third Little Show* that Bea sang a number which would be associated with her for the remainder of her career. With a perfectly straight face and in her best concert soprano, she rendered "There Are Fairies at the Bottom of Our Garden," a popular legitimate concert piece at the time. Bea claimed that Ethel Barrymore urged her to perform the number. The reviews were not as good for the show as they were for Bea and it was never a success. The spectacular opening soon after of *The Band Wagon* eclipsed whatever interest there might have been in the show.

By then, however, Bea was involved in something more important to herself and her future. Through the Wimans she had met a man eight years younger than she who for the next few years would occupy a place in her life and career. His name was Rupert Bloomfield McGunigle. His college nickname was Doc, a sobriquet which remained with him all of his life although the Rupert evolved into Robert as time went on.

Writer Nancy Hamilton knew him well. "He was very tall and he was handsome in a seemingly strong way but he was the gentlest man, like a big bear. He'd been a great football hero at Yale, the Great McGunigle."

Doc was a scholarship student during his first two years at Yale where he studied general science. He did indeed excel at football and won numerals as a member of the Freshman Football Team, the University Football Squad, and, in his senior year, the University Football Team. Doc sang with the Glee Clubs and belonged to the Dramatic Association. However, he intended to enter the advertising business.

"He married the sister of a classmate of mine," said Nancy Hamilton. "Steve [Mrs. Dwight Deere] Wiman took him over, she thought he was very funny. He was employed by Dwight Deere Wiman because he needed a job. He got into the theatre, which he really didn't want to do at all."

Nancy had written a song called "I Hate the Spring" and through Doc it was submitted to Wiman, who optioned it for Ernest Truex. Truex turned it down but *The Third Little Show* served to introduce Bea to Doc.

"She adored him and he adored her," said Nancy. "He was a very, very funny man, so attractive and powerfully built. He was the darling of the girls without much wanting to be. Doc wouldn't have taken such lovely care of Bea in a very special way if he was simply hitching his wagon to a star."

"Doc was dedicated to her," added Marc Connelly. "He was one of the dearest human beings and Bea loved him, too. It was a very gentle love affair, I don't think it had anything to do with the physical. He was a thoroughly incandescent human being." Doc became a writer and remained in the theatre for the next few years.

The Third Little Show managed to keep running for 136 performances and in October the production attempted a road tour which made it to Philadelphia where it closed permanently. Once again, Bea agreed to do two a day at the Palace. Milton Berle, Fifi D'Orsay, and the Mills Brothers were the other headliners. Bea was making good money at the Palace and the audiences loved her there. When the Sutton Club beckoned, Bea responded and for a time she appeared in cabaret each night after her two shows at the Palace.

Doc continued to remain close to Bea and when she discovered that Warner Brothers had separated *Show of Shows* into single segments which were being exhibited as short subjects in motion picture theatres throughout the country, he advised her to sue them for breach of contract. Bea sued for fifty thousand dollars claiming that Warners, by showing her comedy scenes as single comedy episodes, had "presented her to the world as a cheap and inconsequential performer."

When Bea promised the Theatre Guild she would appear as the nurse in the world premiere of Shaw's *Too True to Be Good*, she was stepping into her second book show. Unfortunately, Shaw's efforts were received with mixed emotions by the press in all of the out-of-town theatres they played. Pittsburgh stated, "It is a gorgeous entertainment for people who like to have tin cans tied to their illusions." Washington, Cincinnati, and Buffalo were more or less along that line.

Shaw, announcing the piece as "A Collection of stage sermons by a Fellow of the Royal Society of Literature," discussed the state of the world, modern young women, medicine, the aptitude of British army officers for their jobs, the beneficent qualities of fresh air and exercise, and post-war conditions. Bea had sworn an oath to herself earlier on that she would stay in the character.

"Miss Lillie makes music-hall fun of her duties as the chambermaid countess," declared one viewer, "and why shouldn't she considering both Miss Lillie and the duties." So much for her oath to herself.

"I didn't mind so much learning those frightfully long speeches. In fact it was fun, rather, because I hadn't the faintest idea what they meant at first," Bea explained. "I feel very legitimate. Noël Coward said I was about as legitimate as Snoops the Lawyer but he is very sniffy about Shaw anyway. He said the play was tripe. Of course, I do think Mr. Shaw had a nerve to call it a play but I wouldn't go that far!" Bea had to sit through one very long speech delivered by another actor and she felt anyone that long onstage with nothing to do belonged offstage.

Hope Williams, Leo G. Carroll, and Claude Rains were among the actors who strove to make the play into something. Shaw seemed to be saying that the rich were no better off than the poor although many audience members failed to grasp that piece of wisdom. Shaw insisted that the balcony tickets sold very well as opposed to orchestra seats, which went slowly. George Bernard Shaw and the Theatre Guild had an excellent working relationship. *Too True to Be Good* was not included in it, alas.

On June 4 Bea sailed for France to meet Bobbie for a vacation on Cap d'Antibes. She told the press she was learning to speak French on the way over because Bobbie, who spoke it very well, demanded too much candy for acting as an interpreter. Bea obviously did not spend too much time with Berlitz. In Cannes she attempted in pidgin French to contact Elsa Maxwell at her hotel. The operator's command of a second language was as lacking as Bea's but she managed to convey the news that Elsa was out and asked who was calling. "C'est Lady Parle qui Peel," answered Bea, terribly pleased with herself. Elsa dined out on that one for the rest of her life.

In England, Bea and Dolin arrived at her home one day and saw Bobbie playing in the backyard. He answered Bea's call and appeared in the kitchen with dirty face and hands.

"What on earth have you been up to?" asked Bea.

"I've been in the garden," smiled Bobbie, "playing with the fairies."

"Fairies? Elves, dear," said Bea as she patted him on the head and went into the other room.

On another occasion, Pat arrived to escort Bea to a dinner party in time to hear the charwoman involved in a heated argument with her little daughter, who had been missing for most of the afternoon. When the woman demanded to know where her child had been, the terrified girl managed to stammer that she had been to London

Bridge. As Bea strode into the room, the char shouted, "London Bridge! I'll give you London Bridge!"

"Oh, no, you won't!" cautioned Bea. "It's not yours to give."

One evening Bea was escorted to a show called *Over the Page*, a revue written by Dion Titheradge and featuring Violet Lorraine and June (later Lady Inverclyde), both friends of Bea's. Although the show was not destined to be a hit, Bea was impressed by a young comedic impressionist, Reginald Gardiner. His imitations of inanimate objects such as wallpaper and buoy lights were hilarious and Bea could not wait to meet him. She discovered when they met that Gardiner was not only handsome, debonair, and amusing but one of the great storytellers of all time as well. Their professional admiration for one another was mutual and Bea swore at the time that they would certainly work together. Soon after, Bea took her son to the Riviera for a few weeks and then she packed once again and was off to America, leaving him in Lucie's care.

SIX

The year 1932 was not to be Bea's year on Broadway. Her next venture, *Stop That Clock*, later changed to *Walk a Little Faster*, allowed her the fun of working with Bobby Clark and his partner, Paul McCollough, who had made a huge hit in *The Music Box Review of 1922*. The show offered Doc (now Robert) McGunigle an opportunity to write for Bea and for the Broadway theatre. The production was Vernon Duke's first full Broadway score. Evelyn Hoey was presented in Duke's "April in Paris," a song which was interpolated into the show after rehearsals had begun. Miss Hoey, desperately infected with laryngitis on opening night, was barely heard out front and the song was hardly noticed and did not become a hit until many months later. Bea and Clark did a spoof of Clifton Webb and Tamara Geva doing their "Alone Together" dance from their show, *Flying Colors*. She also impersonated a 1906 college girl, a belle of the Yukon, and a radio singer. One bit of business she invented became part of theatre history. She was discovered on stage in a long evening gown, announced the next act and then, lifting her skirts daintily, she roller-skated off stage. To prepare herself for the exit she prevailed upon good friend Hope Williams to teach her how to skate. For days she could be seen rolling down East End Avenue.

"There was a little park and she'd go around that park and then we'd start down the hill," recalled Hope Williams. "I had a terrible time catching her. She'd get going and couldn't stop. There was traffic down at the bottom so I really had to catch her. It was very funny."

Monte Woolley directed the show and it was the first production to open at the newly named St. James theatre, on December 7, 1932. The show ran for nearly four months during which time Bea and Sam Walsh appeared at the El Patio Club. When Bea returned to England, Doc went with her after it had been agreed he would supply the book for a new show C. B. Cochran was planning for her. It was called *Please*, and Doc and Dion Titheradge created sketches and the lyrics. An American, Jack Donohue, was engaged to choreograph.

Bobby Peel was no longer living in Tamworth, or in London for that matter. Drayton Manor was being dismantled and the property was being sold. In August, Bea received word that John Lillie had died in Ireland. She and Muriel traveled to his home and in the attic they discovered a small box with Bea's name on it. Inside was all the money she had sent her father over the years with a note saying, "For my daughter, Beatrice Lillie, for a rainy day." Before her rehearsals began, Bea took Bobbie with her to Cap d'Antibes on the Riviera for a short but well-earned rest.

Lupino Lane, who was enjoying a film career, was coaxed back to the stage by Charlot, and he and Frank Lawton were signed to appear opposite Bea. Doc and Titheradge gathered together a ream of Broadway material and Bea appeared as an American blues singer and as Josephine opposite Lane's Napoleon. She and Lawton did a brother and sister dance number called "Hoops," a routine originally performed by Fred and Adele Astaire in *The Band Wagon*. Audiences enjoyed the show and *The New York Post*, on January 2, 1934, reported, "Beatrice Lillie is being rediscovered in London. Her brand of comedy is said to be drawing large crowds to the Savoy Theatre." On January 30, Hitler became chancellor of Germany's Third Reich.

Then Arthur Weigall died suddenly and Muriel was inconsolable. "When Father died, it was a kind of finish for Muriel," said Alured Weigall, Arthur's son. And it was. Sometime later, Muriel stated she was deliberately killing herself. She became a heavy drinker and depended upon Bea for finances and from then on Arthur's son and daughter watched over her.

In February, Bea was having a painful problem with hemorrhoids and went into the hospital the day after *Please* closed. She later told friends, swearing it was absolutely true, that a few weeks later she attended a party and suddenly found herself face to face with her doctor, who had no idea who she was. When Bea reminded him, she claims he apologized and said, "I never remember faces."

In April Bea was notified that her husband was in need of surgery owing to an appendicitis attack. Bobby was rushed to the hospital where it was discovered he had developed peritonitis. Despite all efforts to save him, he died. Bea found herself a widow and her son the new Sir Robert Peel, Sixth Baronet. There was a service at which a great many friends of Bea's appeared, and Bobby was laid to rest with the Peel family in Drayton Basset, in the church where he and Bea had been married.

It was a bittersweet mourning period for Bea, and her heart went out to Bobby far more for his loss than hers—for the dreams and ambitions that never reached fruition in his life. While Bea continued to earn money hand over fist and had gained international fame, nothing her husband attempted proved lucrative. Unfortunately, the Peel talent had come to a halt with his great-grandfather. Eventually all that remained of Drayton Manor was the clock tower. Many years later when I asked Bea if she and Peel would have remained wed had he lived, she said ruefully, "God, no."

Bea had little time for regrets, and in May of 1934 she played the fashionable Café de Paris in London with great success. And then it was off to New York once more. The restlessness that plagued Bea stemmed not only from a career drive but from a childlike belief that if she kept moving the problems of everyday living could be left behind her. She loved fame and needed it. The stage infused her with the power to make decisions all her own. Once in front of the audience she became a complete person and depended upon no one to advise her what to do or to shoulder her responsibilities. She said, "When anyone tells me my name is in the paper I rush to buy it." She meant it.

Muriel and Lucie hovered about constantly, and Bea was aware that she needed Lucie to watch over Bobbie. At times, when Muriel was in her cups she became morose and bitter, often taking credit for Bea's career or fighting with her mother. Bea's relationship with Doc was important to her and she depended upon his advice and support. Doc, no longer married, had no intention of marrying again.

Lest history mistakenly assume 1934 was a banner year for Beatrice Lillie, she paid a visit to her good friend Fanny Brice, who looked at Bea for a split second and asked, "What's wrong with your neck? You better see a doctor, kid." Fanny was correct. Bea's doctor found she had the beginnings of a goiter on her neck and she was operated on at Lenox Hill hospital on July 9. The surgery was successful but Bea never could fathom Fanny's uncanny diagnosis. Bea carried a pencil-thin scar at the base of her neck which became apparent only when she was suntanned. On July 17, Bea was informed that her appeal in the suit against Warner Brothers had been turned down.

Bea consoled herself with a visit from Bobbie. She later attended a performance of Leonard Sillman's *New Faces of 1934*. There was something catchy and vaguely familiar about a song called "I Hate the Spring," written and sung by Nancy Hamilton. Bea went backstage after the show and introduced herself to Nancy, who reminded her of Wiman's interest in the song in 1931.

"Then she said she wanted a book show very badly and wouldn't I write her a book show," remembered Nancy. "So I got the rights from Mr. A. P. Herbert for *The Water Gypsies*."

In the meantime, Bea appeared as a guest on the Rudy Vallee radio show, and several networks began courting her as a possible star for a radio series. Bea settled on NBC, and after agreeing to begin early the following year, she returned home in order to enter Bobbie into Harrow in September.

In spite of an impressive list of staff writers submitted to her by NBC, Bea felt Nancy Hamilton had the sort of humor she could work with. Combined with Doc's particular style, Bea was certain Nancy and Doc were the perfect writers for her. When Bea returned to New York in November, Nancy, who had worked herself to a frazzle, had *Water Gypsies* ready for her only to learn that Bea had no intention of doing it and never had any. Bea was constantly in the habit of saying yes instantly to invitations or requests, promises from which she depended on someone else to save her. Over the years, she did the same thing with writers or dressmakers, often exclaiming how much she would like something and then forgetting about it almost immediately. Few people were ever disturbed by it because Bea was completely lacking in deceit, but those who were meeting her for the first time were often flattered and impressed and hence became the victims of her impetuosity.

When Bea announced that she would be hiring her own radio writers all hell broke loose in the industry. Howls of protest from professional scriptwriters were heard throughout broadcasting and letters to radio editors poured in.

"It has been a long time since any radio event sent so many argumentative letters to this desk," wrote Alton Cook of *The World Telegram*.

In an interview, Bea casually remarked, "Some of the radio writers have submitted scripts but they are the sort of things my people could turn out standing on their ear." What Bea probably meant was scripts suited to her particular style and talent. "We have simply given up eating and sleeping. All of our time is spent worrying about what to do on these radio programs!" For years, whenever an eager writer approached Bea with the news that he was writing a script for her, Bea would answer, "Don't write one for me, write one for Helen Hayes or Katharine Cornell and then give it to me."

But the war of the writers continued. "Miss Lillie will discover that radio is the greatest consumer of material. A new radio writer approaches his job with enthusiasm and freshness. After a few programs, the veneer has worn off and the fun begins." The newspaper scribe who penned this article ended up by saying that it was just this new breed of writers who submitted most of the scripts worth bothering about. He, it would appear, was on Bea's side.

Undaunted by the hubbub she was creating, Bea, trusting her own instincts, went ahead as planned and the radio series began on January 4, 1935. After some insignificant early mishaps, Bea took to radio easily although she found it taxing. The endless stream of new scripts and numbers meant a week's labor in preparation for the broadcast. In 1935, radio shows were done live and in front of an audience. It meant spending a great deal of time with Doc and Nancy Hamilton.

"The first year it was really Doc McGunigle and I doing the shows," said Nancy Hamilton. "We were being paid directly by Bea, not a great deal, and Doc was living with her in her apartment. I was up the street on East End Avenue in a five-floor walk-up so I was very handy. Bea could call at four in the morning to tell me to get there quickly."

She appeared with guest stars such as Benny Goodman and Fanny Brice. She and Fanny were a huge success. Later, there was talk of the two women doing a Broadway show together called *The Whoopee Sisters* but it never came to fruition. Bea created a character known as the Honest Working Girl and read the comic strips as Auntie Bea. The comic strip routine was a satire on the popular Uncle Don radio show.

With Sam Walsh at the piano, Bea made her debut at the Rainbow Room a week after her first radio show. Since it was her first cabaret appearance in some time, the room was jammed with celebrities and friends, among them Noël Coward. During the act Bea introduced Noël, who then sang two duets with her.

With each passing year, Bea was earning increasingly larger sums of money. She was now included in a list of top money-makers in the theatre world on two sides of the Atlantic. One writer described her "transatlantiveness" as a major key to her success. While Bea was busy raking in the chips, her friend Gertie Lawrence was struggling with the bankruptcy courts in England. Gertie's assets were far outnumbered by her debts. A few years before, during Gertie's New York hit *Oh, Kay!*, a reporter commented on her success to Bea, who prophetically replied, "Gertie is riding the crest of the wave, I hope she's saving her money!"

"Gross extravagances," lamented the Official Receiver in London.

Bea's fame, while satisfying her emotional needs, was keeping her separated from her son.

Nancy Hamilton recalled, "The first summer I met her, her mother and Bobbie were over. Bobbie was just adorable. Mrs. Lillie was as serious as she could be. She sang, "Fairies at the Bottom of

Our Garden" and meant every word of it. Bobbie was a very attractive little boy. She was so thrilled with him but as with all great artists it wasn't a complete relationship. He had to be somewhere else instead of with her all the time. He had to be in school."

Bobbie admired Doc enormously and was greatly influenced by the older man. But his closest ties were with Lucie, whom he loved very much. When his grandmother was sixty he taught her to ice-skate, and he always discussed his problems with her. Lucie became an intermediary between himself and his mother, especially in areas concerning his allowance or extra money. When he entered Harrow, his visits with his mother were confined to holidays.

Bea hit the news columns in March of 1935 when a Mrs. Doris Draper initiated an action to recover two fur coats from a dressmaking firm in London. Mrs. Draper, it turned out, had been living as Lady Peel with Bobby for five years prior to his death. The firm claimed they were holding the coats until Mrs. Draper settled an account but the lady insisted that she had only left the furs for safekeeping. Mrs. Draper contended that Bobby Peel was being divorced at the time he died and informed the judge that she had been known in their village as Lady Peel. Although Bea denied knowing of Mrs. Draper's existence, she was aware that Peel was living with somebody else. Since Bea really had no direct connection with the case, the news value decreased rapidly and no more was heard of the matter.

Radio was bringing Bea a wider audience than ever before and she was now a household name thanks to Borden's and Lyon's Tooth Paste, among others. Because of her stage and vaudeville appearances, she was recognized in the street and in restaurants. Soon after she began broadcasting, Bea received a visit from Noël Coward. Rather airily she exhibited a stack of fan mail she had yet to peruse. Noël smiled sweetly as he picked one up.

"May I?" he asked as he opened it. He scanned the note for a moment and then turned to Bea. "This is from the president of Harvard. It says, 'Oh, boy, do you stink!' "

Fanny Brice remained her closest female friend at the time although she adored Elsa Maxwell, Lynn Fontanne, Tallulah Bankhead, Helen Hayes, and other women she had known since before the Charlot days. Over the years, Bea's cropped head, her campy material, and her many gay and lesbian fans and friends gave rise to the supposition that she herself might be a lesbian. As Odette Myrtil once reflected, Bea did not seek out her friends, they sought her company, and, straight or otherwise, if they had charm and humor Bea was not at all interested in what their sexual proclivities might be. It has been said she invented "camp," and her appeal was to admirers from all walks of life, all ages, and both sexes. Bea Lillie, for all the highjinks, was a sensual human being who loved men. Charles MacArthur, Doc McGunigle, Eddie Duryea Dowling, and Rolf Gérard were the men she truly loved; the other affairs were simply other affairs. Even though all four men drifted away later on, Bea never lost their friendship or forgot them and on all occasions became good friends with the spouses of those who married.

"Bea always lighted up a room when she came into it," asserted Marc Connelly. When she was comfortable with the crowd Bea was enchanting. She drank only beer at the time, albeit a great deal of it. One of Bea's great attributes was her ability to fit in everywhere, whether at 1040 Park Avenue at Condé Nast's vast penthouse where his parties included as many as two hundred or more guests dancing to one of two orchestras and imbibing at either of two bars, or simply poking around in somebody's kitchen searching for pans and some eggs to cook for a few friends. The taste and texture of the eggs depended upon the amount of beer Bea consumed. She had little tolerance for alcohol and the tiniest amount could affect her quickly.

According to Nancy Hamilton, "She would get falling down and then when she'd come to, she'd say, 'It was that one beer, you know, it's on account of that plate in my head.' I think that this was her way of accounting for it. She said that in the First World War she had been hit by a piece of shrapnel or something from a dirigible. She always talked about it but I never knew." Over the years, many of Bea's friends heard and believed this to be true, but Gladys Henson was unable to recall any such incident during the war.

"She never told me that! She never had a plate in her head. We were together all through the first war. She was never in bed except at night."

"She had that fall from the horse. After that she could never drink. One and she'd be cross-eyed," said Alured Weigall. Bea began drinking as a means of alleviating her nervousness in public. As Charlot remarked earlier in her career, in the dressing room Bea was completely relaxed and outgoing and backstage she felt secure and in charge. Away from the theatre she had very little to say to anyone not connected with acting. Beer loosened her up and for the early years of her career that was all she drank. It took very little of it to affect her, possibly because of the skull fracture in Hyde Park.

Toward the end of March, Bea agreed to appear at a gala celebrating the retirement of opera impresario Gatti-Casazza, longtime head of the Metropolitan Opera. The intent was to bid au revoir and raise money for the opera fund. The first half of the program consisted of arias and duets performed by stars of the company such as Louise Homer and Lawrence Tibbett. Then Lauritz Melchior and Lily Pons appeared as an aerial act, both in tights and blond wigs. This was followed by Bea and Paul Althouse as Carmen and Don José in a scene from the first act of the opera. Bea descended the stairs, rose in teeth, looking for all the world like a sybaritic Gypsy factory worker until her scarf snagged on a nail and nearly throttled her. From then on it was mayhem as Bea in a frenzy of Castilian jealousy proceeded to annihilate her suitor, his beloved, and a great deal of the scenery before a hysterical audience.

Bea's radio contract was extended for an additional thirteen weeks after which she returned to England. Before she left, however, the Shubert office approached her with an offer to star in a new revue early in the fall to be called *At Home Abroad*. Ethel Waters and Herb Williams were mentioned as possible co-stars. Bea quickly suggested that Reginald Gardiner be contacted for the show.

Bea vacationed once again on the Riviera with Bobbie, where they were joined by Fanny Brice and her children. Bobbie Peel managed to develop a crush on beautiful Cobina Wright, Jr., who was vacationing with her mother, Cobina, Sr. Bobbie, Cobina, and another friend took sides against the Brice children, Billy and Frances, in games, contests, and general torture. One day, Bobbie and friend took little Cobina, hair in long curls and attired in a fancy frock, for a rowboat ride. Billy and Frances lurked on shore plotting some sort of revenge. With a war whoop, they rushed the waterside and overturned the boat, submerging all three carefully dressed children.

Cobina ran screaming in tears to the hotel, hair plastered over her face and the dress ruined. She found her mother, Fanny, and Bea on the hotel terrace where Cobina poured out the whole sordid tale.

"My daughter would never do a thing like that," sniffed an irate Cobina, Sr.

"Bobbie certainly wouldn't," Bea replied testily.

"Hold it!" ordered Fanny, "My kids *would!* And in twenty minutes they'll all be friends again and we won't be speaking if we don't cut it out right now!"

"Very good advice," said Cobina, Jr., many years later. "I never forgot it."

Bobbie returned to Mumsie, and Bea, with Reginald Gardiner, sailed on the *Barangaria* for New York. Reggie set foot on American soil for the first time when the ship docked on July 22, 1935, a week before the show went into rehearsal.

At Home Abroad boasted a cast large enough to require three rehearsal theatres; and when the show traveled to Boston for a September opening, a heretofore unheard of seven railway cars were required to carry the scenery, costumes, and lights. Dancers Eleanor Powell and Paul Haakon, Eddie Foy, Jr., Vera Allen, and Woods Miller were among the cast members when the show opened at the Winter Garden Theatre on September 19, 1935.

Vincente Minnelli, who was currently art director of Radio City Music Hall and responsible for many of its greatest spectacles, executed scenery and costumes and was overall director of the production, which was staged as a "Musical Travelogue." When the show opened, Minnelli's reviews matched those of the stars. Reviewers felt his innovative use of colors and lighting, without resorting to opulence, "filled the stage with rich glowing colors that give the whole work an extraordinary loveliness."

In Boston he revealed a knack for dispensing with extraneous material and retaining only the best-suited for his performers. Bea had a terrible time with a number called "Antonio," done with an Italian accent and with the speed of a *Barber of Seville* aria. She found it impossible to do and it was finally cut after much haggling and a few tears on Bea's part. As a result of Minnelli's guidance, the Boston reviews were so excellent that *At Home Abroad* went straight to New York rather than to other cities.

The opening night audience was crowded with celebrities, among them Bert Lahr, Burns and Allen, Ira Gershwin, Bob Hope, Sophie Tucker, and Lorenz Hart. Bea appeared as a harassed shopper attempting to purchase "One Dozen Double Damask Dinner Napkins," a sketch written in 1927 for Cecily Courtneidge. As a mountain climber she yodeled a number called "Oh, Leo," tuneful enough to top the sheet music sales a few weeks later. She satirized the Merry Widow as the Toast of Vienna by singing a waltz and later as a saucy French lady singing "Paree," which became a standard of hers. When the chorus ladies did a number called "Get Yourself a Geisha," few of the audience noticed a shy and retiring chorine until Bea stepped out suddenly and sang, "It's better with your shoes off!" and brought down the house. The "Geisha" idea came to Bea after she watched the number from the wings in Boston. She persuaded Minnelli to try it and he let her put it in.

Bea once again garnered valentines from the press. "One of the greatest woman fun-makers on the English speaking stage"; "No one else can hover so skillfully between beauty and burlesque"; "Funnier than I have ever seen her before"; "Miss Lillie is shattering in satires." Business was extraordinary and extra holiday matinees were added. The Thanksgiving matinee broke the house record for a holiday matinee and the weekly gross at one point topped any in three years. Reginald Gardiner found himself a career in America on stage and in films and never left.

Bea felt he deserved his kudos. "He's as mad as a March hare and can't help being funny. Who else but a loon," she raved, "would imitate wallpaper, the fog settling over the Flushing Flats, or a swinging door? I can imitate Reggie but only Reggie can imitate a swinging door!"

In December Bea and Reggie were booked into the club Montmartre adjacent to the Winter Garden theatre. They were so well received that Bea promised to remain as long as they wanted her. Their opening was attended by Fanny Brice, May Murray, Tallulah Bankhead, Cobina Wright, Elsa Maxwell, Ray Bolger, Lee Shubert, Xavier Cugat, and Ira Gershwin.

With Bobby gone and Doc writing in Hollywood, Bea desperately needed somebody to help her in running her affairs now that she was making more money than ever before. He turned out to be Edward Duryea Dowling, a Shubert stage director and former dialogue director for Paramount Studios in Astoria. Dowling, a close friend of John Shubert, son of J.J., made headlines a few years before by running off with dancer Betty Compton, known to be the paramour of New York's flamboyant Mayor Jimmy Walker. The marriage lasted exactly thirty-three days. After the divorce, Compton eventually married Walker. Eddie Dowling was handsome and debonair with a practical business sense and exactly what Bea needed. They would be lovers and remain good friends for the next twenty years.

Lucie Lillie arrived with Bobbie during the Christmas holidays. Bobbie, Billy Brice, and Cobina Wright, Jr. were seen at the hockey matches and riding in Central Park. Bobbie and Cobina attended a few holiday parties together before he returned to Harrow.

At Home Abroad moved in January to the Majestic Theatre, vacating the Winter Garden in favor of Fanny Brice and Bob Hope in their *1936 Ziegfeld Follies*. After the show closed on March 7, Bea toured with the production but not before she was able to squeeze in an endorsement for Welch's grape juice, which, she stated, "Is found on my breakfast table every day. I use it for making punch."

The tour presented one major problem. Bea signed to do a ten-week radio series with Walter Wolfe King and Lennie Hayton's Band. To add to the problem, Nancy Hamilton was appearing as an actress in *Pride and Prejudice* on Broadway. It was decided that Bea would broadcast by remote from whatever town she was appearing in and King and Hayton would do their segments in New York.

"I did that one single-handed," related Nancy Hamilton. "In *Pride and Prejudice* we didn't have Monday shows so I would go up every Saturday night on a train to Chicago, Boston, or Washington and we would decide what I would be writing about. Then I would come home, write it, play in *Pride and Prejudice* and it would go on Friday night. Saturday night, I'd jump on a train again."

Nancy explained to Bea that unless some of her old sketches, her English sketches, were available she would not be able to continue. Bea informed her that all of her old sketches and any of Noël

Coward's were hers to do with as she pleased. Nancy then wove Coward and some English music hall sketches in with her own, which relieved the pressure a great deal.

"Noël had written a song called 'Lilac Time,' " Hamilton recalled. "It was an idiotic song, very funny, so I introduced that as a song of two cities. Bea sang her part from Washington and Walter Wolfe King sang his from New York. It was a very funny effect. I ran into Mr. Coward and asked him if he had caught the broadcast. He said he never listened to the radio and I said that we used that lovely song of his, 'Lilac Time.' He wanted to know by whose permission and I told him that Bea had told me we could use it. 'Bea told you that? She has stolen from you too I can see.' But he said it very kindly."

Noël might have been kind about it but later, toward the end of the series, there was the threat of a lawsuit from various writers whose sketches had been used but fortunately it was withdrawn.

When the show played in Toronto, Bea was informed that the mayor was going to present her with the keys to the city.

"I got there on a Sunday morning, and on Monday, the thirtieth, Bea was just furious," Nancy recalled. "She didn't know what was happening or why we were being driven around in the rain. She didn't even remember where she'd been born, it was very very funny. Bea said, 'I hope they don't expect me to make a speech!' Then we were in a little office and she didn't know what to say and the mayor, who handed her the key to the city, didn't know what to say. Then we all got into an open carriage in the rain and were driven somewhere."

During the week in Toronto, the son of Alice Grosjean, Bea's childhood friend, went backstage and introduced himself to Bea. They subsequently met many times after that. Grosjean's son, John Springer, went on to become a highly respected press agent in Hollywood and New York. It was Springer who escorted Bea during one of her final public appearances thirty-seven years later.

After her radio stint ended, Bea went again to the Riviera and enjoyed a holiday with Pat Dolin and Bellita, the skating star, who was with Pat. Bobbie joined them and he and Bea were able to have a short visit during which she promised him a trip to New York at

Christmas. However, after she did a very successful appearance at London's Café de Paris beginning on July 7, she changed her mind and took him back with her in August for a few weeks before he returned to school. Bobbie met Eddie Dowling for the first time and was able to renew his acquaintance with the Brice children before returning to his grandmother.

SEVEN

Eddie Dowling, now officially Bea's manager, had arranged her contract with the Shuberts for a new show called *The Show Is On*, in which she would be starred opposite Bert Lahr. Meanwhile, she and Eddie were seen everywhere together, the Stork Club, Toots Shor's, Tony's, Leon and Eddie's on Fifty-second Street, and the famed 21 Club. Most of the places were famous holdovers from Prohibition days and had now gone legit. Bea enjoyed them mainly because the Broadway crowd, actors, columnists, and audiences, frequented them. Sardi's, which opened on West Forty-fourth Street in 1927, in time became her favorite restaurant. Bea claimed it was the only place in New York where she could obtain roast beef sliced paper thin, as they did it in England.

Vincente Minnelli was in charge of *The Show Is On*, in which Bea and Bert Lahr were referred to by one reviewer as "two of the hardest working, as well as among the most satisfying, performers on the musical comedy stage." Minnelli gathered music from the most popular composers of the day, Rodgers and Hart, "Rhythm"; Arlen and Harburg, "Song of the Woodman," which would be forever associated with Lahr; the Gershwins, George and Ira, "By Strauss"; Fetter and Duke, "Now" and "Casanova"; Adams and Carmichael, "Little Old Lady." There were sketches by Moss Hart and David

Freedman. Reginald Gardiner appeared once again with Bea and Paul Haakon, and Mitzi Mayfair supplied the dancing. For this production Minnelli obtained the services of young Gordon Jenkins as musical director. Bea's material was top drawer. In one sketch she appeared as a latecomer to a production of *Hamlet* in which Gardiner, as John Gielgud, is reduced to a psychotic mess. She floated out over the audience on a crescent moon dispensing her garters to the spectators, and appearing as a French actress she attended the reading of a new play. When the reading was finished and the actress was questioned as to what she thought of it she answered simply, "I didn't understand a goddamned word." As Josephine Waters she did a take-off on Josephine Baker, sang "Rhythm" with a large corsage bobbing on her chest, and played a burlesque queen stripping for a living. Bert chopped down a tree with wood chips hitting him in the face from every direction and fought with the IRS over a one-hundred-dollar rebate.

A few days before Bea left New York for Boston, she was profoundly moved by the voice of King Edward VIII on her radio. "Now at long last," began the monarch in one of the most famous radio addresses of the era. Her friend, the Prince of Wales, now King of England, was abdicating in favor of Wallis Warfield Simpson. At the time, Bea took it as a great personal loss, but years later, in retrospect, she felt it had all been for the best. When Hitler attempted to destroy England, Bea firmly believed the presence of King George VI, Queen Elizabeth, and the young princesses was an extraordinary and heartening moral support for the nation. She and the Duke remained friends but she found it difficult to warm up to the Duchess because of an incident that occurred in the Waldorf Astoria. Bea, on her way to a party, turned into the foyer of a suite where she encountered the Windsors in the midst of an argument. "If you want to go, then go! Here's the key," the Duchess was iterating and she threw what was obviously their room key on the floor. Bea stepped back quickly as the Duchess stormed back to the party and the Duke leaned over and retrieved the key. They did not see Bea and she remained out of sight as the Duke walked sadly down the hall to the elevator.

Bea drove herself to Boston for the tryout of *The Show Is On* and was arrested on the Boston Post Road for racing at eighty miles an hour with a Massachusetts driver. Both drivers put up twenty-five-dollar bonds which were forfeited when neither one showed up for trial. According to the gossip columns, Boston was supposed to have been shocked by the show's dialogue, mainly Bert's, but the Boston papers denied this. After postponing twice in that city for technical reasons, the show was well received. It opened in New York at the Winter Garden on Christmas Day and ran for 237 performances.

"Neither Miss Lillie nor Mr. Lahr has been funnier," "One of the great women of the theatre," "A super comedienne," were among the tributes printed the day after.

Fanny Brice went on tour with her 1936 edition of the *Ziegfeld Follies* and Bea replaced her on her *Revue de Paree* radio series. Because of the time element involved, Bea found a system which enabled her to arrive at the theatre in time for *The Show Is On*. She dashed into a special Radio City elevated train at 8:30 that reached Fiftieth Street and Sixth Avenue in time for her to catch a taxi and a green light to Seventh Avenue and Fiftieth Street, whereupon she did a quick change into a costume and went on stage at the Winter Garden.

In January of 1937 there was a terrible flood in the Mississippi Basin. A huge benefit was arranged by Leonard Sillman, the first-ever rehearsed benefit performance, and Bea, joined by Bert Lahr, Reginald Gardiner, Noël Coward, Gertie Lawrence, and a hundred others, appeared. It was a gala performance before six thousand people at Radio City Music Hall and raised eighty thousand dollars for the flood victims. Bea then signed for three pictures at Paramount and sailed for London after telling reporters, "I'll know whether I shall be in the last two pictures after the producers see my first picture." The remaining two were never filmed due to the war.

The first picture was *Dr. Rhythm* with Bing Crosby. Bea returned to the United States on the *Queen Mary* and during the trip was supposed to have asked, "When does this place get to New York?" In New York Bea managed to see *Pins and Needles*, the Garment Industry revue. She went backstage afterwards and knocked on the men's dressing room door, shouting, "Close your eyes, I'm coming out!" An odd experience awaited her when she saw *Hooray for What*, the Ed Wynn show. Mr. Wynn substituted Bea's name for Mae West's in some blue-tinted comedy. Bea did not react either way to it but suddenly Mr. Wynn, later on in the performance, walked to the floodlights and publicly apologized to Bea.

During her New York visit, she gave a party in order to see all of her friends at one time. Donald Ogden Stewart, George Schlee, Elsa Maxwell, Grace Moore, Condé Nast, Helen Hayes, Reggie Gardiner, Lillian Gish, Hope Williams, Marc Connelly, Charlie MacArthur, Gladys Swarthout, and George Abbott kept the place jumping throughout the night.

In Hollywood, Fanny Brice insisted that Bea stay with her, an uneasy situation for Bea in that she was forced to share a room with Fanny's daughter. Bea felt she was intruding upon Frances's privacy and worried about coming in late and disturbing her but Fanny would not take no for an answer. Fanny had the fridges stocked and Bea was able to raid them at all hours of the night, and, since Fanny seldom left her bed, they did not get in each other's way. When Fanny inquired if she didn't find filming much easier than working on the stage Bea responded, "Good heavens, no, it's twice as hard. In the first place I miss the audience. When you are doing a scene you don't know if you're flopping or not or if the gag you are doing is any good in the first place." Bea hated getting up at six. "I've been used to rising about eleven, like any self-respecting person. At two in the afternoon, I think it's dinner time." In Bea's case that was certainly true. Like Winston Churchill, Bea was a "belly-time" eater. She ate when she was hungry, not when the clock told her it was the hour. Consequently, it was not always easy to stroll into a major restaurant at four or four-thirty in the afternoon and ask for dinner. Sardi's never failed to serve whatever she wanted whenever she ordered it, which is another reason she loyally frequented the place.

The living arrangements at Fanny's were working as well as could be expected until the night in November Bea appeared on radio with Al Jolson and Martha Raye. Bea arrived home and asked Fanny's opinion of the program. Fanny told her that frankly she felt Bea had been too "La dee dah" grand, too Lady Peel, and not very funny. Bea took the criticism in good grace by exiting the room in a cloud of invective, locking herself in the bedroom for the next few days, and refusing to speak to anyone in the house. Fanny left orders for Bea's food to be left outside the door. Finally, when the snit wore off, she and Fanny were friends once more.

One of Bea's great memories of that visit was a party given by Cobina Wright. Cobina decided to host an elegant affair strictly for her Hollywood society friends and to omit the show business crowd. Because of her title Bea was invited and arrived dressed formally and on her best behavior. Bea thought the party was boring, as did most of the other guests. Everyone sat about the rooms making small talk and trying their best not to yawn. Halfway through the endless evening, the butler admitted Polly Moran, the comedienne, who bustled into the room brimming with apologies for her lateness and informing Cobina that obviously her invitation had been lost in the mail. Wright struggled to keep her temper and politely introduced Polly to her guests. Polly was served a drink and the party quickly sank back into its former torpor. A few minutes later the butler interrupted Moran to ask if she wished another drink. "Sure," said Polly, handing the man her glass without looking around, "I'll have another glass of this piss!" There was a huge laugh, the radio was suddenly playing music, guests began to dance, and, before she knew it, Cobina had a highly successful party on her hands.

Bea made the opening of the new Le Ruban Bleu in December with Len Hanna and then returned to England. Charles Cochran contacted her and asked her to appear in his forthcoming *Happy Returns* opening in May. Then she was informed by Harrow that her son was in deep trouble and a candidate for immediate expulsion. It seems Bobbie and a friend came into possession of a pornographic movie and a projector. In the privacy of one of their rooms they invited a few chums to view the exhibition. For want of a screen, somebody unwisely selected a window shade, which was lowered and utilized for the showing. Two or three Masters, out for an evening's stroll, were treated to a rip-roaring sex pageant plainly visible through the shade. Bea could not believe her ears. She was furious with Bobbie for not realizing the film would be seen through the blind and after she stopped laughing, she convinced the school that Bobbie meant no harm and should remain.

A second family crisis arose when Muriel suddenly married Napper Dean Paul of the rather odd Paul family. His mother, Lady Dean Paul, was thought by her son to have had three personalities, and Brenda Dean Paul, his sister, after a horrendous bout with drugs, finally died of an overdose. It was again an impetuous move on Muriel's part brought on by her increasing loneliness and heavy drinking since Arthur's demise. They were together for only a few months but never divorced. When he inherited a title sometime later Muriel was able to jokingly comment that she was now "a Lady in her own wrong!"

Cochran planned on using material from *At Home Abroad* and *The Show Is On* and contracted Eddie Dowling to stage the show. The popular Crazy Gang team of Bud Flanagan and Chesney Allen were signed opposite Bea. Dancers Phyllis Stanley and Patricia Burke as well as Constance Carpenter appeared in the principal line-up. "Mr. Cochran's Young Ladies," Cocky's answer to the Ziegfeld Girls, were now an integral part of his revues and eighteen of them joined in the festivities on stage. Bea, once again, sang "Rhythm" and "Paris" and acted in the sketches she did in New York; in fact whatever was not from the American revues could be traced back to former Cochran shows. Even with Bea tossing her garters from the moon and destroying Hamlet, the show was not a roaring success. Bea did manage to find an endearing friend in her dresser, Daisy Flanagan. "Daize" would remain with Bea for some time and become an important part of her life.

Cyril Ritchard was appearing at the same time in a show called *Nine Sharp*.

"Bea used to come quite a lot because she was mad about a young man called Michael Anthony. She came practically every matinee and of course it made our day because we adored her," said Ritchard. "One afternoon a lovely girl about nineteen knocked at my door and said, 'I had to come 'round because I enjoyed the show so much. I'm Maude Fain's daughter.' And she was a darling. Maude Fain had married a man in the navy who had adopted her. Bea's reaction was, 'She's got to meet Bobbie!' I said, 'Well, you work *that* out, dear, I'm not going to do that for you!' It was that strange quirky mind of hers."

New York producer John C. Wilson was to produce an American

version of Coward's 1932 London success, *Words and Music*, and signed Bea to star. The show was to be renamed *Set to Music* and rehearsals were scheduled for November. Bea once again returned to the Café de Paris in September and was a tremendous success. Later in the month she had been booked into the Embassy Club. As it turned out her last week at the Café de Paris overlapped the Embassy and Bea was bumping into herself as she sped from one club to another each night. One night Alured Weigall went to see Bea at the Embassy Club.

"After the show, everybody was congregated around the bar at one end. Bea went and sat at the other end saying absolutely nothing and not moving. Gradually, one, twos, threes came over, like some sort of magnetism, the entire room was around her. I've never seen a woman with more poise."

MGM approached Bea about an appearance in their forthcoming *The Great Ziegfeld* but the timing was wrong and she turned it down. She was given material in *Set to Music* which would become part of the Lillie legend. Noël wrote "Weary of It All" and "I've Been to a Marvelous Party" for her, and "Mad About the Boy," which had been done earlier, became associated with her especially after she recorded it. There was a plaintive little number in which Bea represented a pawnbroker's daughter about to be presented at Buckingham Palace. Seated in a luxury automobile with her escort and beautifully gowned, three white feathers in her hair, she sang, "Today it is three white feathers, yesterday it was three brass balls!" In the cast were Anthony Pelissier, Fay Compton's son who had been ring bearer at Bea's wedding, and replacing Nora Howard was Gladys Henson, formerly Gladys Gunn, who had married actor Leslie Henson and was Bea's close and intimate friend.

Nora Howard was a cockney-type comedy actress who worked along the same lines as Gladys. Nora and Bea had been friends since Noël Coward introduced them. She later married pianist Stuart Ross in America. One night a few years later she and Ross invited some friends, including producer-director John Fearnley, to dinner. Nora was carefully supervising everything as they sipped cocktails when the phone rang. Gertie Lawrence and a friend, on their way to a dinner party, were calling from the corner, and wished to stop by and say hello. After they arrived and were having a drink, Fearnley noticed that Nora was checking her watch and casting an anxious eye toward the kitchen from time to time. She successfully concealed her relief when Gertie announced that they were on their way and dashed for the kitchen as soon as they departed. A moment later a somber-faced Nora appeared in the door, hands on her hips. She looked at her guests and sighed sadly, "Well, the potatoes is fucked!"

The show opened in Boston two days after Christmas.

"Noël had gone off someplace as he usually did," recalled Gladys Henson, "but he was coming back and everybody said, 'Noël's coming in tonight so let's do the show like a house on fire.' When the curtain came down the stage director came on stage and said, 'Everybody stay onstage, Mr. Coward wants to speak to you.' We were expecting him to say how wonderful we all were. He said, 'This is the most disgraceful thing I have ever witnessed! How dare you, every one of you, behave in this outrageous manner!' Beattie wasn't down on the stage, she would not be called onstage. So then he went in to Beattie and you should have heard the language. We were across the hall listening. Bea told him to get out and he did. 'Never to return, dear girl,' he said."

Later that night Len Hanna was giving a party for the company at the Ritz.

"We weren't going to miss it," said Gladys. "So we all got dressed up and went to the party. Beattie arrived later with a box of Kleenex, her face absolutely ravaged with tears. She sat on a stool outside the party room. Len Hanna went out and got her to come in. Then Noël came in and later they made it up."

For her first entrance Bea was discovered sitting on a big white horse. "I told her ages before that she ought to do a Brünnhilde," remembered Nancy Hamilton. "And she said, 'Write me one!' I answered, 'You almost don't have to have a Brünnhilde written. And then she was coming over in *Words and Music*, so I wrote my own story of the opera during which I turned into a Brünnhilde in *One for the Money*. And she opened two weeks before coming in on a horse as Brünnhilde. It was unbelievable. I'd been to Boston to see it because

I'd heard about it and I went back and said, 'You are a wretch!' and she replied, 'Well, you could have let me have your sketch.' "

The show opened at the Music Box Theatre January 19. Critics felt that both were at their best with *Set to Music*. "Although Miss Lillie has been synonymous with perfection in comedy for quite a long time, an old admirer might be forgiven for believing that she also is more incandescently witty now than before," wrote Brooks Atkinson.

During his curtain speech at the end of the show, Noël Coward referred to Bea as the greatest comedienne in the world. The compliment registered heavily with Bea, who felt that the man who uttered it was without equal.

"All their lives they'd been doing this," said Gladys, referring to the Boston incident. "Gertie and Noël always had those fights. Noël and Gertie were together in a show once and the same thing happened in the dressing room. A woman in the cast ran in and said, 'You must stop this, I love you both and you can't go on like this!' Noël turned to her and said, 'Well, you're fired for a start! How dare you interfere when I'm talking to my friend!' "

EIGHT

As audiences crowded into the Music Box events were changing the face of the world. A few months before, England and Germany had signed an anti-war pact. Germany was moving into Czechoslovakia as the Poles were preparing to fight for their lives. New Yorkers were not as optimistic as their English cousins and tension was building in the States. Bea told Lucie to bring Bobbie for a visit and they arrived on the *Aquitania* on March 30. Bobbie now sported a moustache, which gave Bea an opportunity to joke with the press. "Look at him, people will say he's eighty-one instead of eighteen!" When they had difficulty finding his luggage, it was discovered that Bobbie had checked it under L for Lillie. Bea introduced him simply as Bobbie Peel to friends. He informed Bea that he hoped to attend Harvard Law School as soon as his status with the military was established.

Another topic of discussion was the rumor that Bea and Eddie Dowling were married or at least thinking of it. Bea denied it quickly, and when it was hinted that perhaps the reason they were not was her title, that Bea would never relinquish it, she instantly retorted, "No title could ever mean so much to me if I wanted to marry." Bea had also never been sufficiently in love to test her statement.

"She always had extremely nice men that were mad about her," said Cyril Ritchard. Whenever Bea needed somebody there, somebody was always there. She could always depend upon her friends.

One night at a party, she and Nancy Hamilton were talking about material and stories that could be converted into musicals. Bea went on at great length about a book called *Mary Poppins* which she thought would make a stage show. Without saying a word to Bea, Nancy wrote to the author. She explained that Beatrice Lillie had introduced her to the book and she felt it would make a wonderful musical. Nancy asked for the rights for one year to work on the idea.

"This was in 1939," recalled Nancy. "Bud Lewis, who had worked with me on *One for the Money* as my composer, and I did a musical version of *Mary Poppins* for Beatrice Lillie."

In 1940, author Pamela Travers and her son arrived in the United States. By that time Katharine Cornell and Guthrie McClintic were interested in producing it. It would have been Cornell's first venture into producing.

"Pamela Travers was thrilled with it. At that time the war was on and Bea couldn't come over," said Hamilton. But letters and cables were exchanged. I'll never forget one cable I got from her that said simply, 'What do you mean goes off on the end of a balloon!' I think for a while she thought she was going to come over in the middle of the war. Pamela Travers then went back to England. Meanwhile, we were being paid advance royalties but it was perfectly obvious we couldn't do it until the end of the war."

The World's Fair opened at the end of April and Bobbie, Lucie, and Daisy, who had come to America with Bea, were taken to see the exhibits from around the world with the exception of one from Germany. The young ladies passing out leaflets and samples were reminders of Bea's days with the Canadian National Expositions. "I think some of the same girls were still around," joked Bea. The war was temporarily forgotten when the King of England arrived in Washington with Queen Elizabeth for a state visit. They went to Hyde Park with the Roosevelts and ate hot dogs and drank beer. Their visit made Bea homesick, and as soon as the show closed she followed Bobbie and Lucie back to England. She was booked into the Café de Paris once again for twelve weeks beginning in July.

Dowling arrived to discuss a new show in which she would play opposite Charles Butterworth but Bea would not budge until she was sure of what was in store for her son in the event war was declared. She rented a country place on the estate of Lord Jersey and bought Bobbie his first sports car, an MG. Her one and only ride with him began in Montreux, Switzerland, and ended, after an eighty-mile-an-hour ride, in Cannes. The journey left her shaken and she traveled by taxi from then on and let Bobbie drive his friends about.

When the Nazis invaded Poland, England declared war on September 3. Bobbie immediately rushed to sign up but was told by an enlistment officer to go back to school. The country waited for the next move during the period known as the Phony War. A moratorium was called on all debts owed, and liens against anyone were put aside for the time being. Women and children were moved to those homes with extra room in the country and others left for Canada, Australia, and the United States. There were also those who were determined that the Germans were not going to alter their lifestyle and continued to run their businesses as usual. One of those was Sir Reeves-Smith, who owned Claridge's. He gave orders that the hotel's shops were to go on as if nothing was happening. In some cases he suspended rent payments until after the war. The shop of Jane Ross, mistress of haute couture, remained opened for regulars, which included Bea.

At the Savoy Hotel, a basement banquet room was converted into an air-raid shelter. There were changing rooms for ladies and gentlemen and almost everyone carried "siren suits" in small bags, clothes in which to change the following morning if they were confined through the night. The bags also contained toothbrushes and shaving equipment for those heading straight for the office.

Cobina Wright and her daughter passed through London on the way to the States and visited Bea and Bobbie in the country place. Young Cobina's escort was Philip of Greece, the future Duke of Edinburgh, who had been attending school in Scotland. The Wrights then joined hundreds of Americans on their way home. The Phony War dragged on so long that those who had moved away began moving back into the cities, imagining that perhaps nothing was going to happen at all or if war came it would not last very long.

Bea entertained the navy for two weeks at Scapa Flow, appearing in two and three shows a day on battleships. She was one of the first to volunteer her services. In London the Lord Mayor had ordered all theatres closed when war was declared, so consequently many actors were out of work and, as in Bea's case, bored. During the lull, Hugh "Binkie" Beaumont, the producer, decided to throw together a revue utilizing songs and sketches by Coward, Novello, and Arthur Macrea, sung and acted by the best available and willing talent in London. He approached Harold French and asked him to direct the production, which he planned to open at the Embassy Theatre. Bea agreed quickly and was joined by Fred Emney, Hugh French, Bobby Howes, and Gladys Henson.

Bea decided to do her spy sketch from *Set to Music*, four or five chorus girls were hired, and rehearsals began at a leisurely pace until Beaumont suddenly decided to open the show in Brighton first and then at the Queen's Theatre in London. *All Clear*, as the show was to be known, hired more chorus girls and everyone worked night and day to pull the piece together and meet Beaumont's new deadline. French, in a race against time, begged Bea to stage a Noël Coward finale in which she had appeared. Bea, Bobby Howes, Fred Emney, and those concerned met at the Globe Theatre where they rehearsed while French lighted the show at the Queen's Theatre. When Coward phoned and asked to watch a rehearsal, French agreed.

"I said, 'Yes, fine.' We got to the end of the first half and he thought we were doing very well. Then we arrived at the production number, which was entirely in the hands of Bea. I went and sat in the dress circle and Noël remained in the orchestra. Suddenly, this thing started. Bobby Howes did not know one line, Bea was sort of humming through it, and then on came Fred Emney, meaning to be funny, in a toga and suspenders, and a pipe. I thought, 'How extraordinary, this is supposed to be rather gracious and grand!' "

There was a roar from the orchestra and Coward charged up to the dress circle. A nasty row ensued in which French was accused of a gross lack of taste. "I forbid it, I forbid it," shouted Coward. "You'll never do another thing of mine!" French, incensed himself by that time, told Noël to run off and join the navy if he didn't like it, but never once did he let on that Bea had directed the sketch. When word reached her, she offered to explain to Coward what had happened but French would not hear of it.

"Bea was the first to admit she had made a mess out of the thing," said Harold French. "She would have gone to Noël but it really wasn't necessary, we were old friends and it was forgotten. She was marvelous. She worked hard because she knew we were up against it. She went on working because those were the sorts of things that happened in those days." The show did good business during November and December.

The hard work was a device to keep the war apart from her life also. John Gielgud said later that Bea had an almost childlike attitude toward it all, as if the war had nothing to do with her. Obviously this was related to her fears for Bobbie and she did not want to think about it. The deadly truth was difficult to dismiss after the horror of Dunkirk in May and the German invasion of France in June.

Bea followed *All Clear* with *Tonight at 8:30* in which she appeared with Vic Oliver. Proceeds went to the Actors' Orphanage of which Noël Coward had recently become president. Bea and John Gielgud toured the show for some time entertaining the armed forces.

Hitler began shifting his attention toward the English Channel and the air raids over England began in August. Bobbie decided upon the navy and went to Officer's Training School and now the war arrived on Bea's doorstep. Bea increased Bobbie's pocket money to twenty pounds a week and encouraged his visits to London whenever he was given leave. Somehow, she believed that by keeping him close by he would be safe.

"She spoiled him so terribly," remarked Gladys Henson. "He had his car and he was never there for the lectures so they made him an ordinary seaman."

On one visit he informed her that he had fallen in love with a young lady and wished to become engaged to her. Bea warned him that wartime was hardly the right moment to plan an engagement or a marriage and persuaded him to wait. Bea had cancelled an appointment at the Café de Paris that evening in order to talk with her son. While they discussed his future, the Café was demolished by a direct hit, and rescuers later found charred bodies still seated on stools at the bar.

Bea continued to tour bases in the provinces with John Gielgud. They appeared in towns where live theatre had never been seen and performed on makeshift stages. At some performances, Gielgud recited Shakespeare and Bea sang some of her most successful numbers. He convinced Bea to color some of her material a slight shade of blue and the men loved it. On one occasion they were on the bill with an American jazz band. The band was scheduled to open the show but was delayed en route. Bea and Sir John went on first. Gielgud remembered the troops being so eager to hear the jazz group that nothing he or Bea said received the slightest bit of attention. Bea commandeered an ENSA (Entertainment National Service Association—similar to the American USO) bus and took Gielgud to see her husband's grave after which ENSA tried to sue her for the price of gasoline. They relented, however, in light of her willing response to their call for entertainment. Muriel and Lucie accompanied them on one trip and when the orchestra again failed to show up, they prevailed upon Muriel to play for the crowd. Lucie took over and had the lights rearranged and the piano placed in the most advantageous location before she would allow Muriel to go on. Seated finally at the piano, Muriel announced, "I will now play Ravel's *Concerto for the Left Hand* while smoking a cigarette with my right!" As John Gielgud stared in amazement, she did just that and stopped the show in its tracks.

Bea's rapport with her military audiences was phenomenal. She appeared in Aldershot in February of 1940. Gunner John Ellis remembered, "I was a twenty-year-old Canadian soldier who had just missed my very first Christmas at home with my family. We soldiers were all rather lonely and in February 1940, with Dunkirk still three months away, on a Sunday afternoon I attended the Garrison Theatre with several of my comrades and saw in person the great Beatrice Lillie. The theatre was crowded with British and Canadian troops and that lovely lady, not looking much older than ourselves, sang encore after encore. It was as if she sensed our loneliness and she received ovation after ovation. We wouldn't let her go and she gave us number after number. She loved us as much as we loved her. I know I speak for every soldier in that large theatre when I say she cheered our hearts for days, even weeks afterwards.

It has been my good fortune to have attended operas in Naples, Seville, London, Warsaw, the Bolshoi in Moscow and Leningrad, but that performance of Miss Lillie's stands out as the best. It was an experience which will live in my memory always."

Later, when Bea was confined to bed with a cold, Bobbie arrived to inform her that he was off to war. Dorothy Dickson was visiting Bea at the time and witnessed the farewell. Then Dorothy walked him to the door. "The first time I ever saw him as a child he was wearing a sailor suit and the last time I ever saw him he was in a sailor suit."

Lucie received a letter from Bobbie, mailed from HMS *Sultan*. Most of his letters were addressed to Mumsie and this one was dated January 2, 1942.

". . . Nothing of great importance has happened on board so far. Some of the lads brought a piano out onto the upper deck and we all had a sing-along one evening and the other day we made up a tug-of-war game and I was the anchorman. We took on the officers and beat them, too! It was great fun. These last few days I have been sleeping on the upper deck as it has been so warm, so marvelous for January.

"Darling, do write to me immediately and tell me how much of this the censor cut out and I will know next time what to write about. When I get some more news, I will write to you, but please keep onto Mother about you know what.

"Well, my dearest, may God keep you safely in his tender loving care and please know the Truth."

Because he mentioned warm weather, Lucie and Bea surmised he was in the tropics and far from the war. "You know what" was the pocket money Bea willingly sent, and "please know the Truth" was in reference to Lucie's interest in Christian Science.

Charles Cochran signed Bea to appear in a new revue called *Big Top*. Cochran paid for the show in part with royalties from his third book, an autobiography, but the show was doomed to failure. Cyril Ritchard and his wife, Madge Elliott, Patricia Burke, and Charles Hickman were among the players and Elsie April probably never forgot the production because she gave up a role in Noël Coward's classic film *In Which We Serve* to do *Big Top*. Rex Whistler, a very promising young scenic designer, painted his last backdrop for *Big Top* before he lost his life in the war a few months later. The show opened at the Royal Court Theatre in Liverpool on March 18 and then moved on to Manchester. Ritchard felt it was not a very happy company and many were under the impression that Cochran's main interest was in building Patricia Burke into a star.

Although satire was not Cochran's forte, Bea was given some excellent material, much of it written by Herbert Farjeon. As Madam Recamier tossing and turning uncomfortably on the couch, she finally settled down into the classic pose. From a window, she joyfully extolled the virtues of bird song while the shutters kept banging shut in her face. She ended the number by confessing she did not know one damn bird song from another. Her big hit, which became a standard of hers, was "Wind 'Round My Heart" (then called "The Lady in Gray") as she, suffering in the throes of a broken heart, contemplated throwing herself from the London Bridge. Bea's dress for "Bird Song" was designed by a man who would play an important part in her life later on. In Manchester Bea received flowers from a young serviceman on leave.

"She had never met him before," said Ritchard. "He came to the show because he was crazy about her. The company never knew his name; we called him "Brown Eyes.""

After the second performance in Manchester, Bea and some cast members met in her suite at the Midland Hotel for some food and relaxation. They were all well into a word game when the phone rang. Bea answered a call from Lucie. She read a telegram that would change Bea's life forever.

"Able seaman Robert Peel . . . missing in action in Ceylon." Bea heard a jumble of words as Lucie quoted from the telegram she held in her hand.

Across the world, in the harbor at Colombo, Sri Lanka (then Ceylon), the Japanese had bombed a ship at anchor. Bobbie was aboard when they scored a direct hit and he was never seen again.

"She didn't stay off for one performance," said Ritchard. "But the cold steel in her eyes was absolutely terrifying. Bobbie had only just got to Colombo that day and got on board when the Japs arrived and that was the end of that. When the news of Bobbie came, Brown

Eyes stayed through the day so she'd be all right to do the show. Some of us felt he was sent by God during that terrible time. I don't think she ever saw him again after that."

There have been countless versions of Bea's stalwart behavior, but the truth is she was devastated and never for the rest of her life recovered from the loss of her son.

"The day Bobbie died Bea began her own death," said a close friend. For the first time in her life, Bea was forced to shoulder a crisis alone. The burden of grief could not be relegated to another, as most of Bea's problems up until then had been. For the remaining performances in Manchester she kept to herself most of the day with little to eat or drink. Her dresser Daisy was in attendance constantly answering phone calls and fielding questions from reporters. Cochran offered to close the show but Bea would not hear of it. According to legend a note was pinned on the call board advising her fellow actors that Bea was aware of how they felt but Bea preferred to "just get on with it." Ritchard had no recollection of any such note. If there was one, chances are Daisy wrote it to protect Bea.

One thing was certain, "Wind 'Round My Heart" was no longer amusing to the cast, since Bea, at the end of the number, was carried off like a corpse. The show finally opened in London where it ran for just under one hundred forty performances and was Cochran's last revue.

Bea's friends from all over the world rallied around with phone calls and letters of hope or condolence. Anxious mothers of servicemen wrote to her for encouragement, many offering their moral support. Her admirers seemed to feel she had some unique panacea for dealing with the dreadful loss she now shared with numerous other families. Her public show of strength did help many others in the same situation.

"She did a lot for people by the way she took it," recalled American actress Iva Withers. "I was in England in 1942 when it happened. I had lost a brother in the Royal Navy and then my fiancé was killed. When I saw the way she was holding up, it gave me courage as well."

When a second telegram from the Admiralty informed her bluntly that Bobbie was presumed dead she was overwhelmed with grief.

"She wouldn't for years believe he was dead," said Gladys Henson. "Some of her friends, like me, tried to keep her in touch with the outside world saying, 'Darling, you've got to face it, he's dead. You must remember he's not going to come down the chimney one night.' She got quite cross with that, she wouldn't have it." Lucie did little to help matters by reminding Bea, when her mood did lighten, that she was in mourning. "Do you really think you should be seen at parties with Bobbie gone for such a short time?" or "Don't you feel that is the wrong dress for someone in mourning?" were her catchphrases.

Through friends of Lucie and Muriel she sought aid from psychics and mediums by attending séances, hoping for some encouraging sign. On one occasion, a psychic referred over and over again to a "platter": "Your son sent you a platter of some kind." Bea left in a rage, tearfully grumbling that this could have nothing to do with her son. But months later a package arrived from South America. In it was a platter Bobbie had sent when his ship anchored there.

Bea became obsessed with the idea that someone, somewhere, must have news of Bobbie. She put personal ads in the newspapers imploring anyone with information about him to contact her. Whenever she entertained troops in hospitals or camps, she searched for his face everywhere thinking he might be a victim of amnesia. She let it be known that cadets who had trained with him were welcome in her home and friends who visited her apartment were never surprised to see several navy personnel mixing with the guests.

In retrospect, Bea's closest friends felt she was haunted by the memory of the long separations during Bobbie's lifetime. The excitement and the drive that had put her on top had worked against her in the end. Her personal hurt, together with guilt, stemmed from that. The party that had gone on for twenty years was now over.

"She didn't pay any attention to him when he was a little kid," said Odette Myrtil. "Her mother took care of the child. And then, when he died, she became a fiend about him."

"Bea was such a fool. She allowed her mother to bring him up so she didn't have the joy of his growing up," remembered Phyllis Monkman. "It was only when he became thirteen or fourteen and became so attractive that she didn't want him out of her sight. When he was a little boy, she wasn't very interested. She wasn't in love with his father and he eventually went to school and she only saw him occasionally. Lucie latched on to him. She knew when she got Bobbie she was all right as far as Bea was concerned for money."

Perhaps Bea realized the truth of what Phyllis and Odette said. One thing was certain, she found it most difficult to cope with the situation. Bobbie's sea chest, containing cuff links she had presented to him, arrived home packed with his gear a year later but Bea continued to hold out hope for his return. She tried to escape from the proximity of the war by cabling New York that she was ready to work there once more. However, the Home Office notified her that a voyage abroad would be very dangerous and refused her a visa.

The United States was now in the war and Eddie Dowling arrived in England, a major in the Special Services. Bea's apartment at 55 Park Lane became the meeting place for all of her friends.

"We all used to go 'round to Bea's when the bombing began," said Cyril Ritchard. Through Eddie, Bea became acquainted with Bob Goldstein of 20th Century-Fox, who was then in the armed services. John Gielgud arrived at Bea's one night and was surprised to discover Clark Gable shooting craps on the floor under her Modigliani. Gable was a guest of Goldstein's and Bea claimed Gable fell asleep on her couch, awakened later and attempted to seduce her. Bea insisted he was unsuccessful. By that time, the bombings were so systematic one could almost set one's watch by them and nearly everyone remained in bed when the sirens wailed. Bea was one of those who stayed where she was if at home. After spending one night in a crowded subway station, Bea's physician, Dr. Robert Freymann, and his wife made a pact never to leave their home again when the sirens blew. It was a blessing for Bea that he lived through it all since Dr. Freymann assuaged her ragged nerves with a sedative now and then to enable her to sleep through the night.

"During the war a bomb fell on the BBC. We heard it fall," said Ritchard. "There was a short pause and he went on with the news, just in a slightly higher key!"

Muriel was drinking heavily and Lucie was beginning to fail mentally so it was almost with relief that Bea accepted Binky Beaumont's offer to join ENSA.

"The main tour had Leslie Henson, Vivien Leigh, and Dickie Haydn with us," recalled Dorothy Dickson. "Dickie was the biggest success. The audience passed out laughing. Toward the end of the tour, we got out to Suez. When we arrived around nine o'clock, it was coal black. We were standing on a platform with thousands of troops out there in the dark. They couldn't see us and we couldn't see them! Only performers who could really belt out something could be heard and I'm afraid poor Bea flopped that night. It was the only time I ever saw her flop. It was a terrible situation all around because it was a night or two before the invasion of Sicily."

The show was called *Spring Party* and they did three a day many times for the Eighth Army from Gibraltar to Cairo. They performed for General Montgomery in Tripoli and for General Eisenhower in Algiers.

"In Tunis, at one of the shows," Bea said, "the flies were so terrible they gave me some netting around my bed. I waited until all the flies were in and then I got out of bed and had a good night's sleep!" In a room which she shared with Dorothy Dickson, she found a rat drinking from a leaking tap in the sink.

"There was always a joke about me getting into places where there were bedbugs or flies," laughed Dorothy, "but that king rat was a new one, even for me."

In Tunis Bea was downed by dysentery and confined to her bed, forcing her to miss a party given in honor of King George VI. Then His Majesty was laid low by the same malady. Later, during a garden party at Buckingham Palace, Bea was presented to His Majesty. She voiced her disappointment at missing the Tunis party and gave the reason for her absence. H.M. commiserated with her stating his problems with the same disease. The King excused himself and Bea was surrounded by her friends eager to know what she and the monarch talked about. "Diarrhea!" cooed Bea.

From barracks to battleships, Bea gave of her time. In hospitals, she studied the faces of the wounded around her on the chance that Bobbie might be among them. She asked questions hoping that someone who knew him was in the crowd. She was awarded the African Star by General de Gaulle. Passing through Gibraltar she waved at Noël Coward, who was traveling with another unit. Outwardly, Bea appeared much the same. She laughed and joked and never took her hurt onstage. At about this time she switched to Scotch because of the pressures of the war, she said.

In 1944 Bea went into a show written by Robert Morley called *Staff Dance* in which she played a character called Frieda Appleby. In the cast, which included Mr. Morley, was a fifteen-year-old actor named James Grant Tyler. Grant was an attractive, precocious, and intelligent boy whom Bea liked immediately. They became good friends and he filled a corner of her life left vacant by Bobbie. Bea paid him extra money out of her own pocket so that he could live at the same hotels as the other cast members. Grant sent a percentage of his pay to his parents every week and had little left over. Unfortunately, *Staff Dance* did not make it past the critics in Oxford.

"I'll always remember the night when the management came down to tell us they weren't going to bring the show in," said Morley years later. " 'Bea and Robert, you are the greatest artists in the world,' they announced to us. 'We must preserve you! You are national treasures but this one definitely will not be good for you in London. Of course, they'd cheer you to the echo but this one just isn't for you.' We went back to the hotel and discussed the turn of events over a drink or two, and decided the producers were absolutely correct. We were the greatest artists in the world!"

Bea had a war story which she loved to tell involving a bomb that landed in Trafalgar Square and buried itself deep into the earth without ever exploding. The area was immediately roped off and a demolitions expert sent for, a man who had been decorated for bravery and received the Victoria Cross. The man was lowered into the crater by a rope tied around his waist with orders to yank the rope if he wished to be brought up in a hurry. The onlookers remained silent as they watched the man disappear into the ground. Nobody breathed as time ticked by. Suddenly the man began jerking wildly on the rope. The crowd backed away as he was quickly brought to the surface.

"What happened?" an officer called. "Is it going off?"

"No," shrieked the terrified man, "there's a great big nasty rat down there!"

Bea was engaged to appear in the film version of Lonsdale's *On*

Approval, which she filmed in England with Clive Brook and Diana Wynyard. The film, not destined to greatness, is shown now and then at film festivals.

On August 24, Bea was busy recording a radio show called *Nightcap* at the Criterion Theatre in London. The show, recorded on huge slow-moving disks, was presented at a later date over the Allied Expeditionary Forces Network.

"One small little band of Canadian musicians scraped together for Canadian background," stated W. Ray Stephens, a member of the band. "Glenn Miller was on the U.S. side but Bea Lillie, being Canadian, chose our side. The theme was 'Holiday for Strings' played by the saxes, who used clarinets. After that we merely sat on our hands while her accompanist, a very nice chap named Cyril, played. Lady Peel kept clapping her hands and saying, 'Now, now, Cyril! Let's be alert!' Our favorite number was her 'Three Little Fishes.' Later, of course, they brought in the 'big' units from Canada and shipped us off to Italy although I didn't think we were that bad!" Bea's little band of Canadians consisted of a paratrooper, a heavy-artillery soldier, a tank driver, an MP, and a future colonel in the Australian army.

"So Lady Peel was well protected by her musicians although not from the bombs," said former Infantry Sergeant Stephens. The Criterion Theatre was being utilized after the Fortune Theatre, where the programs were usually recorded, was blown up by a buzz bomb.

Eddie Dowling cabled with news for Bea. Billy Rose had optioned a Cole Porter revue and was planning an elaborate production starring Bea, Bert Lahr, Benny Goodman, Alicia Markova, and Anton Dolin. Nancy Hamilton, having agreed to forgo advance royalties for her version of *Mary Poppins*, was also awaiting Bea's decision regarding that show. Certain that the war was ending, Bea accepted the Rose offer.

Grant Tyler, with his parents' consent, was spending most of his time in London and living in Bea's apartment. She introduced him to Noël Coward, who immediately signed him for his new show, *Sigh No More,* for which Noël had written the book and the music and planned to direct. For reasons known only to the Master, he assigned the nickname Clam to Grant, a label he bore for the remainder of his life. On the night of costume parade for *Sigh No More*, the men were given tights to wear in one scene. Grant, who knew nothing of athletic supports or dance belts, appeared on stage with neither. As Cyril Ritchard, Madge Elliott, Joyce Grenfell, and the cast paraded in costume for Noël's approval, the proceedings were abruptly interrupted by his shrill "Stop!" Everyone came to a halt as Coward called out from his seat in the orchestra.

"Clam, just what do you think you are doing?"

"I don't understand, Mr. Coward," stammered Grant.

"Look at you! Your tights! You look as though you were wearing an entire Rockingham tea set down there!" Grant nearly fainted from shock and a ten-minute break followed that outburst.

Dwight Wiman, who was working with the entertainment forces in London, coaxed Bea into appearing with a unit of *Information Please* which he was dispatching to Germany. Clifton Fadiman and Franklin P. Adams, the New York regulars, and Reginald Gardiner went along as the panel. Bea was the celebrity guest with the group, which eventually appeared in Linz across the river from Ens where Hitler was born. A rumor started that Bea was involved with a certain Lieutenant Mills, an American, and that marriage plans could be in the picture. Bea denied this and stated that, in any case, the gentleman in question would have to obtain permission from the United States army before he could marry a foreigner. The rumor was untrue. When the ENSA tour ended, Bea received word from Eddie Dowling that he had remarried.

NINE

Bea arrived in New York on October 28, 1944. She was greeted by a bevy of press who were mainly interested in her opinion of Noël Coward's *Middle East Diary* in which he hinted that Brooklyn soldiers were lacking in courage. There was talk of having him banned from Brooklyn. Bea defended him saying that he had worked as hard as she during the war to entertain troops in hospitals, on ships, and on land. "I do hope it all gets straightened out," Bea said. "He has many friends in Brooklyn and has always adored America."

Pat Dolin was living in Bea's New York apartment. He offered to move but Bea would not have it. She was not ready to face Bobbie's belongings or the memories she associated with 25 East End Avenue. She informed the Rose office that she preferred the Waldorf-Astoria and Billy Rose arranged a suite for her and stocked it with beer. He then arranged a press conference at the hotel.

Somebody asked about the condition London was in after all the bombings and Bea answered, "It is like a movie set, all front and no back! We had a theatre shortage, the buzz bombs took care of that. The Lunts were there doing *There Shall Be No Night*. Finally, they either had to close up or play in blackface there was so much dirt sifting from under the stage from nearby explosions."

Bea went right into rehearsal with *Seven Lively Arts* and had only been reading over the sketches for a day or two when she asked Pat Dolin to return to the Waldorf with her. She and Pat were doing a scene together, a take-off on a popular psychological play called *Angel Street*, and Bea wanted to run over the lines with Dolin.

They began reading the script but Bea appeared to be distracted. Finally, she told Pat that she had a letter she wished him to read to her.

"I know it's about Bobbie so I want you to read it," she explained. Bea gave Pat a letter, obviously from the military, addressed to Lady Peel in care of ENSA at the Drury Lane Theatre in London. Pat quickly scanned the message and then asked Bea if she really wanted him to read it out loud. Bea insisted she could take it.

The letter read:

Dear Madam:

A week or so ago one of my present shipmates informed me that he had read an article in *The Daily Mirror* to the effect that you are seeking information re: your son, Robert Peel. I have no idea how old that paper may have been so, perhaps even before this, you may have had far more information than I can give you.

You will realize, of course, that I must be careful of what I write, especially so, as at present I am on foreign service, and this letter will have to travel some considerable distance to reach you. Perhaps at some time in the future, your profession may bring you to the same vicinity as myself. Should that be the case, I shall make a point of trying to see you.

Your son was a member of the same mess as myself, aboard a destroyer. He was not with us very long but he earned the respect of all of his mess mates mainly because of the fact that he tried to be one of us, and never emphasized the fact that he came from different surroundings than the remainder of us.

At 7:50 A.M. approximately, on the morning of April 5, 1942, we were attacked by dive bombers, and, after the attack that lasted for a few minutes, the ship was struck by one bomb. At this time Robert Peel was carrying ammunition to one of the guns. Mercifully, he must have died instantly, because he was within five yards of the explosion.

Bea rose quietly and went into her bedroom, closing the door. "I sat there without moving," said Dolin. "It was the most awful ten or fifteen minutes I ever spent in my life. I really didn't know if Bea was going to throw herself out the window. Bea returned and said, 'All right, Pat, all right. Let's get on with it. Give me a beer. I know the worst.' "

The letter had a profound effect on Bea, and she was hardly in the correct frame of mind to attempt a Broadway show, especially the lavish overblown extravaganza planned by Rose. She started out by hating the songs Cole Porter had written for her. She had brought with her from London one or two numbers she wished to try out, but Porter's contract stated that he was to be the sole composer except for a ballet sequence being contributed by Stravinsky. Porter was not about to budge. The one saving grace as far as Bea was concerned was her sketches by Moss Hart. Rose boasted that the show was to have no point of view, few important statements to make, and would be all gloss, an old-fashioned Ziegfeld-style revue. He even took to sending telegrams to his cast as the late showman had done. His audacity in spending huge amounts of money in the face of the havoc still raging throughout the world did not endear him to the theatrical community. He appeared as a great show-off instead of a showman.

When Rose interrupted rehearsal one day to correct Bea on line readings she told him to leave the stage or she would call Moss Hart and tell him she was not going to do the show. Bea claimed she was not told about an out-of-town tryout in Philadelphia and went reluctantly. She had some acceptable material, thanks to Hart, such as one in which she tried to buy a ticket to a ballet she mistakenly thought was called "S. Hurok." In order to describe it to the ticket taker she did her own version of the "Dying Swan" all the way down to the floor. Bea fought incessantly with Philip Loeb, the director, and dashed to the phone to call Hart the first moment she was upset. Loeb made the mistake of trying to direct Bea and not the sketches. He criticized pieces of business that Bea invented, which drove her to distraction. One day Bert Lahr walked into her dressing room and discovered her alone and in tears—an image he found difficult to forget. Bea loved her friends and relied a great deal on them, but, with Eddie married once more, she desperately needed a strong arm to lean upon. The experience was never a treasured memory and she renamed the show "Seven Deadly Hours" early in rehearsals.

The conflict between Cole Porter and Bea finally reached a point where Bea advised Rose that she would not appear on opening night if she was not allowed to sing one of the songs she brought over with her. It so happened that the song she hated most was Porter's favorite. When Bea sent word that she was too ill to perform opening night, Billy Rose sent his doctors to the Waldorf but Bea refused to see them. Time was running out and Rose approached Actors' Equity next. At five in the afternoon of opening day, Cole Porter and Bea Lillie were not giving in. Billy Rose reached Bea by phone and she again said no. She did open the door for the president of Equity, who relayed Bea's conditions to Rose. Bea agreed to appear if she could sing her song on opening night and Porter's the second night. Then he could judge by the applause which song would be left in. Rose called Porter, who agreed, and Bea arrived at the theatre a half hour before the show began. For some macabre motive, Billy Rose opened the show on December 7, an unfortunate decision considering the fact that men and women all over the world were still being slaughtered in the conflict. Mrs. Dorothy Hammerstein was credited with supervising the redecoration of the Ziegfeld Theatre, which was owned by Mr. Rose. Mrs. Hammerstein's daughter appeared in the production as one of Rose's "Ladies of Fashion." These ladies were personally chosen by Harry Conover, head of the modeling agency bearing his name. Salvador Dali contributed the murals on the walls of the lower lobby for an undisclosed amount.

When Bea made her initial entrance, she was accorded a hero's welcome by an audience consisting, in part, of Mr. and Mrs. James Farley, George Kaufman, Lucius Beebe, the Gilbert Millers, Libby Holman, Ward Morehouse, the Bennett Cerfs, Mr. and Mrs. William Rhinelander Stewart, and the Oscar Hammersteins. Champagne was served to first-nighters who had paid an unheard-of $24.00 per ticket.

In spite of Rose's ostentation and tasteless waste of money, the show was not successful, although the critics did favor Bea with good reviews —mainly because she was working with the best material in the production. The Playbill stated that in the second act there would be a song sung by Beatrice Lillie, but no title or composer was listed. Lahr struggled with sketches and solos unworthy of his matchless talents. One reviewer complained of being "overfed and underprivileged."

Seven Lively Arts managed to rack up 183 performances, and Bea began a friendship with George Hunter, one of the stage managers and one of the few Rose staff members she trusted. George escorted Bea to the Stage Door Canteen often, where she continued her war work and endeavored to find news of Bobbie. Later, George and his friend Al Jones introduced her to socialite producer James Gardiner, who became a good friend and escort for the next few years.

"On V-E Day several of us thought that Bea might be terribly upset because of Bobbie," said Nancy Hamilton. "We went over to her hotel, and she was. She was alone. She said, 'I guess the time has come for me to do *Mary Poppins*. I will do *Mary Poppins* if the right producer and director are chosen.' " Nancy contacted John Van Druten and asked if he would consider directing the show. Van Druten agreed to do it if Alfred de Liagre would produce it. De Liagre was definitely interested.

"Bea would say, 'Come over, come over,' and he would go over with a contract in his pocket and she'd be all dressed to go out and she would take him out," recalled Hamilton. "Every time he put the contract in front of her she'd change the subject. Finally, I was so embarrassed I said we'd just have to forget it. Vincent Donehue then became interested in it but one day he phoned to say CBS owned the television rights to *Mary Poppins* and that, furthermore, Miss Travers said she would never have anything to do with anything I thought I'd do about *Mary Poppins*. What a shame, it would have been marvelous for Bea." Once again Bea's life was shaped by her inability to make her own decisions and so she returned to England with nothing settled.

Lucie was becoming increasingly absent-minded and Alured Weigall was spending more time at Abercorn Place with her, especially during Bea's absences. Muriel, who had a flat at Hamilton Close, was still drinking heavily and demanding to know why she should not be allowed to live at Abercorn Place as well. Weigall was dividing his time between the two women. Muriel would either fall down or burn herself and was in and out of hospitals. Alured would often sleep over at Lucie's for her protection and many times she would awaken in the night, enter his room, and ask him who he was and why he was in her house. Once she gave him a small check for his kindness and the following day pleaded penury and asked him not to cash it. She took to wearing around her waist a large ring of keys which she mislaid constantly. Weigall kept Bea apprised of the situation and she sent money to both Lucie and Muriel through her solicitor and left the problem with Alured and the attorney.

Better Late was a revue in which Bea starred with Walter Crisham in 1946. Bea sang "Paree" from *At Home Abroad* and the waltz from *Tom Jones* in which she appeared in rolls of mink. There was a take-off of *Lady Windermere's Fan* or "Lady Fandermere's Wind" as Bea loved to call it. In the second half of the show, Bea sang nine songs of her choice with Norman Hackforth at the piano.

"Miss Lillie's art in *Better Late* is seen at its enchanting best," voiced a critic when the show opened at the Garrick Theatre in London on April 25.

Oliver Messel, the famous designer, asked Bea to pay a visit to his nephew at the hospital in Liverpool while the show played there. His nephew, Antony Armstrong-Jones, was recovering from a bout with polio and was in low spirits.

"Bea visited me nearly every day, even between shows on occasion," recalled Lord Snowdon. "She would sing songs and tell jokes to cheer me up."

Grant Tyler played a part in the show and Bea met Murray Matheson with whom she began a long friendship. A thirty-eight-year-old designer with whom Bea worked in *Big Top* was repeating a similar assignment as designer on *Better Late*. Rolf Gérard, a former medical student, was now directing his efforts toward the theatre and painting. Originally from Germany, Gérard emigrated to Switzerland and thence to England. The production, while not memorable, was important to Bea because of Gérard and her subsequent romance with him. As with all of her love affairs, Rolf was seldom out of her thoughts after it ended and they remained close friends and associates.

Nancy Hamilton arrived in England that winter with high hopes again for *Mary Poppins* only to be informed that the author intended to do her own dramatic version of the book, and Nancy lost the rights permanently. *Better Late* enjoyed a respectable run, after which Grant Tyler went into the British army for two years, during which time Bea, through her lawyer, arranged for a small monthly check to be sent to his parents.

Anthony Eden, Dorothy Dickson, Bea, Ivor Novello and his companion, Bobby Andrews, sailed for America on the *Queen Elizabeth* at the end of December. They then boarded a train for Hollywood, without Mr. Eden, and headed west.

Novello and Andrews were forced to leave the train in the middle of the night when Ivor's secretary suffered a heart attack but Bea and Dorothy remained on board and were met at nine in the morning by Gladys Cooper. During a conversation with Cooper, Bea discussed the possibility of purchasing a country home close to London where Lucie could live and be cared for by a housekeeper and where Bea might relax between shows. Gladys, who owned a lovely home at Henley-on-Thames, suggested Bea investigate that area when she returned to England.

Fanny Brice invited Bea and Dorothy to stay with her while they visited Hollywood and shortly after they arrived George Cukor started the round of parties which would be given in their honor.

"Fanny went to Cukor's party, otherwise she stayed in bed all the time. I think she was still doing *Baby Snooks*," recalled Dickson. "People came in to see her, people like Roger Davis. He was so funny, and Fanny loved him. He was the entertainer there, the cabaret in Fanny's house. I don't think I ever saw Bea as near to anybody else as she was to Fanny." Bea enjoyed the visit thoroughly, due mainly to the fact that she was not having to work at that time. Brice had her oversized frigidaires well stocked and everyone helped himself or was attended to by an excellent staff.

"Bea had nobody with her at that time," said Dorothy. "I know I didn't leave any trays around for her. She loved raiding Fanny's fridges and finding herself things to eat."

Bea and Dorothy also spent some days in Palm Springs with Clifton Webb and his mother before Bea returned to New York to appear on NBC radio for a few shows. In order to warm up the audience, the writer originated a character, a woman, who would laugh hysterically in all the wrong places. Bea would then request the lady to present herself on the stage and would ask her what she was laughing about, whereupon the poor woman would burst into hysterical laughter as she tried to explain how funny she thought Bea was. The young lady went on to become a well-known actress and television personality called Arlene Francis.

In April, Bea was aboard the *Queen Elizabeth* once more and headed for home. It was apparent that Lucie was in need of round-the-clock care. Bea, following Gladys Cooper's advice, looked for property in Henley-on-Thames and found a piece of riverfront property that was perfect. Three Queen Anne cottages had been joined together, giving the home a total of ten bedrooms, including servants' quarters, a number of baths, and a wonderful airy and spacious bedroom for Bea overlooking the river and the lawn. There was an old mill on the property and a boat house some distance from the main building. A small island was attached to the acreage by a wooden bridge.

John Brooks, Bea's solicitor, helped her find a suitable housekeeper and Lucie was moved there in late 1947. Miss Eileen Magowan became official housekeeper and she in turn hired laundresses and cooks and maids. Bea breathed a sigh of relief and accepted a new show in New York written and produced by Schwartz and Dietz. She arrived back in the States in early 1948 and went into rehearsal with Jack Haley as her co-star in a review called *Inside U.S.A.*, loosely based on John Gunther's bestseller of the same name. The cast toured the United States in this show with numbers extolling Rhode Island, Mardi Gras, Massachusetts, and Pittsburgh in which Bea, as a choir director, led the group in a song called "Come, Oh Come, to Pittsburgh!" Bea also appeared as a mermaid singing on a rock, an Indian selling souvenirs at a railroad stop, a theatre maid with a Ouija board, and a George Sand type charmer who inspired some great composers. Aiding and abetting Bea and Haley were dancers Valerie Bettis and Eric Victor as well as humorist

Herb Shriner. The show was a big hit and Bea soon forgot *Seven Deadly Hours*.

Most of Bea's good friends were home from the war, and Bea, once again in her apartment on East End Avenue, began having after-theatre parties. With the aid of Bob Goldstein, Bea was able to expedite Rolf Gérard's entry into the United States. Charlie and Helen MacArthur were living across the hall once more and had bought an apartment in the building for their daughter, Mary. Robert Lantz, another close friend of many years, was now married, and had a child, but Bea found it difficult to visit her friends with children. She confessed to Lantz that she made several attempts to visit but could not face a child at that time. Gérard, who was an accomplished artist, began to teach Bea to paint. Once she conquered her initial timidity, she plunged right in and was soon producing paintings of flowers, portraits of friends' children, landscapes, and cats and dogs. She called herself Beatrice Van Gone and liked to paint and exhibit her work under the grand piano where she felt the light was better. Eventually she donated paintings to charity, where they brought in respectable prices. Many went to friends. Gérard went on to become a well-known set designer, beginning with sets and costumes for Katharine Cornell's *That Lady* in 1949 and moving on to the Metropolitan Opera Company in New York.

"She was crazy about Rolf Gérard," said Thelma Carpenter, a featured player in the show, who became part of the after-theatre crowd at Bea's. "He had just come over. He knew Robbie Lantz and that group. I remember one day I was at Saks. There she was buying for him. She was crazy about him. She got him in at the Metropolitan Opera, it was through her. One day something happened, though, and that evening we were going across town in Bob Goldstein's car when Bea suddenly said, 'I'm just not going to have anything to do with those Germans, I'm finished with them.' "

Bea seldom discussed her feelings about the men she loved. She always maintained her affections for Bobby, Charlie MacArthur, Doc, Rolf, and Eddie Dowling over the years, long after the affairs were over. Bea searched all of her life for someone to lean upon, to make her decisions for her. The men she happened to meet and love were all headed for successful careers of their own. As much as they cared for Bea, they could not be there continually advising her and sharing her life's work, so the liaisons ended and her men went their own ways and married other women. Over the years, however, Charlie and the rest remained sympathetic and caring friends.

Bob Goldstein actually asked Bea to marry him, and she had a long discussion with Robert Lantz on her way home one night. She admired Goldstein and enjoyed being in his company but she, true to character, could not make any sort of decision as to what her answer would be. She asked Lantz what he thought. "Sounds like a good idea, Mrs. Goldstein," he replied. Bea stared at him for a moment. "That killed it!" she laughed, as she said good night and went into her building.

During the run of *Inside U.S.A.*, in May of 1948, Bea was awarded a citation by the National Conference of Christians and Jews "for her selfless devotion to bringing joy to the sick and lonely during the war years without regard to race, creed, national origin, or color." Later that same year at the first annual Military and Naval Ball of the Reserve Officers' Association, she received their first civilian award, a citation that read "Her remarkable devotion to the soldiers of the allies and inexhaustible cheerfulness under adverse conditions became a valuable contribution to the morale of the soldiers in several theatres of war."

Bea came down with a bad cold and moved into the Hampshire House where she would be close to the Century Theatre. When she evidenced no sign of improvement, Helen Hayes sent her physician to see her.

"She had a fever and was not well," remembered Dr. Prutting. "The maid opened the door and Bea saw me in the mirror and called to the maid, 'He's handsome, get me my hat!' Then she sprawled out as if she was on a chaise and purred, 'Dr. Prutting.' That was my greeting." The doctor then ordered Bea to bed for two weeks. That was *his* greeting. Prutting was Bea's physician for the next thirty-five years. He was responsible for Bea's friendship with Julia Fitzgerald, the registered nurse he assigned to her case. Fitzy became friend, major-domo, and confidante for many years. While Bea recovered, her standby went on for her at the theatre. The box office receipts dropped twenty-four thousand dollars during the period, which bolstered her morale no end. It proved to her that her absence from Broadway had not lessened her appeal.

Bea's escort at that time was mainly James Gardiner, and when Bea became too dependent upon him he gradually eased himself out of the situation. But Robert Lantz, Hilde Palmer (sister of Lilli) and her husband, Bob Goldstein, and Rolf Gérard were there during the long, difficult period following confirmation of Bobbie's death.

Inside U.S.A. moved to the Majestic Theatre and Bea agreed to go on the road with the show. Replacements were hired for those choosing to remain in New York. One of the new actors was Peter Turgeon, who doubled as a stage manager.

"She was the greatest star I ever worked with. The first night I ever met her socially was on a cold February night as I stood in the alley outside the theatre on Forty-fifth Street. There was a car waiting for her and she offered to drop me. As we drove along she suddenly said, 'I heard the sweetest little story today, a story you might enjoy. A man went to a dentist's office very late one night. The dentist let him in, popped him into the chair and put a bib around his neck. 'No,' said the man, 'it's my penis!' The dentist said, 'You've come to the wrong place, I'm a dentist.' 'No, I haven't,' said the man, 'there's a tooth in it!' "

Peter would shortly make a decision which altered the course of Bea's life once more.

"We got a new bunch of people into the chorus. One of the chorus people we took on was a singer named John Huck. I asked him if he wanted to earn an extra ten dollars a week by carrying Bea, dressed as a mermaid with a fish tail, to her place on stage and carrying her off to her dressing room after the song. Huck agreed. He was engaged to a girl he had just worked with and could use the money. He was hired to carry Bea on and off. Whatever went on in that short trip to and from that stage none of us will ever know."

In the meantime, Doc was back in Bea's life a changed man. He had witnessed the fire bombing of Toyko and the atomic blasts at the end of the war, and the horror of it all left him scarred emotionally. He spent most of his time with Bea and visited her on the road but was having deep personal problems. Eddie Dowling remained her manager but he was in love with somebody else. Just before the show went on the road, Bea discovered that Valerie Bettis painted, and when the show went on tour, she and Bettis painted together in Bea's hotel suites.

"Every night except the night before matinees," said Bettis, "Bea would have thousands of people, it wouldn't matter who, and Bea and I would be on the floor painting and that went on every night." Sometimes Jack Haley and his wife, Flo, would stop by especially when their son, Jack, Jr., was home from prep school. Bea became very fond of Jack, Jr., and nicknamed him Fig Newton.

"The evenings were not like parties, parties, parties," stated Bettis. "There were two things involved. One, when we did not have matinees or interviews, we were normally in a place where there was not that much to do. That meant that I slept and Bea certainly slept unless we had to get up. So our life on another level began after the performance and the fact that the painting was the prevalent thing, it was just a little different than 'Hello, darling. How are you, darling? blah blah blah blah, darling.' It was like an open house where everybody was doing their own thing."

"Since we were traveling from city to city, the stage manager had to give us 'cut offs' and that meant we had to stop or the paint wouldn't be dry enough to pack and move to the next location."

Valerie Bettis also added, "I have never worked with anyone who was more disciplined in working and working on something until it got right. The intensity and the necessity for perfection of that caliber of comedian is extraordinary. Bert Lahr comes to mind also. They never stopped working to make it better."

John Huck began seeing Bea home at nights and arriving with her at performance time. "As far as any of us was concerned there was no sex. Bea needed someone with her and John filled the bill. He danced great attendance on her."

"Good old 'Daize' [Bea's dresser] no longer existed so I suppose he started as a sort of servant," declared Dorothy Dickson.

When the show played Cincinnati, Huck wanted to try out for a new show in New York called *Miss Liberty* with a score by Irving Berlin. Bea called Mr. Berlin and personally recommended John. He obtained a leave of absence and went to New York, leaving Bea alone. Turgeon became her escort involuntarily and often took her driving during the day. Bea would ply him with questions about who was doing what to whom in the company and all the latest scandal.

"Darling, if I should die," she said to Peter one day, "before Gertrude Lawrence, I want you to be very sure in my obituary that they put my correct age, that I am four years younger than Gertrude. Gertrude will lie about it and say I am four years older just because she once was my understudy." In May Bea was saddened by the passing of her friend Neysa McMein.

One night, in Cleveland, her mink coat was stolen and she raised a few eyebrows when she declared that if John had been there it would not have been. "It's summertime and the living is rough," joked Doc, who was visiting at the time. Bea had been given the bridal suite in the hotel.

"There was a sign on the door that said 'Honeymoon Suite.' " recalled Turgeon. "We'd be up till two or three in the morning, not too sober, and all the drunks going by would knock on the door and ask how everything was going." Bea and Peter would wait inside the door and emit erotic noises, panting heavily and shouting obscenities for the benefit of eavesdroppers. Usually Bea would wear her theatre makeup home and remove it as her guests enjoyed food and drink in the living room.

"The suite had an electrical system that must have cost a fortune," added Turgeon. "All sorts of colored lights on dimmers, that kind of thing. There was an enormous divan and one night they played "All the Things You Are" on the sound system. Bea stood on the divan and did a complete striptease right down to the altogether to the song. She was wonderful."

Inside U.S.A. had its own floating poker game, headed by dancer Kazimir Kokic, which met in rooms of the various players.

"There would be a knock at the door," recalled singer Iva Withers. "Somebody would open it and there would be a bottle of Scotch in a hand, followed by an arm, followed by Bea Lillie. She would ask to join the game. She was a terrible poker player, but nobody cared because everyone had such an uproarious time."

Bea received a two-and-one-half-minute standing ovation opening night in Chicago. Huck did not make the chorus of *Miss Liberty* and returned to the show, never to leave Bea's side again.

"He knew exactly what he was doing," said Hubert Bland, a dancer with the company. "He was engaged to another girl. He knew exactly where he was going."

"She became tied in with him. He was as unimportant as a totem pole," remembered Bettis. "Except that it was obvious . . . he was there!" The first of many rows occurred at a matinee and Bea threw a huge vase of peonies at Huck in her dressing room. Turgeon was onstage waiting for Bea to make her entrance. He ad-libbed as long as he was able and finally had to leave the stage and the curtain came down. Haley went in front of the curtain and told some story to the audience and when Bea was finally cooled down, she went on and they began the sketch all over again. Nobody knew exactly what prompted the flower incident, but Bea, not caring who heard her, walked down the hallway in the Shubert Theatre reciting, "John Huck, if he could only f—." Bea returned to her hotel between shows and failed to appear at her usual time for the performance. Turgeon was rushed off to the hotel when she refused to answer her phone. Peter found her in a state of nerves and claiming it was impossible for her to work that night. Applying home-grown psychology he told her she was perfectly right and ought to remain at the hotel and to hell with the show. Bea spun around and laced into him for being so completely unprofessional and demanded that he take her to the theatre immediately.

A great deal of Bea's frustration that day stemmed from the fact that Valerie Bettis had given her notice and was leaving the company that night.

"I was no longer there and the ritual was broken," said Valerie. "There was the fire in the apartment and a lot of the paintings were burned. There was a very happy communal spirit because of our mutual activity. Never once did Bea ever act as if I were some subservient person to her, we were always peers."

That night after the performance Bea invited some friends up to the suite and drank a good amount of Scotch. After Bea had been asleep for a short time, her hotel room caught fire and Bea chipped a tooth and picked up a few bruises in her flight out of the suite. She was hospitalized for a day or two and the show shut down during her absence. The fire was blamed on electrical problems but Bea felt that either she or one of the guests had left a lighted cigarette which burned down and fell into an overstuffed chair.

John Philip Huck was a tall, good-looking man, twenty-six years of age. He had worked one or two chorus jobs before joining *Inside U.S.A.* John harbored great ambitions but exhibited limited talent. He possessed a high baritone voice adequate for the sort of work he had been doing, although his sights were set on opera. He had no acting training, but his ego overcame all of his shortcomings and he was determined to make his mark in the arts. For the remainder of his life John would be convinced he had abandoned a brilliant career on Beatrice Lillie's behalf, a fantasy he verbalized over and over to anyone who would listen. Huck was dominated by an erratic temperament and a vicious temper, a "white rage," as Bea referred to it. He retained an almost pathological belief in everything he said whether it was true or not. Later on in their lives, John would be totally unrealistic in the absoluteness of his talent for personal management, directing, producing, and performing. The credit he took for the first three was completely in his mind, since he never accomplished any of them; and in addition, he did very little as far as the performing was concerned. When John began getting little extra parts to do or a singing bit here and there, he voiced his hope that the company would not feel it was happening because of his friendship with Bea—which in actuality it was.

TEN

Inside U.S.A. closed in Chicago but after a few weeks' layoff continued on with Lew Parker replacing Jack Haley. John Huck continued his fetching and carrying for Bea and she was leaning heavily upon him day by day. He saw her to and from the theatre, arranged for her meals, and accompanied her after theatre. With many of her close friends he was out of his depth, having little in common with them. But because of their love for Bea, they tolerated him as a passing fancy. When *Inside U.S.A.* played Los Angeles, Flo Haley, Jack's wife, gave an elaborate party for Bea that included scores of her friends to which Huck escorted her. He now used John Philip as his stage name and would continue to do so for the rest of his career.

Bea was stricken by the news of the death of Mary MacArthur, the daughter of Charlie and Helen Hayes MacArthur. She cried for them, especially for Charlie, who was ill in the hospital himself at the time. She knew exactly what Helen was suffering as a mother, and knew she would never get over it, just as she had never recovered from losing Bobbie.

When the show ended, Bea went back to England, and in April of 1950 she appeared with Bob Hope on his television debut, a ninety-minute special on NBC. They had a wonderful time together, and *Look* magazine reported that "Beatrice Lillie, one of the guest stars, helped him give the show real pace and sparkle. Her face and delivery were so funny that even an experienced scene stealer like Bob Hope had his own show stolen right out from under him."

Lucie was contented in Henley with Miss Magowan but Muriel continued to oppose all efforts to remove her from Abercorn Place. Alured Weigall continued to watch over her. Bea arranged for Muriel to receive a small allowance each week but left the living arrangements to her lawyer, Alured, and his sister, Philippa Moore.

Christmas of 1950 was spent in Jamaica with Ivor Novello, Olive Gilbert, Bobby Andrews, and Phyllis Monkman, and New Year's Day they all gathered at Noël Coward's home for lunch. From Jamaica Bea went to New York to appear on television. The newly rebuilt Café de Paris beckoned once more and, after attending a party at the Stork Club in New York with Rex Harrison, Lilli Palmer, Mary Martin and her husband, and a cluster of others, Bea departed for England, this time taking John Philip with her. She lost Charles Cochran, followed by Ivor Novello, who died of a heart attack in March. Both deaths saddened her deeply.

Agent Ronnie Waters handled Bea's contract for the Café de Paris. Waters, a good friend, managed to secure one thousand pounds per week for Bea, an unheard-of salary. Then he took Bea to lunch to discuss the particulars. Bea drank far too much and refused to sign the contract. The club followed up by attempting to rescind the agreement because of the salary. It was finally covenanted and she opened at the Café de Paris.

Norman Hackforth, Noël's accompanist, played for Bea and she was resolved to perform new material. Unfortunately, there was not enough time to rehearse. It was a gala opening and all of Bea's friends attended. Coward introduced her and she entered to tumultuous applause.

"She got the most wonderful reception," said Phyllis Monkman. "Ivor gave a party with Ty Power, the whole lot. We all stood up as she came down the stairs. She started off, sang a line and dried up. She asked Hackforth to begin once more. She dried up again and said, 'I'll sing another song.' She sang another new song, about three words, and dried up again. She did it three times and then she said, 'It's no good, I'll sing an old song,' and went back to her old songs."

Bea was badly upset and would not attend Noël's party in her honor until a friend convinced her to join them.

John Philip and Bea went to Venice for a holiday. On the Lido one day she enjoyed a brief chat with Winston Churchill and met for the first time Ellen Blume (now Graham) and her family. Ellen and Grant Tylor met and later dated a few times and she and Bea became close friends although Ellen was never able to warm up to John. Probably one of the greatest problems in the friendship Bea established with John was his lack of anything in common with her friends. Grant Tyler became convinced that something occurred in Venice which changed the underlying structure of their relationship.

"I don't know if she accidentally took too many sleeping pills on top of the Scotch and he saved her life or what it was," he stated later. "Suddenly John took over her sleeping pills. She could no longer carry them with her. He doled them out, two or three at night."

Lucie was hostile toward John but she was also suffering from a persecution complex at the time. She phoned for the police time and time again imagining herself to be in danger of some sort. And Muriel took an active dislike to John, too, mainly because he was threatening her position with Bea.

Bea accepted an invitation to appear in Buckingham Palace at a Royal Command Performance in honor of Queen Juliana of the Netherlands on November 3. When she nervously asked the Master of the Household what she should do, he replied, "About ten minutes!" Noël Coward was there and Princess Margaret recalled Bea beginning her song by announcing, "I will now sing 'Marvelous Party' by Noël Coward, who shall remain nameless." Later Bea taught Her Highness the pearl trick. In *Inside U.S.A.*, while she sang a song "Come, Oh Come, to Pittsburgh" Bea wore a long string of pearls. During a matinee performance one day, on impulse, she flung the pearls over her shoulder. To her surprise, the string flanged straight out from her neck, continued twirling, then opened up like a Hula Hoop and circled down her body onto the floor, whereupon Bea stepped out of them like a fallen pair of drawers. Needless to say, the exhibition brought down the house and remained a standby and foolproof gag of Bea's from then on.

During the Command Performance, Her Highness, Princess Margaret, entertained at the piano and did some imitations. When a reporter asked Bea what she thought of the Royal Talent, Bea came back with, "She's good. She could be competition!" Bea had been whisked to the palace in a limousine and when she left, an attendant called for Lady Peel's automobile. Bea nearly sank into the ground as she observed John approaching in her tiny Hillman-Minx. He had talked his way past the guards and waited to take Bea home. Bea stared stonily ahead as the car passed through the gates. Ordinarily, she might have laughed at the incident but where the Royal Family was concerned, she strictly adhered to formality.

Bea returned to New York with Grant Tyler in tow. His parents sent him off with Bea with their blessings. Unbeknownst to Grant, for some time Bea continued to send the Tylers the small allowance she had set up during his military service. When reporters questioned Grant's relationship to Bea, she simply passed him off as a nephew. The East End Avenue apartment was being painted, so Bea and Grant checked into the Plaza. On the phone the following morning, Bea cautioned Grant about leaving his shoes in the hallway to be polished, an old English custom. The warning came too late. Grant had put his shoes out when he went to bed and they were now missing.

Bea lost Doc in a way she never expected. The fire bombing and atomic blasts prompted him to seek peace in a religious order. He visited Bea to explain his feelings and to bid her good-bye. Then he left the world they both knew permanently.

By 1951 most of Bea's male friends were married and out of circulation although they all remained staunch supporters. Eddie Dowling was still functioning as her manager and they were no longer lovers although his mother retained her dream that Bea and Eddie might someday marry. Rolf was busy with his career and would soon marry.

In the spring of 1952, Bea fell madly in love with a young man forty-eight years her junior. She had noticed him first in *The Member of the Wedding* and found him irresistible. He was ten-year-old Brandon DeWilde, and he was appearing with Helen Hayes in *Mrs. McThing* when Bea met him. Bea and Grant had left Sardi's and passed the Martin Beck Theatre as the show was letting out. Bea swept backstage and knocked at Brandon's door and, under the pretext of a broken zipper, she used his mirror while pretending to repair it. She acted as if she had known him all his life and they became intimate friends. Fritz DeWilde, Brandon's father and the stage manager, explained who Bea was and eventually Fritz, his wife, Eugenia, and Brandon became part of Bea's life.

Brandon's simplicity and sweetness, combined with his passion for electric trains, baseball, firecrackers, and the theatre, became the basis for scores of phone calls to and from Bea. She relished the long drive to Baldwin, Long Island, where she and Brandon would disappear into his room to look at books or down to the basement to watch his electric trains weave in and out of tunnels or over mountains. They began meeting at Sardi's for dinner and Bea never tired of Brandon's accounts of his week at school or what happened at summer camp. Coney Island became one of their favorite haunts and they loved the shooting galleries that took your picture when you hit the bull's-eye. Bea absolutely refused to ride the cyclone, however, and Fritz had to accompany Brandon on that one. Bea and Brandon did journey into the tunnel of love one day and later a radio commentator asked Brandon what Miss Lillie did in the tunnel of love. "It's very dark in there," he explained patiently as if the man were six years old, "so naturally she doesn't do anything!"

Eddie Dowling called Bea to discuss the idea of a show built around Bea's career, a small revue with some of her best sketches and songs. Gertrude Lawrence's husband, Richard Aldrich, owned the Cape Playhouse and promised to book it into his theatre. When Eddie referred to it as a concert Bea retorted instantly, "I hate the word 'concert'! The only good thing about performing in concert is that you can get out of town the minute the show's over!" Eddie suggested *An Evening With Beatrice Lillie*. "Or *An Off Evening With Hamlet*," Bea quipped. *An Evening With Beatrice Lillie* became the working title. Bea did not relish the thought of spending an entire evening alone on the stage nor was she willing to subject an audience to two hours of only Bea. Eddie contacted Reginald Gardiner in Hollywood and he was very interested in appearing on stage once more, especially with Bea. When the word was out, Eddie was besieged with offers from every summer theatre in the East. John

Shubert promised him a New York theatre if Bea was ever interested in presenting herself in New York. Howard Reinheimer, Bea's lawyer, and Eddie worked out a contract whereby Bea would be paid a handsome weekly figure and own over sixty percent of the show. Eddie would be titular producer and director. Milton Stern, hired as stage manager, would be directorial assistant. When the sketches were decided upon, Bea asked for Xenia Bank, an actress who had worked with her in *Inside U.S.A.*, to appear in the sketches. Xenia's unique ability to remain poised and in character in the face of Bea's outrageous impersonations and a hysterical audience made her an invaluable foil for Bea. For years Bea attempted to break up Xenia on stage and she respected her self-control enormously.

Florence Bray and Shannon Dean were added to the cast and Bea asked Rolf Gérard to execute the sets, simple folding flats that would work easily in summer theatres. Bea gave John Philip a bit part in the production. Between songs in the second act John, who had now become slightly overweight, was dressed in evening clothes and wore a long black cape. He entered singing "Come Into the Garden, Maude" and sang into Bea's eyes as she remained poker-faced throughout. When the song ended and he exited Bea would turn to the audience and ask, "Who was that? I thought he was with you."

The summer tour was highly successful and Bea received reams of publicity all over the country. The show was innovative and began a series of "Evenings With" that are popular even today. *Theatre World* noted, "The heroine of the season was Beatrice Lillie, who began an extended tour of *An Evening With Beatrice Lillie* at Richard Aldrich's Falmouth Playhouse, Coonamessett, Massachusetts, to break all existing records at every theatre she played. Not only did she deserve the plaque awarded her by the Stock Managers' Association as 'The Most Cooperative Female Star of the Season,' but she seems to have provided the only competition Eisenhower, Stevenson, Truman, and the rest of the nation's political figures had."

When Bea was questioned about the political race she told the interviewer, "The last time I was interested in things like that was when Truman beat Dewey. I was delighted . . . for Tallulah!"

One happy customer noted, "It may be an evening with one person but it has the feeling of a full-blown Broadway production."

Consequently, when the Palace Theatre made a bid for the show, Bea argued against it. The Palace was instituting a new star presentation policy but Bea felt the show belonged in a more intimate theatre. Eddie discussed this with the Shubert office and the Booth Theatre seemed to be the place to open.

Bea and Reggie enjoyed their first venture into summer stock immensely and Bea took the small inconveniences in stride. When her car didn't show up in Falmouth, she simply hitched a ride in a truck and learned the rudiments of farming from the driver. Reggie declared he had discovered a place called *Lookout!!!* mountain and was going to build there if it was the last thing he did. The summer circuit kept them close enough to New York for friends to see the show. Helen Hayes saw it in Falmouth and laughed so hard she hit her head on the back of the seat in front of her. Brandon DeWilde saw Bea onstage for the first time in Princeton and discovered what all the shouting was about. He loved her performance and caught her every nuance and lift of the eyebrow. Brandon proved her theory that children understood her humor better than anybody.

Olney, Maryland, proved to be the high and the low point of the tour for Bea. The theatre was notified that on September 6, President and Mrs. Truman and their daughter Margaret would attend the matinee. Excitement ran through the company as everyone geared up for the event. Then, on Saturday, before the matinee, Eddie received a phone call from New York informing him that Gertie Lawrence was dead. She had succumbed to cancer early that morning and the news was being flashed around the world. Eddie was faced with the dilemma of when to tell Bea. If she was told immediately, chances were there would be no shows that day and what to do about the presidential party? He ordered all radios removed from the theatre and Milton temporarily disabled Bea's portable which she kept on her dressing table. No newspapers were to be delivered to Bea, a customary practice when breakfast was served, and she was to be shielded from strangers who might allow the news to slip. No unauthorized person was to be let through the stage door. He briefed the theatre staff on the importance of his orders. He only wished Bea to get through the two shows and then she would be free to make her own decisions as far as handling Gertie's death.

Bea was slightly perturbed that there were no papers and asked someone to try and fix her radio but she appeared at both performances none the wiser. When the matinee ended, Eddie intercepted the presidential party on its way back to see Bea and explained the situation to the Trumans. Gertrude Lawrence was not mentioned during their short visit with Bea. After the final performance that night, Eddie went to Bea's dressing room and broke the news. Bea reacted as Noël had in London: she went completely to pieces. Later there were thousands of people outside the church on Fifth Avenue for Gertie's funeral. Bea thought it all terribly garish but reckoned her friend would have enjoyed the tribute.

Bea's back was bothering her before the show opened, the result of a fall she had on the Ed Sullivan show. She called Dr. Prutting, who gave her a shot of painkiller and massaged the area. Bea called him later and informed him that two tickets would be at the box office for opening night and she hoped he would be there. He went thinking Bea might need him but when she sang a song in which she had to kneel, she kneeled and straightened up with no effort. She then looked straight at Prutting and winked as if to let him know everything was all right.

Everything was more than all right. *An Evening With Beatrice Lillie* was a smash hit and Bea was showered with praise. Richard Watts wrote, "There is apparently no one who doesn't concede that Beatrice Lillie is the funniest woman in the world," an observation with which few people disagreed. Other opinions: "One of the world's funniest gals"; "She is the first woman clown, or comic, of all time;" "She is still the funniest, most delightful, and altogether enchanting woman in the world"; "The youthfulness of her spirit remains untouched, the brightness both of her person and personality untarnished." A few weeks later the American Federation of Women's Philanthropies awarded her a citation as "The Greatest Comedienne of all time."

The Booth Theatre rocked with laughter every performance. "For the people who want Lillie this will be fine, for the others it's just too bad. Once they get there, they'll get me," stated Bea.

Reggie Gardiner scored a great personal success and comple-
mented Bea perfectly mainly because of their close friendship.
Reggie could do no wrong as far as Bea was concerned. For the New
York run, Eddie acquired the services of Eadie and Rack, one of
America's foremost piano teams. Eadie and Rack (he had been
named Rack by John Murray Anderson, the director; it was short for
Rachmaninoff) were a married couple who had been a phenomenal
draw at Hollywood's Club Gala and the Blue Angel in New York.
They were musicians' musicians and numbered Frank Sinatra
among their admirers. When they played, Eadie never took her eyes
off Rack and the effect was intimate and personal and became their
trademark. Thanks to intelligent casting, Bea was surrounded by the
best.

Bea brought her Hillman-Minx to the States and the Shubert
office allowed her to park in Shubert Alley. She began regular visits
to Sardi's less than a block away, and often Brandon and his parents
joined her for dinner. Grant was inducted into the United States
Army but was stationed not far from New York and was home often.
Fitzy looked after Bea at home, and Rene Diggs, an ex-vaudevillian
now in the wardrobe union, was Bea's dresser in the theatre and took
care of the wardrobe. Ellen Graham was an assistant stage manager.

Ellen and Grant Tyler dated occasionally when he was on leave
from the army. One Sunday evening they dined at 25 East End
Avenue with Bea and John. Fitzy prepared dinner consisting of
vegetables and salad surrounding a leg of lamb.

"It was a huge leg of lamb," recalled Ellen. "I don't know how
much it weighed. Something happened between them, I can't
remember exactly what it was, and Bea picked up the lamb and
threw it at John. I think he ducked but it hit him. It was the first time
I ever saw anyone throw a whole leg of lamb at anybody. I thought
it was Bea's moment of triumph until he picked it up and started to
eat it!"

Christine Jorgensen, probably the most famous name in the world
at that moment, dined at Sardi's one evening where Bea was waiting
for the DeWildes. Christine had left the United States a few years
earlier as George Jorgensen and, after a series of operations in
Denmark, emerged as Christine. As they were being seated, Genie

DeWilde knew something out of the ordinary was going on in the restaurant.

"What's all the excitement about?" she asked Bea.

"C.J. is here," whispered Bea.

"Oh, my God, where?"

"There," Bea indicated with her head.

"Who's C.J.?" piped up Brandon in a voice heard round the room.

"Nothing, darling, let's order dinner, shall we?" Bea pretended to peruse the menu with great interest.

"I want to know who C.J. is." Brandon was now standing and looking around the room. Bea glanced nervously at the adjoining table, where the patrons were enjoying the scene. "What is everybody looking at? Who is C.J.?"

"Guess what I have in my dressing room, Brandon," Bea exclaimed gaily.

"Isn't anybody going to tell me who C.J. is?"

"Two turtles!" sang Bea.

"Is C.J. somebody's name?"

"Live ones, darling," said Bea rising and snatching up her purse. "And you and I are going to see them right this instant, aren't we?" Brandon was out of Sardi's and looking at turtles in record time. Genie and Fritz did explain C.J. to Brandon in due time and it took some days for Brandon to figure it out.

An Evening With Beatrice Lillie (or *An Evening Avec* as Bea referred to it) became a hot ticket and Bea's dressing room became the center of her life as the Duke and Duchess of Windsor, Marion Davies, and nearly everyone she ever knew dropped in at various intervals. Tallulah Bankhead arrived roaring, "Darling, you are Duse, you are Bernhardt!" Bea had appeared on Tallulah's *Big Show* radio show in London two years before and, in an exchange of comic insults, Tallulah told Bea she had seen her on television and in the close-ups her face had looked like four yards of corduroy!

Bea was on top of the heap once more, at least professionally. John drove her to and from the theatre every performance, and as far as her co-workers and friends were concerned, he was still "the new boyfriend" and not to be taken very seriously. Philip had high hopes for a career in opera and hoped that Bea would be able to pull some strings and open doors but she never did. It is doubtful that he would have succeeded in that career since he was lacking any formal training. What John believed was real and what was actually real would cause both of them a great deal of unhappiness as time went on.

Shannon Dean was making up one night when Milton Stern came to her dressing room and told her the performance was cancelled. He said that after an argument of great proportions John struck Bea, who, in falling, had hit her head against the sink in her room. Eddie Dowling called the police, according to Milton, but Bea did not prefer any charges against him. For many years, when Philip lost his temper, Bea would shake her head sadly and say, "Poor John, it's that awful frustration thing he has." She never elaborated, mainly because she did not want to face it, but his problem was his ill-concealed desire to be accepted by her friends and her profession as the talented performer and erudite businessman he imagined himself to be. Occasionally, to make John happy, Bea would drive to Connecticut on Sundays to visit his family, a duty she was not particularly fond of carrying out. As nice as they might have been, Bea had little in common with them and was never able to visualize herself and the Hucks as "one big happy family."

An Evening With Beatrice Lillie ran for 275 performances. For the 50th, 100th, and 200th performances, the stage crew threw parties on stage after the show. The 200th party was especially festive, with a banner announcing the performance number, food-laden tables, and a fully stocked bar.

Bea Lillie and I first met over drinks. Milton Stern, my best friend, asked me to bartend at the party. I was an out-of-work stage manager at that moment and eagerly accepted his offer of free drinks and the once-in-a-lifetime opportunity to hobnob with one of the greats of my profession. I had seen Beatrice Lillie on stage, on the screen, owned many of her records, and had memorized most of the classic Bea Lillie stories. Once, I sat near her at the theatre.

Miss Lillie approached my makeshift bar that night escorted by a male friend. She was dressed in a cerise evening gown with matching pillbox hat.

"Scotch and water for the lady, please," said her friend, "very little water and one piece of ice. And I'll have vodka and tonic, without lime."

"I'm sorry, sir," I began, as I iced two glasses, "I have no lime. Will you have it without lemon?"

The world's funniest woman caught the joke immediately, threw back her head, and laughed heartily. Five months later I was working for her, and we were friends for the next thirty-six years.

The audience had left and friends of the cast and crew gathered for the occasion. Reginald Gardiner shaved off his famous mustache for the party and painted false ones on most of the male guests. Rene Diggs, dressed as Bea, impersonated her in one of the maid sketches, Reggie told a few of his most famous stories, and Shannon Dean and Milton Stern portrayed Eadie and Rack to taped music. Bea wound up the evening with a blackout sketch which she performed with Ellen Graham.

Two secretaries seated at their typewriters:

BEA

"How do you like the new boss?"

ELLEN

"He's very good-looking. He dresses so well."

BEA

"Yes, and so quickly!"

BLACKOUT

Bea received a special Tony Award for her efforts in *An Evening With Beatrice Lillie* and when the show closed she went to Europe with John after promising Eddie she would tour with it in the fall. Dorothy Dickson and Phyllis Monkman visited Peel Fold, which Bea now called her Henley home, at various times during the summer. In London Bea, along with all of England, was caught up in the excitement of the coronation of Queen Elizabeth II and sat next to Noël Coward at the actual event. She saw Noël in *The Apple Cart* and later attended his performance at the Café de Paris. She was thrilled with the news of John Gielgud's knighthood and, in general, had a fine summer.

Bea rehearsed with Eadie and Rack in her New York apartment and Eadie immediately noticed a few distinct changes in Bea's relationship with John. It was evident that John was living at 25 East End Avenue and Eadie saw that he was answering all phone calls and speaking for Bea in many cases. Appointments were referred to John and she checked with him before accepting dinner dates and most social engagements. She obviously did not deem it necessary to explain John to friends or new acquaintances and usually introduced him to people with an offhand, "You know John . . ." Undoubtedly it rankled him when surrounded by Bea's important theatrical friends to be rated as the boyfriend. Ironically, Bea obviously did not know how to rate him either. Unlike Doc or Eddie, John found little to talk about except Bea, which he always did at great length to those who had known her longer than he had. As Valerie Bettis said, "He was just *there*!"

ELEVEN

The road tour of *An Evening With Beatrice Lillie* would be Bea's final nationwide excursion, one that would take her from coast to coast and to her native Canada three times. Eddie Dowling had arranged the tour through the Shubert office with nothing less than one-week stands and, in some cities, as many as four to six weeks, which assured Bea of an easy journey. She arranged to have her Hillman-Minx car with her for most of the trip, thereby enabling her to leave for each succeeding city at a convenient hour with John driving.

My job was to act as secretary, sell the souvenir book, from which Bea derived a profit, answer her mail, and other secretarial duties which would be relayed to me by Rene Diggs. The faces surrounding Bea were the ones she knew from New York and her relationship with cast and crew was, as always, warm and friendly. I had my dog along, and Milton Stern, whose wife, Janet Medlin, now understudied the women in the show, had their four-year-old daughter, Victoria, with them. Victoria Stern was a gregarious, imaginative, and amusing child with whom Bea fell in love almost immediately. My dog, Kennedy, and Victoria became part of Bea's dressing room troop.

Unlike many performers, Bea enjoyed company in the room before and after the show. Most of the actors stopped on their way in with a bit of news or a story. After the show it was a good-night drink unless we were all meeting elsewhere. There were also nights when Rene would steal in and out of Bea's room warning the company that there had been trouble between Bea and John and it was not an opportune time for a visit. Usually the arguments were over Bea's drinking or John's goal to be appointed her "personal representative," a title he preferred in lieu of "manager." Bea continued to rely on Eddie Dowling in that capacity mainly because John had no experience or knowledge of the theatre. Their disputes became stormier as time passed and the *Evening With* company bore the brunt of these fracases. Company manager Louis Epstein, elderly and ill, complained that John was harassing him to death over bills, percentages, and business matters which did not concern him. John usually made demands in Bea's name and often Eppie found himself in trouble with Bea, who insisted that he was not to listen to anything John said. She failed, however, to relay those orders to John. When an altercation took place in the theatre, there would be considerable shouting and door slamming followed usually by Reggie Gardiner singing at the top of his lungs from his dressing room.

There was a terrible row in Detroit when John exited Bea's dressing room in a jock strap shouting that he would call the newspapers and tell them "just what kind of a bitch you are." He had approached Harry Davies, the show's advance publicity man, with a change he ordered inserted in his biographical paragraph in the theatre programs and the souvenir book. Harry in turn was required to obtain permission for any changes from Bea directly. The information John submitted read:

> Even though busy as a performer, John Philip has not neglected his aptitude for business and, it should be stated—once and for all time—for the official record, that he is the authentic personal manager of one Miss Beatrice Lillie. . . .

Bea, of course, would not treat Eddie Dowling in such an unprofessional manner and refused to allow the insert to be placed in the programs. As far as the souvenir book was concerned, Eddie was listed as her personal manager.

Rene was the focal point of all the socializing, self-appointed, and was almost impossible to exclude from any merrymaking. Short and dumpy with a slight limp, the lady had a vocabulary that outdid Mrs. Malaprop but she worshiped Bea and spent her days as well as performance hours with her. Rene's special language was a mixture of New Yorkese and Bryn Mawr with most of her words ending with the letter L. Reggie Gardiner was Reggil, Eadie and Rack became Eadle and Rackle, I was Brucel and so on.

Bea always arrived early at the theatre, a pattern she had followed for most of her career. She would either make up slowly and then rest on a couch or she would nap until the cast began arriving and then get on with the makeup. During the show's New York run she developed a fondness for her stage carpenter, Mac McCort, a grizzled older man who usually arrived for work early and dozed in a quiet corner until showtime. Bea felt he was lonely and would often sit and talk with him backstage.

On performance days Bea never went near liquor, a rule she instituted years before and religiously followed. It was folly to expect Bea at a cocktail party for that reason although as she grew older she disliked cocktail parties in general. However, when the final curtain fell, she walked quickly to her dressing room where Rene stood just inside the door holding a full tumbler of Scotch mixed with a drop or two of water. This Bea would drain in one motion. Then she would change into a dressing gown and remove her makeup as Rene prepared another drink.

After the Boston opening, Bea invited the cast to her hotel for food and drink. I instead took Ellen Graham out for supper near the theatre. I could not have been more surprised when Milton called me the following day to tell me that I had been fired. Bea was hurt and angry that we had skipped her party in favor of a restaurant. Later that day, Milton and I met Grant Tyler at the railroad terminal. He was on leave from the army and his surprise visit delighted her so he was able to square it with Bea and I was rehired. It was not long before Bea and I were laughing about the incident.

The Latin Casino in Philadelphia was presenting Nelson Eddy and Bea took a group to see him. He knew Bea was there and played much of the show to her and at one point broke her up by donning a cowboy hat and informing the audience that he would sing "There Are Prairies at the Bottom of Our Garden."

In Washington, D.C., Bea was suddenly besieged by phone calls from Washington hostess Gwen Cafritz. Cafritz was tossing a Washington-style bash and wondered if Lady Peel (always Lady Peel to Mrs. Cafritz, never Miss Lillie or Bea) would consent to grace the affair as guest of honor. Since nobody else in the cast had been invited Bea decided not to attend without an escort. Shortly before the gala evening, Reggie happened to cross paths with Tyrone Power, who mentioned in passing that he was to be guest of honor at the same party. When Bea heard the story she asked me to phone her regrets. The major-domo at Chez Cafritz had no idea who Beatrice Lillie was. A quick switch to Lady Peel brought Mrs. Cafritz to the phone in a flash. Surely Lady Peel could spare a few hours? Would the caller please try and talk her into it? "Even you come!" was her final solution. As it turned out neither Bea nor Power attended, which was just as well since a very heavy snowfall that night forced guests to abandon their automobiles and walk to the party. The morning newspapers carried glowing reports of the evening, including a squib about the two illustrious guests of honor, Lady Peel and Mr. Tyrone Power.

The following Sunday was Eadie's birthday and Rack invited a small group to celebrate in their suite. The hotel phoned to announce that a Mrs. Cafritz was in the lobby seeking Miss Lillie. Gwen arrived in the suite and bore down on Bea, ignoring everyone else in the room. Bea attempted to introduce her around but she was not particularly interested. When Bea introduced her to the guest of honor, she asked Eadie what she did in the show. Everyone was stunned to learn that she had not even bothered to see a performance. She and Bea then had words which resulted in Gwen's hasty and tearful exit.

When Bea toured she enjoyed opening night conviviality in her hotel suite whenever possible and the Pittsburgh opening led to a memorable one for all concerned. Everybody gathered in Bea's sitting room. Sandwiches were everywhere and Scotch flowed copiously all evening. Toward the end of the night Bea, feeling no pain, was helped to bed by Rene after insisting everyone remain and whoop it up. She loved to sleep for an hour or so after taking her sleeping pills and then join the crowd once more for a nightcap. Then it was back to bed for another nap followed a short time later by her night lunch which had been ordered hours before and was usually laid out in her room. I named her return to the parties her "comeback," which she loved, and each party night she would admonish everyone not to leave before she made her comeback.

Because it had been an opening night, most of the cast was exhausted and finally the guest list was whittled down to Eadie, Rack, John, and me. Rack and I were having a conversation when suddenly Eadie and John began an argument. There were loud and not terribly friendly words being bandied about. Eadie proceeded to rise from her chair and start for the door. John followed her and barred her exit. Eadie shoved John with all her strength and stormed out into the hallway. Rack quickly followed with me behind him. Rack went to Eadie and was grabbed and pinned against the wall by John. I approached John and asked what was wrong, my first mistake. My second was placing my hand on his arm trying to get his attention.

Suddenly I was on the floor, John on top of me slugging away and totally out of control. Eadie and Rack struggled in vain to remove him but it took Bea, making her comeback and screaming the place down, to divert John's attention long enough for me to escape into a crowded elevator which had the good sense to arrive at that moment. Bea was returned to her bed and dozed until time to eat.

The following day I discovered a long red bruise running down the side of my jawbone. I had a few aches and pains and difficulty hearing in one ear. Milton rushed me to the theatre doctor, who did not believe me for one moment when I told him I had fallen down. I had a splitting headache and Milton insisted we report the incident to Louis Epstein. We went to Eppie's office at the theatre. He already knew about the trouble, which he was reporting in detail to Eddie Dowling by phone as we strolled in.

"Here he is now!" growled Eppie as he handed me the phone.

"Why didn't you have the son of a bitch arrested?" screamed Eddie into my good ear.

With skull throbbing, I explained that it was over and forgotten as far as I was concerned and all I wished to do was get to bed.

"I would have had the son of a bitch arrested," persisted Eddie, making my head ring like Big Ben. "If it ever happens again, have the son of a bitch thrown in jail!" I returned the phone to Eppie before Eddie was able to squeeze out one more "son of a bitch" and went home for a peaceful rest. Not for long. I had barely snuggled in when the phone rang. It was Lady Peel and she was demanding to know what had occurred the previous night in her suite. I reminded her it was in her hallway and it was nothing important. I could understand her anger but not her rage at me. Bea phoned back two or three more times and her tone became increasingly nasty with each conversation. Finally, with my head about to take off like a rocket engine, I hung up on her. John called next demanding to know how I could hang up the phone on Beatrice Lillie. To demonstrate how easy it was I hung up on him, then ordered the phone shut down for the duration.

It came as no surprise that I was once again headed for the bread lines. In fact I accepted the news of my firing with relief. Milton refused to give up and I was told to stay out of sight and not to leave town. After the performance that night, Rack invited a few of us to the suite for food and drink. Eadie tried hard but could not remember what she and John had been arguing about in the first place and, after a few salty remarks concerning John from others in the room, there was a moment of silence during which Reggie spoke seriously,

"It's the fucking finger sandwiches, you know."

Everyone stared at him as if he had become unglued.

"What did you say, dear?" asked Eadie gently.

"Every time we have those bloody finger sandwiches all hell breaks loose." Reggie proceeded to name other parties which had ended in mayhem. He became aware of everybody's scrutiny. "Well, let's face it, kids, we must steer clear of finger sandwiches from now on."

"A little difficult, old buddy," said Rack. "If it's Bea's party there isn't a hell of a lot we can do about the food."

"It'll be up to Bruce or Rene, whoever does the ordering. Remember, no finger sandwiches ever again. Have them cut in half and let it go at that. One of you had better tell Rene and caution her, for God's sake, that mum's the word. And now I think we should all leave here one by one under the cover of darkness and retreat to our beds. Don't reveal your names even if they nab you and force you to devour thousands of finger sandwiches. Bruce, dear boy, get some rest and I trust by tomorrow this will all be over. If I know my Bea it will." One of Reggie's most endearing qualities was his imagination.

Bea had been decidedly upset by the trouble in her suite, especially after Milton explained exactly what had occurred. She was also not well enough acquainted with me to know I would not carry it any further. Her fear of adverse publicity conjured up visions of headlines and reporters. Consequently she went to the theatre at night, remained alone, and returned to her hotel with Rene after the performance. She and I avoided each other like the plague. Victoria Stern saved the day. Bea had nicknamed her "Old Vic," and one night I mistakenly wandered backstage as she waited for her first entrance. She and Old Vic were seated on chairs near the wings whispering to each other as I attempted to pass by unnoticed. As luck would have it, Victoria spotted me and cried out, "Oh, Uncle Bwuce, how is 'or poor 'ittle ear?' " Bea and I stared at each other for a moment. Her lower lip trembled and we dissolved into gales of laughter. The war was over and I, to quote Bea, was back in the will.

As the Pittsburgh run came to an end, I approached Bea's dressing room one night at a point where I knew she would be completely dressed. I knocked and opened the door, whereupon Bea threw her entire weight against it, slamming it shut and nearly leaving my arm inside. Just as quickly, the door reopened and Bea appeared wildly flinging Tweed cologne, the only scent she ever wore, about the room as if she had gone mad.

"What the hell is wrong now?" I demanded.

Bea tilted her chin up, handed me the Tweed bottle as she sailed grandly by, and said, "I just farted!" as she went onstage to sing "Wind 'Round My Heart."

On Thanksgiving night in Cincinnati Bea bundled into her car with John and sped through the dark to the town in Kentucky where Doc McGunigle resided with his religious order, "no longer in the world" as he put it. Bone weary, she managed to sit through a high mass before being ushered into a small room where Doc waited to gather her into a bear hug. Bea was delighted to see that the old McGunigle sense of humor still existed and in no time she and Doc were screaming with laughter as she relayed news of old mutual friends and other theatre gossip. Doc asked Bea if she would say hello to a friend who had been a great Beatrice Lillie fan and when Doc opened the door his friend fell into the room. He had been listening at the keyhole the entire time. Bea and Doc bade each other a warm farewell, somehow realizing that they would never meet again. In spite of the long drive back to Cincinnati and a performance that evening, Bea was happy she had made the trip. Doc arranged for Bea to receive bread and cheese from the order and Bea continued to keep in touch by mail, but they never did meet again.

Late in life, Doc was operated on for cataracts, which made it necessary for him to wear strong lenses, and then he lost his hearing but never once did his eagerness or interest lag for the life he chose. A week or two before Christmas in 1983, Doc fell and broke his hip, which was operated on in a local hospital. Nothing could keep him from celebrating Midnight Mass on Christmas Eve with the rest of his community. After breakfast on Christmas Day, he complained of shortness of breath and died immediately afterward. He was four weeks short of eighty-two.

Grant Tyler, on leave from the army, joined Bea for Christmas in Cleveland. Rudy Vallee, who was appearing at a local club, was registered at the same hotel and Bea and Rudy walked Vallee's dogs together. There was a company party backstage at the Hanna The-atre on Christmas Eve attended by the cast and crew, and there were some smaller frolics in Bea's suite during the holiday.

Reggie Gardiner tiptoed into Bea's dressing room one evening when she and I were alone and announced in a whisper that he was having a small get-together at his hotel for author Louis Bromfield and his daughter.

"Why are you whispering?" Bea wanted to know.

Reggie silenced her quickly, looked around the room, then closed the door. "Because I have not asked Rene to this one. I adore her as you know but I don't believe this is really her sort of gathering if you know what I mean, so please, for God's sake, just show up and don't say a word." When the show ended, everybody who was invited quit the theatre by any devious route they could. Bea thought seriously of escaping via the bathroom window but decided against it and fled the premises when Rene made a trip to the wardrobe room.

The party was a huge success. The bar was well stocked and food was plentiful and the sandwiches were halved. Bea had known Bromfield before and she sat next to him on a couch for most of the evening. Everything was in full swing when Reggie answered a knock at the door and found Rene smiling happily in the doorway. It was evident she knew she had been deliberately slighted and, as in the case of Polly Moran, was having none of it.

"Hi, Reggil!" she trilled as she wafted into the room with a few libations under her belt. "Hi, everyone!" Reggie for once was speechless but with true English manners he introduced her to the Bromfields and offered her a drink. Rene then waved at Bea and wiggled her rather ample bottom between Bea and Mr. Bromfield, who regarded Rene with suspicion. Rene winked at Bromfield and said, "Hi, got a cigarootal?"

"Do I have what?" asked the renowned author.

"A cigarootal, hon. You know, a Chesterboot!"

Bea quickly offered Rene one from her cache. Rene helped herself, looked around expectantly for a moment and then dug her elbow into Bromfield's ribs, eliciting a sharp intake of breath from the guest of honor.

"How about a matchel?" she asked. Bea came to the rescue as Mr. Bromfield rose swiftly from the couch and repaired to the bar where he treated himself to a cold drink of some sort. The party continued until the wee hours but it was days before Rene forgave Reggie for the snub.

Throughout the holidays Bea remained in a happy frame of mind mostly because of Grant's visit. Then he returned to the army and the show moved on to Chicago for a six-week run at the Blackstone Theatre. When Mac McCort did not report for work one night, a bellboy who was contacted by phone reported that Mac was drunk in his room. Bea flew into a rage at the accusation and sent Harry

Davies and me to Mac's hotel. The bellboy opened the chained door a crack and it was obvious Mac was deathly ill. We had the safety chain removed after first sending for a doctor and Mac was rushed to a hospital. As we returned to the Blackstone, Milton had just been informed that Mac had died. Bea returned to her dressing room and closed the door and remained alone for the rest of the evening. Mac's death followed closely on that of Lee Shubert, Bea's former producer, who had died Christmas Day.

After the performance, the cast went to Gibby's, a popular hangout some distance from the theatre, and Bea drank heavily. John told me to see her home. In the taxi she said very little except to mention Lee Shubert and Mac. I helped Bea get ready for bed and we enjoyed a nightcap or two as she settled under the covers. I then cleared away the glasses and bent over to kiss Bea good night when she suddenly leaned into me and kissed me passionately on the mouth. I managed to ease her onto her pillow but she refused to let go and I realized she was serious. I argued that John might lumber through the door at any time but that did not deter her for a moment. I disentangled myself as gently as I was able until Bea, realizing it was all in vain, said angrily, "Well, for Christ's sake," and rolled over and went to sleep. I sat near her until I was sure she was asleep and then left quietly. Bea never mentioned the incident again and it made no difference in our friendship if she remembered.

Bea received a call from actress Estelle Winwood, who was passing through town. Winwood asked for two tickets for the performance that evening. However, Miss Winwood insisted, not very tactfully, that she would prefer not to pay for them. Bea obliged by paying for them herself. On her way in that evening, Bea explained to the doorman who Estelle was and asked him to please have her wait a few moments while she changed into a dressing gown after the show. Miss Winwood, according to Bea, would be backstage before the final curtain hit the floor. When the show did end, a tall lady swathed in mink approached the doorman and asked for Bea. I signaled to him that it was not Winwood and he asked her politely to wait, whereupon the lady seated herself upon a trunk near the door and waited. Winwood and a young man were right on schedule. Although armed with Bea's instructions, the doorman was not prepared for Estelle's entrance.

"I'm here to see Miss Lillie," boomed Miss W. in a voice they certainly heard at the Shubert Theatre some blocks away. The doorman repeated Bea's orders. "Young man, I am a great star in the American Theatre!" Estelle persisted in a pitch akin to Bankhead's, "and I am here to see Miss Lillie." With that she marched toward the hallway leading backstage. The confused doorman put up his arm to block her entrance and Winwood became Medea in the last act. She started screaming Bea's name until Bea ran down the hall pulling on a robe and led her to the dressing room. Shortly after, the lady in mink descended from her trunk and told the doorman she would come back some other time. I happened to be close by and asked her if she wished to leave a message.

"Just tell her Irene Castle stopped by," she smiled warmly. I ordered her not to leave and informed Bea who her other guest was and Estelle was left to her own devices as Bea ran down the hall to greet Castle. Amid shrieks of laughter and delight the two women returned to Bea's dressing room. Outclassed, Miss Winwood departed soon after. Irene Castle invited the cast to her pied-à-terre on Michigan Avenue and later sent Bea a photograph taken a few weeks earlier of Irene in a dress she had worn in *Watch Your Step* forty years earlier. It fit her perfectly.

Bea Lillie and Bert Lahr clowning around in *The Show Is On* (1937) (Photo: Billy Rose Theatre Collection. The New York Public Library at Lincoln Center, Astor, Lenox and Tilden Foundations)

Bea Lillie (right), with Mary Carlisle and Bing Crosby, in *Dr. Rhythm* (1937) (Photo: Pictorial Parade, Inc.)

Left: Beatrice Lillie and friend

Right: Sir Robert Peel, Sixth Baronet. Beatrice Lillie's son Bobbie, circa 1940. (Photo Courtesy of Alured Weigall)

Above: Beatrice Lillie, Clark Gable, and Madeleine Carroll in the Cub Room at the Stork Club (1948) (Photo Courtesy of the Stork Club)

Below: Beatrice Lillie, Jack Haley, and ensemble in a scene from *Inside U.S.A.* (Photo: Will Rapport. Courtesy of Hubert Bland)

Left to right: Grant Tyler, Reginald Gardiner, Bea Lillie, and publishing executive
Cass Canfield celebrate with Tallulah Bankhead at the Stork Club (1952)
(Photo: Stork Club)

Nelson Eddy (center), shown here with Bea Lillie and Reginald Gardiner, sang "There
Are Prairies at the Bottom of our Garden" to Bea in 1953. (Photo from Author's
Collection)

Right: The author, with "Herself"

Below: Beatrice Lillie as the harassed customer attempting to purchase "One Dozen Double Damask Dinner Napkins" from Fred Keating (Photo: George S. Bolster)

Top: Beatrice Lillie and the author performing "Milady Dines Alone" (1956)
(Photo: George S. Bolster)
Above: Bea Lillie and John Philip Huck (right) on the beach at Monte-Carlo with friends.
That's Dorothy Pasternak peering around Bea. (1959) (Photo: Bruce Laffey)

Above: Tony Randall, Tammy Grimes, Beatrice Lillie, Cyril Ritchard in "Four for Tonight" (1960) (Photo Courtesy of the National Broadcasting Company, Inc.)

Left: Beatrice Lillie and Noël Coward during rehearsals of *High Spirits* (1963) (Photo: Friedman-Abeles)

Left: Beatrice Lillie, at age ninety.
Henley-on-Thames, England.
(1984) (Photo Courtesy of
Shaun Duffy)

Below: The Beatrice Lillie Building, Toronto, Canada. Dedicated
by H.R.H. Prince Philip, Duke
of Edinburgh, March 11, 1989.
(Photo: Mahmood Khan)

TWELVE

Bea was drinking more than she ever had before and Rene was replenishing the Black & White Scotch more often. John switched her to beer and every night Rene made sure there was an ice bucket with beer in it, cold and ready for Bea, but she was not ready for it and stuck to her Scotch while Rene and I drank the beer. Then John changed her brand to Dewar's, believing it to be milder. John either chose to believe otherwise or simply did not care that Bea was obviously alcoholic now. Gone were the fun parties of years ago where Bea painted or friends entertained. Bea was now drinking solely to get drunk. Unfortunately, those who were aware of the problem could do nothing. If her drinking was mentioned to John he simply blamed those who gave her a drink when she requested one, hosts or waiters who had no idea that Bea needed help, or fellow actors who ordered her a drink if she asked.

Rene constantly complained of arguments between Bea and John at night and sometimes continuing for most of the following day or until Bea and Rene left the hotel to shop. John reprimanded Bea about her drinking and then Bea would get furious and continue on after the show the following night. One night at the Pump Room in the Ambassador East where she had gone with one or two company members, Bea had to be carried bodily from the eatery.

Playwright Maxwell Anderson attended a matinee and Bea received him in her dressing room afterwards. I happened to be there, and John was lounging on Bea's chaise. Bea introduced Anderson to us, and John reached up limply from his position on the couch and shook his hand. I noticed Bea stiffen. When Anderson left, Bea, white with rage, turned on John and shouted, "If my son had done that I'd have slapped his face!"

Another friend of Bea's, a Catholic priest, came to see her one evening. He was with a strikingly handsome younger cleric who resembled Tyrone Power. Bea invited the priests and a gang from the show to her suite at the Blackstone Hotel. The younger priest proved to be a talented jazz pianist and entertained the crowd at Bea's piano. Everyone was so enthralled with the concert they failed to notice that Bea was becoming very intoxicated and morose. All at once she burst into tears and, sobbing pitifully, she told the older priest of Bobbie's death and her own personal heartbreak. Rene helped her into bed and the priest sat with her until she fell asleep. The following day he phoned to inquire after Bea and I apologized for the scene, reminding him that we were actors after all.

"I understand," he replied. "We're all in the same business!"

Reginald Gardiner's wife, Nadia, arrived from Hollywood. She and Bea were polite to each other but Nadia could not seem to break through Bea's reserve and the two ladies treated each other with a surface cordiality. In spite of the problem, Nadia promised Bea a party when the company played in Los Angeles. Bea had a small group for drinks in her suite shortly after and the Gardiners attended. Bea drank steadily and all evening observed Nadia sullenly through half-closed lids. Then suddenly, for no apparent reason, Bea crossed the room and confronted Nadia.

"You are a shit!" she yelled. The room became silent instantly. "You're a shit! A shit!" With that Bea went into her room and closed the door. There was a dreadful moment as everyone stared at their shoes after which, since there was nothing more to say, guests drifted out. Reggie, understandably, was in a rage. Nadia, to her credit, carried it off with great dignity and said nothing as they went to their rooms. Reggie was so angry he could not sleep and later that night he returned to Bea's and listened for signs of life inside. Hearing none, he slipped a note under Bea's door in which he demanded that she apologize to Nadia. Bea never mentioned the note and Reggie always felt that she either chose to pretend she did not read it or that John had confiscated it when he returned to check on her. Nadia confronted John in the theatre the next day and proceeded to let him know how she felt about the terrible shape Bea was in and then she left for home.

Reggie, unable to brush the incident aside, then faced Bea and loudly told her exactly how he felt. As a result, Bea took to her bed and the show closed down for the next few days. A doctor was called and Bea remained secluded in her room, seeing only a few of the company. Famous opera soprano Mary Garden, then in her eighties, had come to Chicago to give a lecture and was stricken with the flu in the same hotel as Bea. They shared Dr. Collins, the hotel doctor, who carried messages back and forth between the two stars.

Finally Bea agreed to appear at a matinee and I went to the hotel to escort her to the theatre. As we waited for the elevator a very old lady came along the passage and introduced herself to Bea. It was Mary Garden and the two ladies boarded a crowded elevator to- gether. On the way down Mary Garden turned to Bea and blurted out clearly, "You know, my father was a great admirer of yours. He had your pictures all over his workshop." Bea smiled frigidly and made a fast exit when the car reached the lobby, waving a quick good-bye to Garden.

"Just how old is that supposed to make me?" Bea muttered huffily under her breath and before I could answer she added, "And if you ever mention this to anyone I'll kill you!"

True to her word, Nadia did honor Bea with a party after the show opened in Los Angeles. *An Evening With Beatrice Lillie* played the Biltmore Theatre and many of Bea's friends arrived to say hello, including Vincente Minnelli, Claudette Colbert, Bob Goldstein, Gracie Allen, Harpo Marx, Clark Gable, who sent flowers the next day, and Cary Grant. Nadia and Reggie went all out at their home on North Crescent and produced a star-studded affair. A band of strolling balalaika players, in keeping with Nadia's Russian back- ground, kept guests entertained all evening. Early arrivals were greeted by the sight of a slightly inebriated Louella Parsons trying to keep her balance by employing the arm of five-year-old Peter Gardiner as a lever. Peter, teeth gritted bravely, held his ground until rescued.

Bea had been previously booked on a late-night television interview show and Reggie obligingly turned on a set in the den for anyone who wanted to see the program. By the time the interview ended, the Gardiner house was jammed with guests. The affair was in full swing when Reggie realized that Bea had not arrived. She was in the car with Rene and John. For some reason, perhaps the confrontation with Nadia in Chicago or her subsequent suggestion, delivered by Reggie, that he forgo the party, John elected to drive Bea and Rene through most of Southern California in a deliberate attempt to make Bea late for the party. Nobody ever knew what he hoped to accomplish, but most of the company assumed he felt he was destroying the evening by keeping Bea in absentia. As John sped aimlessly through the night, Reggie and Nadia's guests were gawking at the likes of Elizabeth Taylor, Grace Kelly, Bing Crosby, Michael Wilding, Darryl F. Zanuck, Louella Parsons, Hedda Hopper, and Brian Aherne, to name but a few. It seemed Reggie was the only person aware that Bea was not in attendance.

Meanwhile, in the car Bea was close to hysterics, and only when she threatened to open the door and leap out did John turn around and head for the Gardiners. Bea arrived in terrible disarray and retired posthaste to one of the guest rooms to pull herself together. She met Shannon Dean and inquired if she had any sort of stimulant she could take to perk her up or something to calm her nerves. Dean slipped her a Dexedrine. Later Bea was to discover that no matter what she drank the pill kept her sober, and for years after, Shannon would receive an unexpected call from Bea when she felt in need of a "pick-me-up" or a "stay-sober."

Unfortunately, John added fuel to an already smoldering fire at the Gardiners' party by quietly but firmly passing the word along to the *Evening Avec* cast that they were not to hang around Bea or bask in her light with the intention of being introduced to celebrities, most of whom everyone had already met and talked to in any case. As luck would have it, somebody slipped the word to Reggie, who flew into a rage and threatened to evict John from the party. Nadia, cool as always in a crisis, calmed everyone down, and the party, according to the papers the following day, was the hit of the season. Many years later, Nadia stated that she felt that Bea had once been in love with Reggie, probably in the thirties, which accounted for Bea's lingering coolness toward her.

Anna Russell, the famous Australian satirist, came backstage one night to see Bea. Reggie, Ellen Graham, and I were in Bea's room having a drink when the "Down-Under Diva" arrived. Anna, toujours effervescent, swept into Bea's room extolling the merits of the performance in a voice fit for a Valkyrie.

"My darling, you were wonderful, magnificent!" she expounded, "Whoever did the casting for this show? Reggie is perfect! Eadie and Rack are superb!" Then before anyone could stop her, Anna shrieked, "And where did you ever find that great big fat tenor?" Reggie nearly choked on his drink and fled the room with Ellen and me close on his heels, leaving Bea to cope with the situation. Bea closed her door quickly and I hoped fervently that John had not heard the remark.

Before the show closed in Los Angeles, Bea received a visit from Jack Benny. Rene remained close by while the two great comedians met in Bea's room. After some time Benny left but not before he located Rene. "Is anyone around to see Bea home?" he asked sadly. "She's had a lot to drink and she'll need help." Rene assured him there was and Mr. Benny departed.

Gordon MacRae saw the show and looked Bea up in San Francisco. Gordon was appearing in a show, awaiting news of the birth of his new child in Los Angeles and praying to be notified that he would be the star of the forthcoming film version of *Oklahoma*. Bea promised to have a small party for him before he left. She invited members of the cast to Finocchio's, a world-famous female impersonator nightclub. Most of the cast played the show to her and she visited the performers backstage afterwards. During nightcaps, someone mentioned that Christine Jorgensen was living in the penthouse at the Fielding Hotel, where most of the cast were staying. Bea decided that Christine must be invited to Gordon's party the following night. Christine's manager did not agree readily when I contacted him, insisting that if Bea Lillie requested the

presence of Christine then Bea Lillie should do the inviting. A
telegram was immediately sent in Bea's name. No answer was
forthcoming, and the following night Bea insisted that Janet Medlin
and I visit Christine and invite her personally. I could talk to
Christine, and Janet would add the proper air of refinement, according to Bea. There was resistance once more from Christine's
manager but eventually he ushered us into a room where the world's
most famous transsexual was preparing to do her act. It was not easy
but we finally convinced Chris that we were on the level, and she
agreed to show up for a drink after her last show that evening. Crazed
with success, we relayed the news to Bea.

Bea was so anxious to meet Jorgensen that she forwent any liquor
all evening and was completely sober when Christine arrived with
her manager and his wife. The cast and crew and other guests were
quivering with suspense, but Christine very quickly put everyone at
ease. She and Bea liked each other enormously and remained friends
from then on. In 1954, three years after world headlines announced
Christine's sex change in Denmark, she still attracted crowds wherever she went. Purchasing a specially built fire-engine-red Cadillac
convertible did little to aid her anonymity in San Francisco. There
was little likelihood of the car's being stolen, since wherever Chris
chose to park it the automobile was immediately surrounded by
hordes of people; nobody stole either ruby installed over each
headlight.

When John Brooks, Bea's London attorney, came to see Bea,
Chris lent me the car to meet him at the air terminal.

"My God, I hope this isn't Bea's car," he gasped. "It must have
cost the earth!" I assured him it was not his client's wagon, and we
headed for the city with the top down. En route Brooks became
increasingly alarmed at the number of cab drivers, pedestrians, and
police who called out to us whenever we stopped for a light or crossed
an intersection. Finally, after a few hundred "Where's Christine?"'s,
Brooks glanced at me as if I might be kidnapping him for ransom and
timidly inquired, "Christine who?"

"Jorgensen," I called out gaily and Brooks nearly fainted. He did
not faint, however, when Bea took him to see Christine's act that
night. Instead, as Christine approached Bea's table after the per-

formance, Brooks leaped to his feet, pumped her hand vigorously, and stammered, "Oh, how do you do. We have one in England too, you know!" Nobody laughed harder than Christine.

Christine called me one day, puzzled by John Philip's offer to be her personal manager. Chris was being represented by a perfectly able manager and declined the offer. She also was confused as to how he planned to be with Bea and her at the same time. Nothing was ever mentioned about the offer again, and it is not known if John intended to leave Bea for another position. At that moment, for a career move, it would have made sense since Eddie Dowling was still Bea's manager, and Howard Reinheimer, her attorney, handled her financial affairs and contracts. Jorgensen was also attracting huge sums for appearances throughout the world.

Shortly before the show left San Francisco, Bea and Christine were alone in Chris's suite. Chris informed Bea that she was contemplating a book about her life, whereupon Bea suddenly grasped Jorgensen's arm, and in a voice shaking with emotion said, "Don't ever tell anyone everything about yourself!"

"To this day, I have no idea what she meant by all that. I do know the effect was chilling. Then, a second later, everything was back to normal," claimed Christine.

John brought a man named Albert Taylor to see Bea in San Francisco. John introduced him as a waiter from the Palace Hotel who had served with Bobbie in the navy. Taylor told her that he had been a member of the burial squad when Bobbie was laid to rest with his shipmates. All of this came as a surprise to Bea, who had been officially notified only that Bobbie was missing and presumed dead. This information arrived as Easter was approaching, heralding the anniversary of Bobbie's death. In retrospect it is interesting to note that the only Albert Taylor on record at the Palace Hotel went to work there eight years after Bea played San Francisco.

Bea fell completely apart in Vancouver shortly after Easter, the anniversary of Bobbie's death. A guest discovered her sleeping on a loveseat in the hallway near her suite. Totally disoriented, Bea found her way to the lobby attired only in a sheer nightgown, where she confronted a startled desk clerk. The clerk contacted John with great haste and John responded by phoning other members of the cast and asking them to run to the lobby and rescue Bea from her predicament. He received little cooperation from slumbering co-workers but steadfastly refused to leave his room. John's reluctance to go to Bea probably stemmed from the fact that she usually turned on him when she drank, whereas with others she was docile and friendly. Finally, Rene was roused and ordered to the front.

The perplexed hotel employee tried his best to convince Bea that she would be more comfortable in her room. As he was arguing the point with her, an airline bus drew up in front of the hotel and discharged members of a crew. Bea chose that second to groggily ask the clerk where she was.

"In the lobby of the Georgia Hotel. Vancouver," stated the man.

"Fuck Vancouver!" caroled Bea as the flight crew entered the lobby. Rene arrived with Bea's mink coat, and wrapping it securely about Bea bundled her off to bed before the amazed group recognized her. As a result of Bea's problems the show was cancelled once again for a few performances.

Eddie Dowling was forced to join the company in Minneapolis when Louis Epstein died suddenly. Eppie had been complaining about ill health for some time. When he failed to show up for the payroll, Milton and I found him dead in his bed, a book in his hand and a smile on his face.

"Poor Al Jolson," said Bea sadly. "Imagine what he is going through right now!" Eppie had been Jolson's friend and manager for many years. When Jolson died, he left Eppie nothing in his will and broke Eppie's heart. Eppie claimed he was forced to sue for his final year's salary because he had no money. Jolson was not a name one mentioned to Eppie.

Dowling arrived with Abe Cohen, another Shubert company manager and good friend of Bea's. Eddie's appearance seemed to upset John to the extent that he lost his temper and went after Rene, nearly choking her and frightening Bea half to death. Eddie's cavalier attitude toward John enraged him. Eddie was as always still Bea's personal manager. Everyone breathed easier when Eddie returned to New York and peace was restored. Happily Rene cared enough for Bea to forget the experience.

Bea, when intoxicated, began more and more to send for hotel doctors. When she took to her bed after a night of socializing, she would take her sleeping pills which John left each evening in her turtle-shaped pillbox. However, when she arose later to have her night lunch, she would insist that she had not taken them. This would be followed by phone calls to John or the hotel desk demanding to see a doctor. Bea would then explain to each doctor that she was unable to sleep and would request Demerol. Many of the doctors obliged since they were dealing with an international star with a spotless reputation, and Bea would sleep through the night. When John switched to placebos, it only made matters worse and Bea was up most of the night. She would also hide her jewelry on closet shelves and under mattresses, making it necessary for Rene to search the room carefully when Bea left it.

Abe Cohen's presence lifted Bea's spirits a great deal. He insisted upon introducing her as "Lady Cohen" to strangers and would storm into her dressing room and demand that she begin the show if she was behind schedule. Bea would pretend anger but she enjoyed it. When he burst in one night and shouted at Bea and Ellen, "Will you two bitches shut up and get this show on the road," Bea quickly dressed screaming with laughter and got the show on the road.

On one of her trips by train, Bea drank too much in her stateroom and Abe had to have the car switched to another station in Chicago. A well-known columnist arrived to interview Bea and found himself in a verbal altercation with John, whom he later referred to in his paper as Bea's Svengali. John resented the implication deeply and ever after denied any such motive when interviewed. Unfortunately, during the argument, Bea removed an expensive ring and hid it in the berth. It was never recovered.

Rene set fire to her hotel room in Buffalo and Fitzy arrived in Baltimore with her sister to look after Bea for the closing week. Everybody celebrated on closing night in the theatre, so much so that Bea had to be carried up the freight elevator in her hotel. She then called for a doctor, who after listening to her refused to give her any Demerol.

"I refuse to contribute to Miss Lillie's dependence upon Demerol," he declared sorrowfully. John was furious but the doctor was adamant. Actually, Bea never mentioned Demerol unless she had really been drinking heavily.

The Hugh Beaumont office in London contacted Eddie and agreed to present Bea in *An Evening With Beatrice Lillie* in the fall of 1954. Ever since San Francisco, John had toyed with the idea of flying with Bea to the Far East to visit Bobbie's grave now that she was aware there was one. Bea never for one minute believed Bobbie's body had ever been found, but John persisted.

Because of the long and involved trip, Bea went to Howard Reinheimer to have her will updated. I was in the apartment when she arrived home in a rage. She was furious with Howard, who had asked her in the privacy of his office if there was a possibility that she and John might be secretly married.

"How dare he! How bloody dare he!" she raged. It took a few moments to calm her down enough to explain to her that Howard had to ask her the question in the event something happened to her on the trip. She finally cooled down but it took a few days for her to forgive Howard for putting her on the spot. Plans were made for the trip, although Bea was not keen on the flight around the world, which would terminate in England in time to rehearse the show.

A few days before the flight, Bea called and asked if I wanted to go shopping for some last-minute items. We toured Fifth Avenue and decided to dine at Sardi's later. She suggested we go to a film to kill time. I knew she did not want to have anything to drink early in the day so we did just that. Considering the enormity of the flight she was about to embark upon, Bea and I may have been the only two members of the audience who laughed our way through *The High and the Mighty*, a somber film about passengers aboard an airliner in trouble. John was angry that I had taken Bea to see such a picture before the flight, but Bea and I could only giggle harder at the absurd coincidence. Just before she left, Bea asked if I would like to live in her flat at East End Avenue while I searched for an apartment of my own. Her only stipulation was that I not inform John of the arrangement. Grant was still serving in the army, and since the flat was vacant I agreed, and promised to forward the mail and keep an eye on things.

Grant and I saw Bea off on her double-decker Pan American clipper, which took her to Hong Kong and thence to Colombo. The caretakers of the military cemetery where Bobbie was buried were in the process of landscaping the grounds and the commemorative stones had been placed flat on the grass. When officials were notified of Bea's visit they thoughtfully ordered the memorial to Bobbie and his friends to be righted, adding a measure of dignity to Bea's difficult journey. For a time Bea pondered the idea of having Bobbie's remains flown to England but decided to leave him where he was. If he wasn't really buried there, she did not wish to know about it. When the ordeal was over, Bea and John visited Japan where they attended the Kabuki theatre and flew home from Tokyo.

Before getting into rehearsals Bea went to Capri where she saw Noël Coward briefly and spent some time with Christine Jorgensen, who was on a European holiday. Bea gathered a group together for a farewell party for Noël and, with Gracie Fields joining the group, Bea, Ellen Graham, and a crowd went on board movie producer Sam Spiegel's yacht for drinks. New York socialite Peter Howard was on holiday with Lady Sylvia Ashley, wife of Clark Gable. When introduced, Christine addressed her as Mrs. Gable and received a decidedly frigid reaction. Bea explained that dear Sylvia preferred Lady Ashley while in Europe.

"Being called Mrs. Clark Gable anywhere isn't too bad where I come from," cracked Christine.

Reginald Gardiner decided he had had enough and did not appear with the show in England. Instead, Bea selected a young comedian just out of Cambridge named Leslie Bricusse. Eadie and Rack flew over to join Constance Carpenter and the rest of the London Company which opened in November of 1954.

"I was very moved after the first night of *An Evening With Beatrice Lillie*," recalled Alured Weigall. "When we went backstage and brought her out to go back to her flat, we had to push through a crowd at the stage door. Everybody was saying, 'How wonderful, how wonderful.' She was exhausted and said, 'Well, just wait until we get the critics tomorrow.' She looked drawn and thoroughly apprehensive. As we got into the car she suddenly let everything go. She

released all her worries and said, 'Well, anyway, I did my best.' "
This was Bea's first London appearance in nearly eight years and she
always felt that New York audiences were more responsive to her
style of performing. Her reviews were excellent on the whole, with
one reviewer stating, "To spend an evening with Miss Lillie was to
be entranced all over again by her art." *The Daily Express*, though, felt
that "Miss Lillie is a survival of the cocktail age." London audiences
were happy to have Bea back and business was exceedingly good.

Bea once again was able to spend time in Henley-on-Thames
where Lucie was still being looked after by Eileen Magowan. Bea
divided her time between Henley and her London apartment at 55
Park Lane. Mrs. Lillie was becoming increasingly senile and Bea
complained to friends that she had taken to tossing the patio furniture into the Thames. Although Bea was able to make light of it when
she told the story, it nevertheless worried her. She did manage a
laugh when Christine Jorgensen suggested she buy iron furniture.
Mumsie enjoyed automobile rides through the countryside and Bea
opened an account with the local taxi service. Lucie became particularly fond of one of the drivers and Miss Magowan always requested him. Lucie would greet him genially but after some time
passed would suddenly ask Magowan who the man was and what he
was doing in her car. Miss Magowan would hasten homeward and the
drive would terminate. If Bea encountered Muriel there on a visit it
became doubly difficult for her. Muriel was drinking heavily and
often berated Bea for imaginary offenses. Muriel still emphatically
believed she was responsible for Bea's career. On the other hand,
both sisters, when in their cups, were capable of outrageous statements concerning their mother, brought on in Bea's case by Lucie's
close association with Bobbie, an intimacy which Bea never completely shared, her interference in their private lives, and her constant domineering presence.

Though the show was a hit, Bea's personal life was far from a
success. John was dating another woman, an actress, and Bea was
angry and hurt. She called Pat Dolin one night very late and asked
him to come to her flat at 55 Park Lane. "I can't take any more," she
cried and threatened to do herself in if Pat did not come.

"I went 'round but I had the good sense to check with the porter," said Pat. "I told him I'd had a call from Bea and that I was going up. He said, "I think Mr. Philip's just gone up." I went up, rang the bell, knocked at the door and nobody came." Pat left after telling the porter to note the time.

"The next day around five o'clock," continued Pat, "Bea called and asked what I was doing that night and that was that. She said that John was back. He was having a thing with this woman we always called 'the poor man's Ethel Merman.' " Bea never mentioned her call to Pat or her threat to herself and Pat dropped the matter. Eadie said later that Bea went to the apartment of the lady in question and there followed an unpleasant scene.

One night Phyllis Monkman stopped backstage to see Bea and found she had been drinking. "I went by the dressing room to say hello, I was on my way home. I thought, 'Bea can't go on this evening.' The stage manager came into the room and said it was eight o'clock or whatever it was. She went on and dried up all over the place and then she fell down on the stage and they had to ring down. She pulled herself together, they gave her a cup of coffee, and she went on and fell down again. Then she started drying up. Some woman in the stalls shouted out, 'She wants a cup of coffee, that's what she wants!' So they rang down and didn't ring up again." That was the only time in a forty-year friendship that Phyllis or anyone ever saw Bea drink at performance time. The newspapers reported that Bea had fainted and in a letter to me she stated that she had been off for five minutes, that her illness was exaggerated.

Bea's "illness" brought John home quickly, and Bea divided her time between Henley and London once more. Muriel remained in a flat at Hamilton Close and Bea was assuming financial responsibility for her. The houses belonging to Lucie sat dormant at Abercorn Place at the time.

After her London success Bea toured the provinces to great acclaim and proceeded to record *An Evening With Beatrice Lillie* with Eadie and Rack. There was a slight brouhaha connected with that when Rolf Gérard called me to say that on the first release the *Evening With Beatrice Lillie* album did not carry his signature on the caricature used for the cover. Gérard said he was not too concerned but that his union could take offense. Word was sent to London and the omission was rectified. The album was a great success and became a collector's item later. When the show closed, Leslie Bricusse, who played opposite Bea, married and honeymooned in her New York apartment and then returned to London to write a show called *Stop the World I Want to Get Off* with a talented young man named Anthony Newley. Before she left England, Bea filmed a cameo scene in Michael Todd's *Around the World in Eighty Days.*

THIRTEEN

Bea and John returned to New York early in 1956. She called immediately to ask if I would, first, go shopping with her, and, two, go to Coconut Grove and Palm Beach with another *Evening With Beatrice Lillie*. I said yes to both. Eadie and Rack were booked for the winter at the Roney Plaza in Miami and would not be available, and Reggie Gardiner was working elsewhere, but Ellen, Shannon Dean, and Constance Carpenter agreed to do the production. Since Leslie Bricusse was busy writing, Bea recruited Fred Keating, raconteur and magician, to perform opposite her. Fred had been in *Dr. Rhythm* with Bea and Bing Crosby, and his sense of comedy, charm, and his exceptional magic tricks made him a natural for the show. I arranged for Bea to listen to a young pianist-conductor named Donald Pippen; she liked him immediately. Don brought a shy attractive pianist named John Kander, whom she hired first for his good looks and secondly because he could play piano. Her only problem with her new piano team was remembering names. She had been introducing Eadie and Rack for such a great while that she decided to call them Don and Jack in order not to botch it up. On opening night in Florida she very proudly introduced them as Eadie and Rack anyway.

While readying the show, Bea and Brandon dated at Sardi's with his parents and managed an evening at the Stork Club for the first time in years. Sherman Billingsley sent her perfume the following day. William Hammerstein, son of Oscar, had under option a musical in which he felt Bea would be perfect. Entitled *The Works*, it concerned mystery and love in a wax museum. Bea, John, and I went to Oscar Hammerstein's house on East Sixty-first Street and joined Bill Hammerstein, Albert Hague, the composer, and Herbert and Dorothy Fields, who wrote the book and lyrics. Bea listened to the story and the score and she was definitely interested in the show.

Bea was seeing less and less of Eddie Duryea Dowling since she was being contacted by the theatres directly, but her attorney, Howard Reinheimer, continued to handle contracts and all business. Bea managed a visit to Eddie's mother's bedside in the hospital. Mrs. Dowling continued to hope that Bea and Eddie might marry.

Reinheimer usually received bills and charge account receipts directly and paid them after Bea approved them. John began to change the system and the bills came to Bea directly. Both Bea and John procrastinated so badly that the stores were constantly sending warnings and late charges. Because of the delay, Bea would insist that certain bills had been paid and I would have to dig back into the checkbook to prove to her they had not. John was charging so much in Bea's name that he did not want Reinheimer to be aware of it. Neither did Bea.

Michael Ellis, managing director of the Coconut Grove Playhouse, supplied Bea with a large airy apartment over the theatre. There was a kitchenette, two baths, two bedrooms, and it was a short walk downstairs to the theatre. Bea decided I should sleep on the living room couch. On opening night, there was a party in the restaurant adjoining the theatre and Bea was seated next to Marlon Brando, whom she did not recognize. There was very little conversation until a photographer called Brando by name whereupon Bea plunged into conversation with him. Brando asked to be excused and never returned to the table. Later he told a friend he felt that people should not speak to someone just because they were a celebrity. It was explained to him that Bea was ill at ease with strangers and found it difficult to engage in conversation. When she realized who he was, Bea found a level on which to talk with him. Brando later visited her at 25 East End Avenue. As the evening wore on Bea had too much to drink, and John asked George Campbell, the press representative, to see her to the apartment. George, who hardly knew any of us, agreed out of respect and took her home. Bea made a scene when John did not follow and asked George to call a doctor, which he gladly did. The physician and John arrived at approximately the same time, and a verbal battle occurred during which John physically barred him from entering Bea's room. The police were called and detained John while the doctor tended to Bea.

Although the scene did not sit well with George, he became fond of Bea and held a series of parties at his home for the company, a few at night and some by the poolside during the day. Then one night John disappeared and Bea was in a rage and drank too much. In the apartment, I begged her to forget it and get some rest but she was out for no good that night. Unbeknownst to me, she called the police and gave her name as Lady Peel. In the restaurant downstairs, Ellen and Connie Carpenter were having a late snack, when the officers arrived. When they heard them ask for a Mrs. Ladapeel, Connie and Ellen ordered another drink and kept quiet, although they both knew instantly who "Mrs. Ladapeel" was. The police thundered down the hall, while I prayed Bea would not hear them and that they would not knock at the door. They finally left, and when I informed Bea that they had come and gone she was livid. I then informed her that I was leaving that snake pit and left. I ran into John Kander the following day and poured out the saga of the night before. He suggested we have a quiet dinner a good distance from the theatre and talk it all over. We were hardly seated before Bea and a group walked in and were seated at the next table. Bea and I had our backs to each other. On the way out, a member of the cast stopped Kander, and I was trapped next to Bea. A light tug on my jacket caused me to look down into her face. "Snake pit, huh?" she whispered and grinned wickedly. I leaned over and kissed her on the cheek. "I love you," I mumbled. "S'mutual," she answered.

Palm Beach welcomed the show with open arms. It was Bea's first visit in some time and the first familiar face she saw was that of Channing Hare, the portrait artist. Channing painted a portrait of Bea in the thirties and immediately demanded that she sit for another. Bea agreed and with that settled, the show opened to rave

189

reviews. The George Vigouroux hosted the opening night party and extended Bea and Company the use of their pool while we were there. George had been a dancer in *She's My Baby* but neither Bea nor he mentioned it, Bea having evidently forgotten it and George probably wishing to forget it.

We began using George's pool and every day he had lunch served and Bea sunbathed and swam. John insisted upon sunbathing nude on his stomach, which embarrassed Bea because of the servants.

One day Bea and I were stretched out side by side when George came down for a swim. He was preparing to dive, when Bea asked him where Ethel, his wife, was.

"She's in her room going over her checkbook. She's fifty-five thousand dollars overdrawn," said George and dove into the water. Bea and I sat bolt upright in unison and Bea mouthed, "Fifty-five thousand?" at me. Later he told us all was well, it was only fifty-five cents.

The show played for a week and the company departed, leaving Bea, Ellen, John, and me in Palm Beach. Channing was painting Bea and the party invitations were stacked up. Actors Murray Matheson, Iggie Wolfington, and Eric Rhodes, all friends of Bea's, arrived for the next show, which gave her a further reason for remaining in Palm Beach.

John was still haggling with Bill Hammerstein over *The Works*. He was suggesting under the guise of joking that he might be right for the lead and later, when he was on the phone with Hammerstein, I heard him say, "How much? Oh, come now, Bill, your father paid that secretary from Astoria more than that for doing *Annie Get Your Gun*." The absurdity of the remark would have had me screaming with laughter had it not been such an insult to Ethel Merman.

Then literary agent Harold Freedman arrived with a script of *Auntie Mame* based on Patrick Dennis' book. Bea was enchanted with it. Freedman broached the idea of two companies opening simultaneously, one in New York with Rosalind Russell and one in London with Beatrice Lillie. John was annoyed that Freedman talked directly with Bea and with his eye still on the male lead in *The Works*, nothing came of *Auntie Mame* at that time.

When George Vigouroux took us deep-sea fishing, we met at

sun-up and went to sea for the day. It was a beautiful day but there were no fish. We tried three or four locations and then had lunch. Afterwards, Bea and Ellen dozed in the sun and I continued to fish. Suddenly I had a strike and screamed, "I've got something!" Bea leaped to her feet and grabbed her purse exclaiming, "Oh, dear, how do I look?" and repaired her makeup as I reeled in a thirty-six-pound grouper. It was a record catch and there were pictures taken at the dock later. George took the fish home and invited us to have dinner that evening. George's cook prepared a wonderful meal with the grouper as the star attraction. Bea and I looked at the fish, then at each other and we could not eat it.

One day, near the end of our stay, Bea was making up in her bathroom and I sat on the edge of her tub while we talked. We were making silly chatter and giggling with laughter. I began an off-color story and Bea signaled for me to lower my voice, which I did. Just before the punchline, John strong-armed his way through her front door.

"What's going on in here? What are you two whispering about?" he shouted. Bea and I were thunderstruck. Bea was frightened out of her wits, grabbed her purse, and ran out the door with me close behind. We walked quickly down the street and I held her steady as she fought back the tears. Suddenly John was in the car and driving down the street next to us.

"What's wrong? Why are you acting like this?" he demanded. Bea did not answer. A moment later, he veered to the left and landed on the sidewalk in front of us. He missed us by an inch. Bea was frantic by then and walked around the automobile and kept walking as John called for us to get into the vehicle. Finally, he realized he was not winning and drove off. Bea and I continued our walk and as we began to cross the highway, a sports car headed in our direction changed course and made straight for us. We leaped onto the curb as the car screeched to a halt. There was laughter from within as the window rolled down revealing the face of the Duke of Windsor. He and Bea enjoyed a good talk and her mood lightened dramatically. As he drove off, I mentioned that she called him Sir all through the conversation.

"Well, dear, he was the King," she said seriously.

"Then what do you call the Duchess?" I wondered.

"Mrs. Simpson!" she sniffed and walked on.

Bea had the opportunity to see Mrs. Simpson and the Duke once again at the Red Cross Ball headed by Cobina Wright. There was wining and dining and dancing to Lester Lanin followed by a round of speeches. When the party ended, Bea came across the Duchess's place card in front of Mrs. Wright's place. On it in the Duchess's strong handwriting were the words, "Mrs. Wright. The Duke does not get up ever. *Remember that*," which explained why the Duke of Windsor did not speak that evening.

Palm Beach was locking up for the season as we left. A car rental service offered us two automobiles free if we would drive them to their location in New York. Bea drove with me and John took off at high speed and disappeared almost immediately. Bea, who hated speeding, relaxed and we were enjoying the ride when, in Virginia, we saw a homemade sign advertising Pekingese puppies for sale. We discovered a little house in the woods and stopped. Bea saw a beautiful beige-colored Peke sunning itself in a wire enclosure and scooped it up in her arms.

"This dog is absolutely beautiful. I love him!" cried Bea.

"So do I. She's my prize bitch. Put her down," said a voice from a window.

The lady of the house proved to be jolly and hospitable and took us inside. There we were shown a litter of six- or eight-week-old beige-tinted Pekes with pitch black muzzles. Bea wanted all of them until a fat, sociable little male ran out from under the stove and pushed its way through the others and onto Bea's lap. She was lost. Between us, we managed to scrounge up the ante for the dog and left the house with seventy-five cents between us. A check of the gas meter warned us that we were nearly out of fuel. We bought seventy-five cents' worth and headed into the bank in the next town we passed. The manager obligingly called Bea's New York Bank, and we sped up the highway with a pocketful of cash, a full tank, and a new dog.

When we arrived at 25 East End Avenue, the doorman hurried out to Bea. "I am sorry to tell you this but Mr. MacArthur is very ill in the hospital. He asked if you were back in New York."

When Bea sought additional information the man added proudly, "He would not have an ambulance or a cab. He walked there himself. He wanted you to know that."

Bea spoke with Helen Hayes, who said Charlie was terribly ill. According to Bea, she was told that Charlie pulled all of the tubes from his body, that he wanted to go. Bea kept in touch, and at one point Helen told her that when she leaned close to Charlie in his hospital bed and told him that she loved him, his eyes fluttered open and he murmured, "You should." Bea also learned that at one point he said, "I believe in God, I just wish he hadn't written me such a lousy exit." She was overcome with grief when MacArthur died. A great deal of her past went with him, and she ached with compassion for Helen. Bea, Dorothy and Lillian Gish, Rodgers and Hammerstein, Irving Berlin, and Alfred Lunt were among the many friends who heard Ben Hecht deliver the eulogy for his lifelong friend. Charlie was buried in the cemetery in Nyack, and Bea never forgot him.

When Bea had been home for a few days, I asked her what she planned to do with the dog. By now she was calling him Mr. Lee after the Chinese laundry man from her youth. She decided the dog was for Old Vic (Milton Stern's daughter, Victoria), but each day she grew to love it more.

"Guess what I have in my apartment," Bea teased Old Vic on the phone. Old Vic could not guess. "It's an adorable little puppy."

"What kind?" shrieked Victoria excitedly.

"It's a beautiful little Pekingese."

"Oh, no!" cried Old Vic. "My mother says those dogs are the worst!" Bea was thrilled with Old Vic's sentiment, and Mr. Lee remained with Bea for the rest of his life.

The De Wildes were in town, and Bea picked up her romance with Brandon once more. She visited him in Baldwin and made some sweeps by Coney Island. Brandon hated school and was facing the coming summer with the prospect of a tutor and was depressed.

Christine Jorgensen had invited us to her home for dinner, and we met her family for the first time. On the way to Brandon's one day we stopped by Christine's house, and she sent Brandon a photo autographed. "C. J." Brandon blushed and did not quite know how to respond to the gift.

Bill Hammerstein asked to see Bea in Howard Reinheimer's office to discuss *The Works*. Afterwards I asked her what was happening regarding the production. She said that she told Bill she would give him an answer very soon. When I saw Bill backstage at City Center later, he said, "What are we going to do about Bea?" I repeated Bea's statement and he looked at me strangely. I asked him if she did not say she would let him know, and Bill replied that he had simply told Bea that John would have to remain out of the picture if she agreed to do the show. Needless to say, Bea was not destined to play Broadway in *The Works*. Under the title *Redhead*, Gwen Verdon played the part and won a Tony award for it.

Bea promised to tour with a summer package of *Beasop's Fables*, another evening with some new sketches; the Florida group minus Constance Carpenter would be part of it. John Kander decided to join Fred Ebb and become a famous Broadway composer, and Don Pippen went on to be one of Broadway's busiest orchestra conductors. So Eadie and Rack, back from Miami, rejoined Bea.

Meanwhile, Bea went into Doctors Hospital for a checkup and remained a few days while they ran tests. During that time, Ellen Graham gave a party at her family's apartment on Park Avenue, which I attended. Cecil Beaton was intrigued by one of the female guests, a high-fashion model all in black. She was wearing a black-feathered hat and wore long black gloves. Ellen and I watched, fascinated, as she and Beaton went around the buffet table, while she tasted hot meatballs, shrimp, and all sorts of dips with her gloves on. When I remarked to Ellen that I would scream if she washed her hands with the gloves on, Ellen screamed. And so did Bea when I described the scene to her later at the hospital. The next morning Bea called.

"I have a wonderful idea for a sketch," she said. "You're the waiter and I eat all this food with long black gloves on."

"And?" I inquired.

"I don't know, we'll make it up. Come up to the apartment and we'll talk about it."

"Milady Dines Alone," one of Bea's funniest sketches, was born as a result of Ellen's party. Ellen went right to work on the designs for a gown and the hat. Bea and I were still working on the sketch when we opened at the Grist Mill Playhouse in Andover, New Jersey. The scene opened on an opulent restaurant. There were huge doors upstage. While Schubert's "Serenade," recorded in 1905 by Mischa Ellman, squeaked in the background, Bea opened the doors and was discovered standing in a blinding snowstorm. Wearing the long black gown, a wildly feathered hat, long black gloves, and a huge feathered muff, Bea moved slowly downstage. As she turned upstage, kicking her train and flinging tons of paper snow into the wings, she revealed her back, bare almost to the waist. She then proceeded to devour the asparagus, corn on the cob, lobster, and artichoke, all dipped in butter, with her gloves on. At the end, she rinsed her gloves out in the finger bowl and left after stealing the bottle of wine in her muff.

Margaret, Bea's London maid, came on the tour, but she was not happy having to share a room with John from time to time. The bickering got on her nerves, and the final straw came when she was forced to share a double-sized convertible bed with John. Margaret packed it in and was never heard from again.

John Shubert came to Fayetteville, New York, to talk to Bea about a fiftieth anniversary production of *Ziegfeld Follies*. Tallulah Bankhead had just closed out of town in an unsuccessful edition, and Shubert wished to try it again, this time with new producers and, if possible, with Beatrice Lillie. He promised Bea new sketches, songs, scenery, and costumes. He also offered her any Shubert Theatre she wished on Broadway. Leaving Bea with all that, Shubert returned to the Great White Way while she thought about it.

John was arrested on the way to the Cape for speeding and was forced to go to traffic court and pay a fine. Then he bumped into the rear end of a lady's car. It was not a serious accident but the lady recognized Bea and wrote her a letter. A simple traffic accident had now developed into whiplash, scabies, sterility, or what have you. Bea chose to ignore the letter, and its writer was never heard from again.

When we left Matunik by the Sea, I was getting into my car when the passenger door flew open and Bea leaped into the automobile clutching Mr. Lee to her bosom.

"Get going," she ordered, sounding for all the world like Claire Trevor in a Humphrey Bogart film. I ventured to ask where we were going. "To Boston. John's making a terrible scene and I want to get out of here!" I stepped on the gas and drove straight to Boston without a stop and deposited Bea at the Copley Plaza. John had evidently disagreed with Don Wolin, the producer, over the week's take, and an argument had ensued.

While we played Boston, I received a call from Channing Hare. He was calling from his Ogunquit home and invited me to stay with him while I was in Maine. I declined on the grounds that Bea was his friend and I would feel uncomfortable accepting his hospitality with her in such close proximity. Reluctantly, Channing called Bea and asked her and John to guest with him. They accepted, and then I accepted. Channing hosted a lavish opening night party for Bea and for Bette Davis, who happened to be in Maine with her husband, Gary Merrill. Since Bea's room was on the ground floor, it was used for wraps. Somehow the thermostat in the room was turned up, and the room became very hot. John proceeded to make an unpleasant scene and demanded to know just how the hell Bea was supposed to sleep in a room that hot. Calmly, Channing informed him that there was a very comfortable inn not too far away and that perhaps he and Bea might be more comfortable there. The matter was dropped, and an opened window restored the room to normal.

When the tour ended, Bea returned to England. John wanted her to do the *Follies* and during the winter it was announced that she would appear in the spring under the banner of Mark Kroll and Charles Conaway. She arrived back in January and called to say she would do *Milady Dines Alone* if I would play the waiter. Milton Stern was stage-managing and I went on as his assistant. Bea was slightly piqued with me because I told her I felt the whole thing was wrong and she ought not to do it. She was piqued because she felt exactly the same way but John was insisting. He also was responsible for Bea's breaking a lifelong rule about investing in her own shows. She put five thousand dollars into *Follies* but was not happy doing it. She was happy, however, with her co-star, Billy DeWolfe. They met for lunch and she liked him immediately and was delighted with his Boston accent. The producers followed through with a fine cast, including Harold Lang, the superb dancer, and singer Jane Morgan. Richard Barstow, the dance director, hired some talented dancers and singers. Where the producers and Shubert did not follow through was in the sketch, scenery, and costume departments. Almost everything came from Tallulah's *Follies* but John was too busy finding parts for himself in the show to pay attention to this breach of promise to Bea. When some Tallulah dresses were dragged out for Bea, designer Raoul Pene Du Bois put his foot down and whisked Bea off to Fifth Avenue and found her some superb gowns and spared no expense doing it.

What the production lacked in the physical aspect, it made up for with one of the zaniest, most lovable casts assembled in one show. Billy and Bea set the tone for the company, which consisted of showgirls such as Pat Gaston, who married Tommy Manville while the show was still running, Barbara Hall, who won the $64,000 Question with Shakespeare as her topic (she later changed her name to Feldon and achieved fame on television as Agent 99 on *Get Smart*), and Charlotte (Chotzi) Foley, who won recognition as Electra, one of the strippers in *Gypsy*. While singing and dancing in *Ziegfeld Follies*, Carol Lawrence auditioned for *West Side Story* and got the part.

Bea had some good material to perform and came off well. She did a Kabuki number she had done in *An Evening With Beatrice Lillie* in London, something she thought of after seeing the Kabuki on her trip to the Orient. There was an airline stewardess who wrecked everyone's nerves; "Milady," which she used for her first number; and from *The Show Is On*, her moon number. The producers and director fought her on using the moon number, fearing the critics would fault it as old material. Bea's instincts won out and the number not only stopped the show every night but made the cover of *Life* magazine.

Sketches and songs went in and out of the show as fast as people could dream them up. Billy DeWolfe came with reams of his own material, which the audiences loved. He and Bea appeared as two ladies in a supermarket. Bea rushed through costume changes in order to watch Billy on stage.

Problems began in New Haven when John, without consulting Bea, told the prop man to change a prop. Bea was furious, and rather than face John with her anger, she blamed the prop man for taking orders from John and never spoke to him again. John made some very unpleasant remarks about the stagehands. Milton spent hours in a local pub trying to calm down the carpenter, who threatened to floor John. John Shubert told us that John wanted a door in the Kabuki number changed so that it would slide clear across the stage when Bea flung it open. It would cost five thousand dollars to achieve this. I told him it would ruin Bea's timing and that she would do it just once and then never again. John insisted, however, and the door was changed. Bea flung it open and it took forever for her to retrieve it and she never used it again. John then began asking for more material in the show for Bea to do. She, meanwhile, was insisting she would do only four numbers in each act. When push came to shove, Bea, as usual, demanded to know why they listened to John.

There was a production meeting one day and the director informed us that Bea was asking for more bits for John to do in the show. It meant cutting down material given to two brothers hired as comedy actors. When I was asked for an opinion, I simply said, "Do it." Milton seconded me and John was given the parts. The staff and producers were adamant in their refusal to allow John to sing a love duet with Jane Morgan. John was noticeably overweight and it probably would have evoked laughter if done seriously.

Things came to a head in Washington when a battle erupted between John and the creative staff over additional material for Bea, who continued to not want anything additional to do.

"Let me direct this show and I'll bring you in a hit," he shouted at John Shubert, a senseless remark since John had never directed anything in his life. When Milton tried to reason with him, he told Milton the only reason he had the job with the show was because Bea liked his daughter, Old Vic. Milton stopped speaking to him for some time after that. Thankfully, Bea was spared the anguish of these meetings, at least in the theatre. John would often bring them back to the hotel with him and she would hear about them then.

Critic Richard Coe invited Bea and a few of us to his home one night, but Bea generally retired early during the out-of-town period.

Coe was kind to Bea in his review, but the show, in spite of change after change, did not improve. *Ziegfeld Follies of 1957* opened at the Winter Garden on March 1, 1957. The notices were lukewarm, and the consensus was that it was a tacky rehash of a bygone era. Bea received a telegram from Billie Burke Ziegfeld wishing her well, but the show was not a hit. Brandon DeWilde and family attended the opening, and after the show he ran up to say hello as I was talking to Christine Jorgensen. Brandon was taken completely by surprise when I introduced him to C.J. but carried it off without batting an eye. Later he told his mother he nearly fainted.

There was an actor in the show named Robert Feyte, a close friend of Milton Stern's. Bob appeared in some of the sketches and became a stalwart aide-de-camp to Bea. He took over some of her secretarial work, ordered her food, and walked Mr. Lee during the show. He was friendly and extremely kind to Bea, and she began to depend upon him a great deal. At one point he moved into 25 East End Avenue. Bob's presence was a great boon to John, who felt free to leave and visit his family in Darien or to dine out without having to leave Bea alone in the apartment. The arrangement also relieved Bea from the pressure of accompanying John home. She was not close to his family, had nothing in common with them, and never looked forward with any pleasure to the trips. When John approached Bea with the suggestion that she pay him a ten-thousand-dollar-a-year retainer to act as her manager, she was furious and blamed his sister for putting him up to it. Bea claimed that she was already paying for everything he required in terms of clothing, food, cameras, electronic equipment, and travel, to say nothing of a place to live and an automobile. John had managed to manipulate himself into a Catch-22 situation. He was unable to leave Bea alone long enough to carve out a career for himself and earn a salary, and consequently he was as financially dependent upon her as she was on him to make her decisions and keep her company. The argument was carried into the theatre that night. In the finale of the first act, John was onstage with Bea and the rest of the company in a number called "Song of India." John ruined the number completely by stepping out of character and allowing the audience to see that he was angry. He pushed in front of Bea as if to frighten her and in general behaved unprofessionally.

When the curtain came down and the company was leaving the stage, Bea heard one of the girl singers complain angrily, "That fat son of a bitch!" Bea went to her room without a word, but when the girl left the show a few weeks later she came to say good-bye to Bea. Bea removed the platinum and diamond watch she always wore and gave it to the surprised girl.

Ziegfeld Follies of 1957 limped along until June when it closed after 124 performances. Noël Coward came to see the show and offered no comment although he did visit Bea in her dressing room afterwards. John involved Bea in a lawsuit against the producers and was awarded thirty-eight hundred dollars for an album which had never been produced. The producers then sued Bea for a twenty percent overcall on her investment, which had not been forthcoming at the time. It all ended in a draw. Before the show closed, Carol Lawrence was visiting Bea in the dressing room and sat on the floor playing with Mr. Lee. The dog leaped toward Carol and accidentally bit her on the cheek. Carol was rushed off to a doctor and Mr. Lee was banished to a veterinarian for observation and did ten days in stir for his offense. Both Bea and Carol objected strenuously but it was the law.

Free of the show, Bea posed for *Harper's Bazaar* and then appeared on the Arthur Murray television show in July. There were trips to Coney Island with Brandon and dinners at Sardi's. Brandon wanted fireworks for the Fourth of July and everyone met at Sardi's for dinner prior to a trip to Chinatown to purchase the noisemakers. Brandon was so excited he paid no attention to his parents' orders to finish his meal.

"Can't we go now?" he pleaded.

"We do not leave until you finish everything on your plate," Fritz replied sternly.

Brandon put his fork down, looked his father in the eye, and with great authority intoned, "Don't you realize it is a terrible thing to force a child to eat when he doesn't want to?" Brandon won that round, and everyone made a beeline for Chinatown.

When Bea showed up one night wearing a ten-thousand-dollar marquise-cut diamond ring, Brandon did a doubletake, grabbed Bea's hand, studied the stone carefully, and then announced in awe, "Gosh, I bet that cost a hundred dollars!" Bea joined the De Wildes and thousands of children and parents in Grand Central Station and waved Brandon off to summer camp that year.

George and Ethel Vigouroux invited Bea to visit them on Nantucket Island and with John and Billy DeWolfe in tow, she went. On the second or third evening there, Bea retired early and Billy and George pub-crawled until midnight. They returned to the house and settled down for a nightcap. As they sat talking in the living room, John arrived down the stairs in a rage demanding to know how Bea was going to sleep with all the racket going on in the living room. The two gentlemen went to bed and Billy changed his plans and left the following day.

Lucie Lillie died in November of 1957. Feyte called me and I rushed to East End Avenue to be there when Bea was told. She spent most of the day by herself. She told me later that she did not really know how she felt, but she remained completely calm during the ensuing days, which was characteristic of Bea under this sort of stress.

Bob Feyte remained in charge of Mr. Lee, and Bea and John flew to England, where Mumsie was laid to rest in the cemetery at St. Margaret's Church near Peel Fold.

Muriel had been in and out of the hospital and had moved into Abercorn Place after having the locks changed. Bea's solicitor accused Muriel of squatting and attempted to have her evicted. Alured Weigall contacted Bea on numerous occasions regarding the problem, but Bea, as always, paid no attention, and Muriel remained where she was.

For many many years Bea invested money in an annuity which, when she reached the age of sixty-five, would then pay her a monthly sum on which to live for the rest of her life. When she died, the remaining amount would be absorbed by the company in which she had invested the money. During the run of the *Follies*, John had been discussing a more lucrative plan by which the money would be willed to an heir. The company approached Bea, then sixty-three, and told her that if she forwent the annuity at age sixty-five and agreed to postpone her retirement for ten years, she would be free to leave any remaining money to whomever she chose. She chose the ten-year plan and settled it with her lawyer. By then John was thinking of investing Bea's earnings in saving accounts but a man he met at the time tried to interest him in creating a trust fund for Bea.

John later reported the man as saying, "Do it. It will protect the U.S. estate from possible acquisition from the U.K. estate because Bea's a so-called resident of England even though she's a non-resident resident and over here she's known as an alien." All of the trust talk was delayed by Lucie's death and Bea's ongoing career and so the matter lay dormant until 1971.

Bea was shocked by the sudden death of Eadie in Detroit. Rack was beside himself with grief and Bea paid Shannon Dean's expenses to Detroit and Shannon arranged all the details for Eadie's cremation and saw to it that Rack returned to their home in New York.

FOURTEEN

Auntie Mame raised her head once more. Rosalind Russell was having great success on Broadway with the show and now producers David Pelham and Hartney Arthur were preparing to present it in London.

"I was the one really against her doing *Auntie Mame*," said Hartney Arthur. "I was not in favor of it and I only gave in in the end after Tallulah turned it down. Bobby Fryer came along and brought up Bea and said, 'Suppose I put her in the New York company six weeks ahead.' David Pelham handled that and I did all the contract negotiations with Bea and Howard Reinheimer but I couldn't bear John, I couldn't be bothered listening to him."

When Pelham asked Bea if she would mind replacing Greer Garson for six weeks in New York, she replied, "Of course not, dear, we always open in the provinces."

Once it was agreed, Bea went to California and appeared as a guest on *The Dinah Shore Show* where she had the time of her life. Shore and her staff accorded her the star treatment, and she was looked after with the utmost civility and thoughtfulness, making the entire experience a joy for her. Bea and Dinah sang "Every Little Movement Has a Meaning All Its Own," during which Bea snatched up a prop picket fence and waved it about.

Auntie Mame is a fast-moving show and involves more than a score of split-second costume changes. Bea encountered a few problems on opening night but garnered excellent reviews the following day. She was called an "eloquent actress who sketches a new play in her own ironic image." Her scenes with the character of the young Patrick Dennis and those dealing with bigotry were exceptionally moving.

Before she left for London Bea's friends were invited to a party at 25 East End Avenue. Patrick Dennis, who wrote *Auntie Mame*, Constance Carpenter, the DeWildes, the Vigouroux, and Channing Hare attended. Brandon was a fanatic about Cyril Ritchard after seeing his Captain Hook in *Peter Pan* with Mary Martin. Consequently, Bea invited Ritchard to the party after telling him of Brandon's feelings. When Ritchard arrived, he descended immediately upon Brandon and proceeded to tell him what an admirer of Brandon's work he had always been.

Rather than leave Mr. Lee behind, Bea decided to sail to Europe and to take Bob Feyte along. She planned to settle Bob and Mr. Lee in Paris and work out the next step from there. The *Olympic* docked in Naples and Bea and Bob did some exploring. In one of the piazzas, Bea saw a large Neapolitan woman boxing the ears of a lovely young child. She freed her arm from Bob's and marched straight at the offending woman. Before Bob could stop her, Bea swung her purse and bashed the lady in the side of the head. The woman screamed obscenities, the police arrived, and Bob did his best to explain in his pseudo-Italian that Bea was a famous actress who was defending a child. The police broke up the crowd and urged the woman and child to move on as Bea and Bob hurried back to the ship.

After checking Bob and Mr. Lee into a hotel on the Left Bank in Paris, Bea flew to London to begin rehearsals on July 28. There was a short tour to Oxford and Manchester and then *Auntie Mame* opened at the Adelphi Theatre in London. The producers hosted a "Night in a Turkish Bath" party at the baths in the Imperial Hotel to which the Duke of Bedford, Margot Fonteyn, Michael Wilding, John Osborne, Mary Ure, Gracie Fields, and Douglas Fairbanks flocked. Signs welcomed Auntie Mame and streamers and twinkling lights decorated the rooms. Guests lounged on beds beside lily-filled pools and ate and drank until the early hours of the morning.

The critics loved Bea but hated *Mame*. "Sad disappointment," "Evening of only spasmodic fun," "Only worth seeing for quaint bits of business by the star" they moaned. "Beatrice Lillie is absolute heaven, the play is absolute hell!," "Miss Lillie's presence is a waste of her capabilities," "The Beatrice Lillie show would be a better title over here for this Broadway hit" was said in Bea's defense. Kenneth Tynan gave it "a shrug" in *The Sunday Times* but *The Observer* came through with *"Auntie Mame*'s sheer, bubbling good humor restores my faith in America's sanity." When *The Times* called the show a total disaster, Pelham had a large sign painted with the words ENTIRE PERFORMANCE SOLD OUT—TOTAL DISASTER—HOBSON, TIMES, and placed it in front of the theatre. Bea refused to leave the apartment on Park Lane the following day. She shut off the phone and would not read the notes put under her door. She was scheduled to be interviewed in the park but would not meet the reporter. However, she did arrive at the theatre that night in good spirits. Reporters gathered at the Adelphi where John was fielding questions concerning Bea.

" 'Look,' said a fat man," wrote Robert Robinson in *The Sunday Graphic*. " 'The critical press in England is shocking. You know? They write to policy, it's all policy. Why do you want to interview Bea? You want to ask what she thinks of the reviews? She'll tell you they were wonderful!' " Despite the reviews business was good enough that Bea was asked to remain for six additional weeks after playing over two hundred performances.

Auntie Mame took a publicity jaunt to Paris to bolster business. As a tie-in with British European Airways, the company flew to Paris for a weekend. Along with Bea and her cast were Trevor Howard, Leo Genn, Charles Laughton, Phyllis Calvert, and Robert Morley. Ellen Graham happened to be in Paris and joined Bea, Bob Feyte, and some others at a peep show. Bea insisted Ellen was too young to attend, but Ellen went along anyway. Ellen was flying back to the States and called Bea early in the morning to say good-bye. The two ladies babbled incessantly about every subject that came to mind before Ellen said farewell. Boarding her plane two hours later, she was waiting for takeoff when the stewardess called out her name and handed her a telegram. Puzzled, Ellen tore it open and read "Why haven't you written? Love, Bea." Bea went back to England after spending two days with Mr. Lee and was distressed at leaving him.

Without a word to Bea, John went to Paris, gathered up Bob Feyte and Mr. Lee and took the night train to London. In the stateroom, Mr. Lee was dosed with Scotch and finally passed out. John tucked him under some clothing in a small handbag and headed for customs. Feyte was shaking with nerves as he passed through inspection. When attention was focused on John, he bent over and picked up a suitcase and put it on the counter. He passed his handbag to Bob as he opened the suitcase for customs. Bob nonchalantly wandered off with the uninspected bag in which Mr. Lee was out cold. They rushed into Bea's room in Henley shouting "surprise, surprise" and dragged out what appeared to be a dead Pekingese dog. Bea burst into tears and began screaming for a veterinarian as Mr. Lee lay comatose on her imported carpet. Bea's vet arrived, a young well-mannered and serious man who knelt down next to Mr. Lee and carefully examined him for signs of life. After what seemed an eternity and dozens of tests, the vet pursed his lips for a moment, then turned to Bea and said solemnly, "He's pissed!" Mr. Lee slept it off and later woke up as bright as usual and lived happily ever after in Henley. The young veterinarian never knew how the dog arrived at Bea's home and never asked. Eventually Bea bought Mr. Lee a beige-colored wife named Lady Pearl and they became the parents of three beige-tinted offspring.

John began a renovation program at Peel Fold and Bea went mad. Trees were downed, repairs to the house were started, and central heating was ordered. When John Brooks became alarmed at the expense, Bea told Phyllis Monkman, when she came to visit, that she was dipping into capital and was worried.

"I noticed a lot of trees had been cut down," said Phyllis. "When we went for a walk I said, 'Bea, why did you have all those trees cut down?' she said, 'I haven't, he's done it. I'm afraid he's done it for when I pop off.' Then she said, 'I shouldn't have said that, should I?' I said, 'Yes, you should, because you know it's true.' " Later, in Bea's bedroom, she and Phyllis were talking. "The wall of Bea's bathroom was the wall of his bathroom, the other side. We were whispering and suddenly the door burst open and in walked Huck without any clothes on at all, demanding to know why we were whispering. Now, he looked disgusting when he was dressed but when he wasn't dressed, he looked the end! I said, 'Don't you dare come in like that when I'm sitting here!' I don't think he was all there."

When her contract ran out, Bea signed for the additional six weeks but before the show closed John and David Pelham had words over money John felt they owed Bea but he was proven wrong. He then instituted a lawsuit against the Thames Conservancy for a retaining wall he demanded they repair. Since it was declared Bea's wall, they claimed the responsibility was hers and won the case.

Bert and Mildred Lahr were in London and went to Peel Fold for dinner. Feyte decided to make it a memorable visit and employed a husband-and-wife team who hired out as butler and maid. The table was set with the best plate and glassware and the butler dutifully approached John for a list of wines to be served. Impressed with it all, Bert leaned over to Bea and whispered, "Old family retainer?"

Bea looked him straight in the eye and muttered, "Never saw him before in my life."

"You know, you're just as funny offstage as you are on," said Bert as he roared with laughter.

There is an institution in England known as the Actors' Orphanage Fund, founded in 1895. Its purpose is to provide a home for any child of theatrical parentage who needs it because of the death, illness, or separation of their parents, or by reason of financial difficulties. Funds are raised for the orphanage each year by means of a gigantic stage revue participated in by nearly every actor in England. Bea was invited by Laurence Olivier, president of the fund, to appear at the *Night of 100 Stars* on July 23, 1959, at the London Palladium. She decided to do "Milady Dines Alone" and went to New York to pick up costumes and me.

Bea and I "did" Fifth Avenue as she shopped for items she could not find at home. We hit St. Patrick's for a few minutes, the "emergency room at Elizabeth Arden's," and as we were returning to East End Avenue Bea asked if I had ever heard of a play called *Kind Lady*.

"Yes, I know it," I answered. "It's about this woman whose life is taken over by a family. She's a virtual prisoner in her own home and they have control of her money. None of her friends can get to her. She's trapped." I then noticed that Bea had tears in her eyes. "Bea, why are you asking this?"

She replied sadly, "Because when I was in Darien the other day, one of the family said it was the story of my life with the Hucks." I assured her it was certainly a joke, but it had evidently bothered Bea for days. A few moments later a telling incident occurred that startled us both. As we arrived at the apartment, John's sister was leaving. She carried an expensive-looking alligator purse, and after she left, Bea said, "John, wasn't that my bag?" "Yes," stated John flatly and went into his room without further explanation.

Two amusing incidents reminded Bea that time was truly marching on. She decided to call Brandon, whom she had not spoken to in some time. She paled when they began talking, and gestured and pointed at the phone as if something was wrong at the other end. I noticed tears in her eyes, and she handed me the phone and quickly left the room. I said hello and was greeted with a deep baritone reply. Brandon DeWilde's voice had changed. Later, Helen Hayes called. I answered and relayed a message to Bea. Bea responded and then called out, "Ask her how Jamie is."

"How is Jamie?" I inquired, referring to James MacArthur, her son.

"Jim!" answered his mother firmly.

"I beg your pardon?"

"It's Jim," she repeated. "We're no longer allowed to call him Jamie."

It was around this period that John decided he wanted an apartment of his own once again. He took a terraced place at 10 East End Avenue, diagonally across the street from Bea. Bea's contribution was to furnish it, which cost her a considerable sum. John stocked it with wine but never moved in. It was an arrangement that was doomed to failure since Grant Tyler had for some time been living in his own place. He and John were not hitting it off, and he hated the situation at 25 East End Avenue. It was impossible for John to leave Bea alone at night, and consequently the flat he took was used mostly for parties or to house his family or visiting friends.

Grant visited Bea as often as he was able, and they cooked in and watched television on nights that John was in Connecticut. Bea hated spending the night in Darien, and either Grant or I would stay over when John was with his family. Grant had been seeing a great deal of singer Portia Nelson, who would leave messages for Grant with Bea. "Tell him it was just Portia," earned her the nickname of "Just Portia." Bea was doing very little painting by now, and her only recreation was a visit from Grant or me and one or two friends like Ellen Graham, who was becoming a well-known photographer.

"Bea saw things that other people didn't," recalled Ellen. "When we were at a play or in a restaurant, she would pick up things that I never even noticed. And being around her helped me with what I was doing. It was another sense that most people don't even realize they have. She had that gift. Her mimicking came from that because she not only saw who she was imitating but she picked out the right things, the most important things that enabled her to do it again and better. She looked at things differently and then she'd put it on stage."

Without her friends Bea became bored very quickly in New York. She would sleep until around ten, when her maid would bring her breakfast and the papers. After lolling over the news of the day, she might make a few phone calls and then take a long bath and dress for the day. John, who usually slept late, would be sitting either in his underwear or in an open robe, sifting through papers on the table in the foyer when Bea left her room. If she inquired as to what the agenda for the day might be, John usually answered, "Why don't you take a nap, dear?" Bea would then go back to her room and watch "Password" and other afternoon shows, or she would go shopping.

One day she called and asked if I wanted to meet her on Fifth Avenue. "My street, my people," she joked. It was early in the morning and I knew she was probably propped up in bed reading the "rags," her breakfast tray buried under the *Daily News* and the *Mirror*. "Not the *Times*, though, too heavy!" she complained. Mr. Lee had most likely eaten a great deal of her breakfast since John insisted that the maid ply her with bacon, usually nearly raw, and eggs, toast, juice, and tea. Bea would nibble the toast and drink the tea, flush the bacon down the toilet, and give the leftovers to the dog.

I met Bea in front of Bergdorf's promptly at two. Her mink coat was thrown over an Italian silk blouse and pink slacks. The familiar pillbox hat matched the trousers. We barged into Bergdorf's and headed for the hat counter on the first floor. The saleslady had been selling Bea hats for years.

"I sold her hundreds of hats during that time and she always complained about the price. They were very well made and mostly to order, but she continually felt they were too expensive."

The two women had formed a warm friendship, however, and Bea never began a shopping day without dropping in to see her. Back on Fifth Avenue, Bea noticed an elderly lady following us, trying to sneak a look at Bea without her knowing it.

"That one's got me," she whispered and flashed the lady a dazzling smile. Caught off guard, the flustered woman dropped back.

"Little old lady passing wind," sang Bea softly. "That was from a show I did with Bert Lahr. Of course, those weren't the lyrics. We'd never have gotten away with it in those days."

At Harry Winston's we checked out the baubles. "It's all in the lighting, you know. Nothing looks that good out of the window," cracked Bea. A sharp right took us to her bank. Bea ordered her cash by phone and it was waiting when we arrived. A short conversation with her bank manager ended with a wave of the greenbacks and we were headed for Saks. I pointed out a pretty red dress in the window.

"It's all in the lighting, I just told you. It's not red at all most likely. You'd get it home and find out it was puce or something else."

Once we spotted Mary Martin sitting at the glove counter at Saks. She had her elbow resting on the glass as she waited for a salesgirl to show up. A few feet away, two very young tots were staring at her. Bea slid onto the next stool without a word, nudged Mary, and nodded her head toward the children.

"I know, they think I'm going to fly," said the world's favorite Peter Pan. "Meanwhile, I can't get waited on."

"Allow me, darling," said Bea as she went straight behind the counter and emptied boxes of gloves all over the section. Neither of the ladies could find anything. "Why don't we try someplace else," suggested Bea. Mary invited us back to her place for a drink. That seemed to make more sense than looking for gloves, so we accepted.

"I can only stay until sunrise," apologized Bea, as Ernest, the Hallidays' chauffeur, drove us east.

Tussabella, the family poodle, bounded into the hall to greet us. Then she went through the bag of tricks taught to her by Richard Halliday, Mary Martin's husband. I made mention of the fact that Tussabella had come from a litter bred by my very own mother.

"Aren't you going to say 'Small world'?" I asked Bea.

"No!" she stated emphatically, and that ended that.

Over drinks, Mary told us about her life on the Halliday plantation in Brasilia. There was no phone, and it took a few planes and a jeep to get there. The late Gilbert Adrian's house near the Hallidays' was for sale, and Bea thought for a moment about buying it.

"We even dressed for dinner out there," Mary told us. "The men wore dinner jackets, and Janet Gaynor and I wore long dresses and all the jewels."

"What in the world is that bugle doing on your mantel?" asked Bea, suddenly leaving the jungle.

"It came from a house we visited in Bermuda. It was used to call for help in case of fire."

"Now, don't tell me you play it," Bea ventured. With that Mary picked it up, and after one or two preliminary blasts broke into her own version of "Sunny Side of the Street." Bea was up in a flash and at the piano, where she countered with "Rock of Ages." It was a nice combination, perhaps a trifle loud. The maid was either deaf or approving, because she nodded happily at them as she served another drink.

The melody lingered in our ears as we followed our hostess into the dining room, where we inspected the rug she was making. There were squares of a hooked rug in a closet, but Bea felt she could not wait until it was finished. We did eventually see it in Mary Martin's book on needlepoint. From the activity in the Halliday kitchen, it was evident that a dinner party was in the making, so Bea kissed Mary and we left.

From Saks we went into St. Patrick's Cathedral to sit down and rest our feet. Although Bea had spent much of her youth in church, she had her own version of organized religion. There was some

Christian Science mixed in with Roman Catholic and sprinkled with Church of England, but she never associated herself with any denomination, joined a church, or took part in the sacraments. She enjoyed watching Fulton J. Sheen on television and once ran up to him in an airport and told him how much she adored him. We would talk quietly in St. Patrick's and then I would notice that Bea had withdrawn into herself, and she would sit quietly, not speaking or praying, perhaps meditating, for some time. Then, without warning, she would rise and start out.

"Let's think about what we're going to have for dinner at Sardi's," Bea said as we approached Tiffany's. "I might just have a salad and a small steak. How about you?" I could not think about food at that moment, so we argued about the window lighting in Tiffany's until we reached the Savoy Plaza. Bea had lived there at one time and wanted to go in and look around and perhaps have a drink. I reminded her that I was in casual clothes and was not wearing a tie, but Bea insisted.

"Nonsense, darling, they won't stop me," she assured me as we started into the bar. We were instantly tackled by a decidedly unfriendly maitre d.'

"I'm sorry but I can't allow you in without a tie," he purred happily as he smiled at Bea.

"A tie," cried Lady Peel. "What do you mean, a tie? I've never worn a tie in my life!"

He was not prepared for that. "I mean . . . !"

"Yes, I'm sure you meant. Whoever heard of a tie with a blouse like this?" Bea opened her mink. By now our friend was desperately seeking help from any quarter. "I have never heard of anything so ridiculous. Do you know who I am?" He was not permitted an answer as Bea continued. "We'll just see about this. I'm going to speak to the manager!"

Bea spun around and stalked off toward the lobby, leaving the maitre d' in shock and me wondering if she was really serious. I caught up with her near the phone booths. She was hysterical with laughter.

"How'd I do?" she asked.

"Brilliantly!"

We settled for Reuben's across the street. Bea enjoyed it there and had often spent time in the restaurant with Fanny Brice years before. The management greeted her and found us a table in spite of the large tea and cocktail crowd. There was a good deal of whispering and head nodding as we crossed the room and people recognized Bea. We ordered drinks, and Bea went back to discussing dinner. "Roast beef sounds good, sliced paper thin."

I was well into my martini when a young busboy chose to pass our table on his way to the kitchen. He was toting a huge tray piled to the ceiling with dishes and silverware. His foot slipped, the tray took off, and it hit the floor with a crash that the maitre d' at the Savoy Plaza must have heard. All conversation ceased as everyone in the room froze. The busboy looked around wildly and then dove for the floor. As he reached for the first piece of broken pottery, Bea was on her feet. In a voice that could have been heard in any balcony in the world, she cried, "Wait for the laugh!"

Pandemonium reigned for the next ten minutes as the restaurant rocked with laughter. I picked a hunk of asparagus out of my drink, downed the drink, and ordered another. Bea saw the manager bearing down on the kid. There was murder in his eyes, but she intercepted him and rather firmly explained that the poor child had slipped on something that somebody else had left on the floor. She finally received a promise that the boy would not be held responsible. We left Reuben's happy, Bea feeling that she had saved the boy's job and me from the second martini.

Bea wished to walk up Madison Avenue toward her home. On the way, she saw a black diamond mink coat in the window of the furrier from whom she had bought the coat she was wearing. In a flash she was in the store, the coat was snatched from the window, and by the time I was inside, Bea was wrapped in the coat and admiring it in the mirror.

"Be a dear and write a check for thirty-five hundred dollars, will you? The checkbook's in my bag. Isn't this beautiful?" she said in one breath.

"The sleeves are too long and so is the length," I told her.

"That's nothing. I'll have them taken up. Look at this shawl collar."

I stared as she covered her entire head with it. I made out the check, Bea signed it, grabbed her bag, and started for the door.

"Hey, wait a minute! Where's your other coat?" I yelled.

"That goes with the check. I traded it in."

"What about the length and the sleeves?"

"I just told you. I'll have them shortened. How you do go on!"

"But you can't wear a coat that long!"

"I'll have it shortened. Don't be a bore."

The coat was beautiful in the daylight even if Bea had all but disappeared into it.

"Now you need something really grand to go with it," I told her.

"What about Dover sole?"

"To go with the coat?"

"No. For dinner tonight. Taxi!"

We flew to England in time for the Henley Regatta, which we observed from Bea's electric canoe on the Thames. Miss Magowan prepared a picnic lunch, and we spent the day watching the contest and lounging on large, comfortable cushions.

Noël Coward had just written the story and the music for a new ballet which was premiering on July 14. It was being presented by the London Festival Ballet as part of its tenth anniversary season. *London Morning* was the title, and Pat Dolin was among the leading dancers in the piece. The setting for the ballet was outside the gates of Buckingham Palace, and it chronicled the daily events that take place there—families on outings, schoolchildren, tourists, and an ever-present sentry being teased by a pretty young girl visitor. It was clearly a sentimental journey for Coward. "I have as much right to state my sentimental pride as others have to state their shrill contempt," stated Noël in an interview. It was a gala evening with Noël Coward present in a box with Dame Peggy Ashcroft. The reviews were lukewarm, which infuriated Bea, but the premiere was exciting and star-studded.

During intermission, as we were star gazing, Alec Guinness dashed up to Bea and, after begging our indulgences, led her away for a private conversation. As the evening progressed I noticed that Bea seemed nervous and John had become increasingly silent. We went to Caprice after the ballet and saw Noël Coward and many of Bea's other friends. When Bea was in bed, I sat with her and rehashed the ballet and the evening in general. I asked her what Alec Guinness talked about and she said he mentioned a film he thought she might do with him. As if on cue, John barged through the door screaming hysterically that he was Bea's personal representative and Guinness had some goddamn nerve talking to Bea behind his back and making deals without consulting him first. He raged like a madman and it dawned on me that this was the reason for Bea's nervousness and his silence the latter part of the evening. He left the room and I calmed Bea down and she went to sleep. There was no evident follow-up of the Guinness meeting.

John's father, sister, and niece arrived from America and were staying at Henley. Chaos reigned on the Thames as Miss Magowan and the servants strove to keep the house running on schedule. When Bea complained that her breakfast tray was late most of the time, I suggested that she order breakfast served at a set time instead of at the whim of each individual guest. Rather than cause a scene, she left it alone. The overcrowding did little to aid tempers and John decided to dole out liquor to Bea and everyone else in the house by keeping the liquor cabinet locked and opening it for cocktails which he carefully meted out. Bea and I scrounged Miss Magowan's sherry until we decided she needed it more than we did. Bob Feyte was never seen without a beer in his hand but neither Bea nor I was able to stomach lukewarm beer. One night Bea asked why I liked vodka and I listed among its attributes its ability to leave one breathless as the advertisers shouted. She tried a bit of mine, liked the effects, and switched mainly because John could not detect it on her breath. We then conceived the brilliant idea of having Magowan phone the liquor store for vodka and order it left in the bushes by the back gate. We smuggled it into the larder, hid it behind the groceries, and nobody was the wiser. None of this did Miss Magowan's reputation much good among the tradespeople but John never caught on.

Dinners became a nightmare because we never knew when a blow-up would occur among the Huck family. One night John threw a glass of wine across the table at Bob Feyte, causing his niece to leave the room in tears. He followed that up by ordering Bob from the dining room. Then his sister turned on both John and her father one night and accused them of ruining her life by breaking up a romance she was having with a pilot before the war.

"Know what's on the telly tonight?" I asked Bea as peace descended for a few moments. " 'Kind Lady!' I think Ralph Bellamy's in it." It actually was on; I had seen it advertised. Bea glared at me as she controlled her laughter. Bea and I excused ourselves and hurried to the larder, but we did not watch the film that night.

The *Night of 100 Stars* took us back to London. At the Palladium rehearsal, we were surrounded by Peter Sellers, Hermione Baddeley, John Gielgud, Cicely Courtneidge, Audrey Hepburn, Margaret Rutherford, Ralph Richardson, Paul Robeson, and Edith Evans, to name a few. John decided on the spur of the moment that Laurence Olivier might do my waiter part in *Milady Dines Alone*, wearing large, fuzzy slippers. When I realized he meant it, I took Bea aside and explained that while it made no great difference to me, she for one must realize that I was simply a shill in the act and only fed her the props she utilized in the scene. If Olivier, one of the world's most renowned actors, was there in my place, the entire audience would be waiting for some sort of payoff from him and there was none. Bea, of course, knew all of this and had already made up her mind not to ask him to do it. The show went off on split-second timing and was a huge sensation. Afterwards there was a party at Caprice, where Phyllis Monkman joined us and Bea saw almost everyone else she knew.

She went to see Margaret Rutherford in her show and then we returned to Henley, deserted now by John's family, who were off on a tour of Europe. Bea and I took long walks on the country roads near Peel Fold and often visited the little churchyard where Lucie was buried. The summer weather was beautiful and it looked as if we would enjoy a peaceful vacation at Henley, but Bea had other plans.

FIFTEEN

One day Bea, John, and I were lunching on cold lamb, fresh vegetables from the garden, and Peel Fold trifle under the relentlessly watchful eyes of five beige Pekingese dogs and nine cats. I had decided that a quiet nap by the river might be just the thing when Bea, finishing a cup of tea and touching her lips lightly with a napkin, announced casually that we should go to Monte-Carlo. When I asked why just as casually, she looked at me in astonishment.

"Does there have to be a why?" she asked, answering my question with a question. "Would you rather go to Capri?"

John was quick to suggest that we did not know what the weather was like in Monte-Carlo. "Beautiful," Bea answered quickly. "Ellen phoned from Monte-Carlo before lunch and the weather is lovely. For God's sake, doesn't anyone want to go to Monte-Carlo? I haven't been there in years!"

Resigned, John said, "When would you want to go?"

Bea flung down her napkin like a gauntlet. "Let's go tomorrow."

John headed for the phone to call the travel agent, the bank, and John Brooks, Bea's lawyer. Gray was instructed to have the car checked and refueled. Later, John retired to his room to work out the trip on a road map. I was apprehensive about driving all that distance because John had a bad habit of driving for hundreds of miles without a bathroom stop, a ruse to keep Bea from having a drink. Bea loved riding in the car but, after ten hours of gazing out the windows she became restless. John would promise to stop but he usually drove on until Bea was ready to scream.

I was busy packing when Twanky, one of the daily maids, knocked to tell me that Lady Peel requested my presence in her room. As I entered, Bea closed the door quickly and pressed a roll of pound notes into my hand.

"It's some lolly," she whispered before I could ask. "Hide it someplace and don't say a word to anybody. We are only allowed so much English money when we leave the country. This is for us to play with but for God's sake, don't tell John! He'll have a fit and I don't want a scene."

When I asked why she did not take it, she informed me she had a whole bra full. "Shut up and put it away," she ordered. "I called Ellen and told her we were coming." Bea's room looked like a flicker's nest. Clothes were everywhere and the bureau was covered with pillbox hats. Mr. Lee was asleep in an open suitcase and I knew there would be a death struggle to get him out. He was fully aware of what open luggage signified and excluding him from the trip would be a direct insult. On the other side of the room, Lady Pearl and her puppies were busy eating Bea's shoes and not the least bit interested in traveling.

We spent the first night of the journey at 55 Park Lane, and early the following morning we drove straight to Dover. John had the car radio on, and there was a bulletin to the effect that Buckingham Palace had announced that the Queen was expecting a child. The event was noteworthy in that she would be the first reigning monarch to give birth since Queen Victoria. I glanced at Bea, who had tears in her eyes. When I inquired about the tears, she looked at me proudly and said, "She does all the right things."

We landed at Boulogne and went right on to Paris, arriving in time for dinner at Fouquette's and a drive to Montmartre where Bea's Mark IX Jaguar caused a few minor traffic delays in the narrow streets. It was a lengthy drive to Lyon the next morning, but we broke it up with lunch at the Hostellerie de la Poste, a 257-year-old inn, in Avallon. There we eased our tired muscles with beaucoup de vin with the meal. When we hit the road for Lyon, neither Bea nor I was feeling any pain.

The following day we were on the bridge at Avignon and later, when John was not looking, Bea and I dipped into the lolly and purchased some Basque shirts and a beret or two.

That night we drove down to the Mediterranean under a full moon. The mood was sheer enchantment as we rode through Cannes and Antibes to Villefranche where we decided to dine. We discovered a small place along the highway close to the water. It was charming but with one disadvantage. The kitchen was across the road. Our waiter was forced to dodge traffic as he carted food from the kitchen to our table, all the while shouting obscenities as the automobiles sped past. I made the mistake of ordering a provincial fish soup and we could detect the garlic before it got across the road. They could detect it at the Italian border, according to Bea, who loathed garlic.

"If you eat it," she threatened, "one of us is going to walk the rest of the way to Monte-Carlo!" I returned it for a conventional omelet.

As the meal progressed, a very attractive Frenchman dressed in sailor pants and a Basque shirt appeared with a guitar flung over his shoulder. When he spotted a pair of young lovers, he casually strolled to their table, pulled out an empty chair, settled his foot on it and broke into a Mediterranean love song. Bea was eyeing his performance.

"He's a dish—let's call him over," begged Bea. "Yoo-hoo, Garçon, s'il vous plaît," she beckoned the singer, who then came toward us. Bea flashed a come-hither smile, looking as continental as possible, and cooed, "Une chanson, por favor!" Our handsome, dark-eyed troubadour once again pulled out an empty chair, settled his foot on it, and performed an elaborate arpeggio. Unfortunately, in lieu of a romantic "La Vie en Rose," he chose to break into a hearty rendition of "Hang Down Your Head, Tom Dooley." I dared not look at Bea, although she behaved extremely well during the number.

"Thanks ever so," she shrieked when it ended. She tossed a handful of francs on the table and gathered up her things. We were still laughing as we tore down the pike toward Monaco. When we arrived at eleven-thirty, Monte-Carlo was at full tilt.

"Look, there's the palace up there!" Bea was hanging dangerously far out the window in her excitement.

"Yes, the bricklayer's daughter did very well for herself," sniped John, referring to Grace Kelly. I called him a snob, and Bea was so furious she would not speak during the remainder of the drive.

A stringed orchestra was playing as we arrived at the hotel. Bea and I cruised the lobby while John was registering. Bea noticed a poster announcing that Lena Horne would be appearing at the Red Cross Gala so we located the concierge and booked a table. When I knocked at Bea's door the next morning, she was having breakfast in bed and reading the London papers. She suggested I go to the beach and see who was there. I pointed out that we were a great distance from London and New York and chances were slim that I would run into anyone we knew on the beach at Monte-Carlo.

"Remind me to see *Irma La Douce* when we get back to London," she smiled, peering over her granny glasses. This was Lilliesque for "scram," and so I scrammed to the beach where I immediately ran into Mildred Hughes, Peter Gladke, Gloria Kristy, and Rosemary Williams, all of whom were appearing with the June Taylor Dancers at the Sporting Club.

"I'm here with Bea!" I called to Kristy across the pool.

"Bea who?"

"Bea Lillie, you ass! That's Bea who!"

Richard Ney suddenly appeared from behind a beach umbrella. "Is Bea Lillie here?"

Ellen Graham yodeled from the bar. "When did Bea get here?" So much for being a stranger in a strange city.

Bea arrived after lunch dressed for a swim, smelling faintly of Tweed and Saks Fifth Avenue sun screen. By that time, word of her arrival in Monte-Carlo was out, and the crowd that greeted her would have filled Sardi's. When Gwen Cafritz passed, she merely nodded at Bea and continued on her way. I suggested to Bea that someone must have pointed her out to Gwen as Bea Lillie instead of Lady Peel. Gwen was funny that way.

When Rolf Gérard appeared, Bea forgot everyone else in her

genuine delight at seeing him. He was living in Picasso's studio near Grasse and invited Bea to visit him there. After Rolf left, Bea grabbed Ellen's hand and slipped into the pool, pearls and all. "Aren't those the Peel pearls?" asked Ellen.

"Not now," replied Bea, "they're the pool pearls." With that she struck out in what she called the Peel crawl.

One afternoon we drove to Cannes for dinner and afterwards headed for St. Tropez and spent the night. The day after, Raoul Pene DuBois found us at a sidewalk café and Bea invited him to be her guest at the Gala in Monaco.

During the days prior to the Gala, John was monitoring Bea's drinking. For the most part, we sipped an innocuous fruit drink called a paradis. It was difficult for Bea since she was not working at the moment and everyone around her was knee deep in champagne most of the time. She stuck with the fruit drink during the day but drank Scotch at night. I secretly had my paradis spiked with vodka. Around four in the afternoon as I gazed cross-eyed at her, Bea said one day, "I can't imagine what you find so bloody exhilarating in this lousy drink."

Anton (Pat) Dolin owned a villa which hung on the side of a cliff over the harbor and we were invited for cocktails one afternoon. It happened to be a very hot day and we eagerly accepted Pat's offer of a screwdriver. We found that ever-thrifty Pat Dolin served screwdrivers in liqueur glasses. The only buzzes we got were from the bees trying to get at the orange juice.

Invitations arrived from the palace for Miss Lillie and her guests to join Their Serene Highnesses at a concert in the courtyard of chez Grimaldi. Dressed to the nines, Lady Peel, John, and I arrived at the palace punctually. Prince Rainier and Princess Grace viewed the proceedings from a balcony above while their guests sat in comfortable chairs below. The Orchestre National de L'Opera de Monte-Carlo was swinging through the *Ouverture des Noce de Figaro* when we were startled by a sudden chorus of very highly pitched squeals overhead. It was not until several ladies covered their heads with scarves that we realized we had been joined by a screeching cloud of bats, possibly attracted by the radio waves or the mountainous beehive hairdos scattered about below them. A Brahms violin concerto quieted them down for a time, and when we reached Strauss's *Les Joyeuses Équipées de Till L'Espiegle* the mood was such that nobody cared any longer.

It was at a dinner party hosted by Al and Dorothy Strelsin that we met actress Binnie Barnes. She sat next to Bea and regaled her with tales of her days as a chorus girl in London. Toward the end of the meal, Bea told me that Binnie was anxious to go to the Sporting Club for a little gambling. When the time was right, Bea, Binnie, and I sneaked off to the club. Bea played Dix-sept for a time at the roulette wheel with Binnie, who finally deserted us for greener fields at the baccarat table. Bea claimed that Bobby broke the bank at Monte-Carlo while playing Dix-sept.

On the beach the next day, we were joined by Lena Horne and her two children. She and Bea caught up on what was doing and Bea assured her that all of us would be cheering her on at the Gala. The annual benefit for the Red Cross was a favorite project of Princess Grace but this season the festivities were going to struggle along without Their Highnesses, who were planning to be at their mountain retreat above Monte-Carlo. In spite of this, spirits were high and Lena was raring to go.

Bea received a call from producer Leonard Sillman, who was in Cannes. He was traveling with Huntington Hartford and his wife, Marjorie Steele. He asked for help in reserving a table at the Gala. Leonard was preparing a new show for Shirley Booth and was hoping for a sizable investment from Hartford. I used Bea's name when I made the reservation but there was little or no response from the maitre d' when I told him that Leonard was the famous American producer. However, when I announced that his guest, Mr. Huntington Hartford, was a well-known American millionaire, the results were amazing.

The day of the performance bloomed bright and beautiful and the beach club was packed. Raoul DuBois had arrived and after lunch he joined us out on the point for a paradis or two. Suddenly, the sun vanished and the sky was beginning to look downright ugly. The news of rain, and lots of it, conjured up images of Lena Horne, in the newly decorated out-of-doors stage, singing "Stormy Weather" with the real thing going on around her.

Sure enough, the downpour began, and most of us rushed to the bar of the Hôtel de Paris. Henry Astric, artistic director of the casino, was not to be found and Bea insisted I call to check on the state of our reservations. We were told that the Gala might now be held indoors but all reservations would certainly be honored. Lady Peel must not worry her noble head. The gentleman neglected to mention that the room indoors held approximately half the number of guests as would have been seated outdoors.

High in the mountains, their vacation dampened, Prince Rainier and Princess Grace decided to return to the pink palace below. An equerry phoned the casino and notified Monsieur Astric that the Rainiers would indeed attend the Gala. Before Henry could pull himself together, the word was out, and individuals who never had any intention of attending the show in the first place now attempted to bribe desk clerks, managers, maitre d's—anyone—for the privilege of sharing Miss Horne with authentic royalty. One more check on Lady Peel's reservations confirmed that there was no problem.

There was a mad dash for the beauty parlors. Those with no hair had manicures. What Van Cleef & Arpels did not sell they rented and there was not a tube of Edna Wallace Hopper facelift to be found this side of Port Said. Everything emptied out as people rushed to their rooms to bathe, rest, pluck, curl, lengthen, shorten, or what-have-you.

Beatrice Lillie, aged sixty-five and sans hairdresser or mud pack, looked marvelous that night. She wore an elegantly simple Hartnell with matching hat and her diamond and emerald Peel necklace. She posed for pictures on the way into the casino and stopped to have her fortune told by a gypsy. Then she, John, Raoul, Ellen, and I marched to the velvet rope to be told by the maitre d' that he had never heard of us, especially anyone named Peel. Smiling through clenched teeth, Bea proclaimed that indeed there was a reservation for Lady Peel. She hinted, with raised eyebrow, that since Miss Horne was a personal friend, no Lillie might well mean no Lena. She was so determined, yet so calm that anybody watching might have imagined that she was asking him how the kids were.

Lady Peel was given a table. The ensuing question was where to sit. Except for the Rainiers' table, there was not an unoccupied one left in the room. With the threat of "no Lena" still ringing in his ears, the maitre d' ordered a table brought in from outside and had it placed squarely in the middle of the dance floor. When Bea questioned the possibility of Miss Horne's finding it distracting to work in such close proximity to her admirers or that the June Taylor Dancers could object strenuously to hoofing in our Caesar salads, she was assured the table would be shifted to the side when the production began.

We were halfway through our first magnum of champagne when all hell broke loose outside. Their Serene Highnesses had arrived. The royal party swept regally into the club where the press was given its customary five minutes for photos and questions and then they were cleared out. Princess Grace was stunning in a floor-length white gown accented by a long black lace stole flung over one shoulder.

As the fourth estate exited, Leonard Sillman entered. We had completely forgotten about him. Judging by the expression on Leonard's face he had met the maitre d', who doubtlessly had never heard of Leonard Sillman or Huntington Hartford. When Bea realized there might be another reservation crisis, she tossed it off with, "Darling, I love Leonard but now it's every man for himself. Order me a vodka, will you?"

The dancing began and Leonard disappeared as our table was surrounded by a sea of gyrating hips and derrières. The more resourceful of Bea's friends danced in place at her table as they passed the time of day with her, among them Margot Fonteyn, Aristotle Onassis and Maria Callas, and the Maharani of Baroda, who looked as if she were wearing all of Cartier's. Dorothy Strelsin, the Richard Neys, Elsa Maxwell, Jessie Donohue, the Woolworth matriarch (who was sporting close to a million dollars in jewels), and Dorothy Pasternak, wife of the film producer, all slipped in a word or two. The Strelsins had reserved a table in the rooftop nightclub, and we were invited to join them there after the performance.

Leonard Sillman and his guests were shown to an intimate table for four in the anteroom of the men's john. Gentlemen passed their table all evening zipping up or down depending upon which way they were headed. Word spread to Sillman's friends that he was entertaining the Hartfords in the men's room and Leonard's table became the chicest table of the evening. Friends dropped by to say hello and observe the zipper brigade. It all turned out to be a sort of bird-watching contest. Until the day he died, Leonard swore he was offered a substantial bribe to vacate his table in favor of a wealthy dowager.

Bea was smoking a cigarette when our table levitated over our heads with the help of the busboys, who moved us to the side in preparation for the show. The June Taylor Dancers opened the proceedings, almost dancing in our laps as Bea tried to break them up. When Lena appeared, the place went wild. Sheathed in a black sequined gown, her hair styled in a page boy, she wove her incomparable spell before a jubilant, responsive audience. Her husband, Lennie Hayton, conducted the Sporting Club Orchestra and accompanied her at the piano. What might have been a disaster because of the weather had been turned into a smashing success by the star. When her performance ended, even the most sophisticated jet-setters were on their feet cheering.

Later in the evening, Bea was invited to join the Rainiers and was seated next to Princess Grace. Raoul and John wandered off to the casino but Ellen and I elected to have another drink and wait for Bea. Little by little the room emptied out until Ellen and I and the Rainier party were the only ones left.

The Prince and his guests seemed to sit forever, and it was not until later that we heard from Bea what happened at the table. Bea was introduced to the Rainiers' guests, and, bolstered by a few drinks, almost immediately launched into one of her favorite jokes concerning the Walthamstowe Silver Band.

"It's about a little suburb, Walthamstowe, a suburb of London, as we all know. There's a lovely little suburban house, a path, and a little gate. So this little man knocked at the door. He was in uniform. A woman opened the door and said, 'Yes?'

"He said, 'Pardon me, ma'am, I'm collecting money for the Walthamstowe Silver Band.'

"She said, 'Huh? Beg your pardon?'

"He said, 'I'm collecting money for the Walthamstowe Silver Band.'

" 'I'm sorry, I can't hear. I'll just go and get my hearing aid. I'll be back in a minute.' So she got the thing on and tuned it up and said, 'Now, what is it you're doing?'

" 'I'm just collecting money for the Walthamstowe Silver Band.'

"She said, 'I can't hear a thing, I really can't hear anything. Wait! I'll go and get my other hearing aid. I paid three quid for this thing and it doesn't work.'

"The man waited, somewhat less patiently this time.

" 'Now,' she said. 'What is it you're doing?'

" 'I'm collecting money for the Walthamstowe Silver Band!'

"She said, 'Just move your lips, don't talk.'

"So he mouthed the sentence without speaking.

" 'Never mind, just go ahead and speak loudly because I can't hear a thing.'

" 'I'M COLLECTING MONEY FOR THE WALTHAM-STOWE SILVER BAND!'

"She said, 'I'm sorry but frankly it ain't coming through. I can't hear a thing.'

" 'All right! All right! Never mind!' He turned around and walked down to the little gate.

"She yelled, 'Don't forget to shut the gate!'

"He said, 'F—— the gate!'

"She said, 'And f—— the Walthamstowe Silver Band!' "

Ellen and I heard the upshot of the joke across the room. Then conversation began to run out at the royal table. Some of the guests checked their watches, some discreetly yawned.

"What are you doing for the rest of the evening?" the Prince asked of Bea.

"I'm going to find Lena and join Dorothy Strelsin on the roof." Silence.

"The Prince and I have a table on the roof, also," smiled Princess Grace.

"Lovely," replied Bea. Silence.

Rainier asked Bea if she enjoyed dancing.

"Adore it," said Bea. Silence.

Finally, Bea took charge of the situation and looked His Highness straight in the eye.

"I can't leave the table until you do," she said sweetly.

Rainier stared at her for a moment.

"You're absolutely right! I forgot!" He laughed as he leaped to his feet and the party ended.

John arrived back in the room searching for Bea and escorted us into the casino. We were blinded by the array of spectacular jewels, gorgeous clothes, and international royalty. As we swept into this stream of Beautiful People, John gathered Ellen and me into a football huddle. When he was sure he could not be overheard, he said, "Keep your eye on Bea's necklace." He meant it. I raced to catch up with Bea, and Ellen dashed to the bar where she ordered a Maltese Falcon on the rocks! Bea joined Lena Horne and Lennie Hayton at the bar, surrounded by a sea of fans, and never went dancing on the roof.

When it came time to leave Monte-Carlo, John decided he wanted to make a side trip to Spain on the way back, but Bea and I wished to return to Henley. We flew home and left John to tour with the car. Bob Feyte met us at the airport and nearly caused a crisis when he became excited and ran through Customs in our direction with Mr. Lee in his arms. It was only Bea's name and charm that saved the dog from being snatched away to quarantine. We arrived home in time for cocktails, and Bea invited Miss Magowan to join us as she often did when John was away. Bob dispensed a few hefty cocktails, and Bea, who had indulged on the plane, was soon feeling no pain. Miss Magowan, who only nipped an occasional sherry now and then, was a foot off the floor, with Bob and me not far behind. Feyte finally led Bea upstairs to her bed. They were barely out of sight before the phone rang. It was John checking to see if we arrived home safely. He was in Spain and wanted to speak to Bea. I lied that she was at the far end of the lawn and would take forever to get to the phone and he settled for that.

"Everything else all right?" he asked.

"Certainly, all is well!" I answered gaily. Any further communication was drowned out by a terrible crash behind me.

"What the hell is that?" demanded John as I spun around to look. Miss Magowan, with a smile on her face, had passed out backwards straight into the fireplace. Andirons, coal scuttle, and pokers were all over the room.

"It's the dogs, I have to go. Have a nice trip," I bellowed and hung up. Bob ran into the room and we set Eileen Magowan on her feet. As Bob led her upstairs to bed she was singing a bawdy music hall song at the top of her lungs. We cooked our own dinner and ate in the kitchen that night. There followed lazy rides in Bea's electric canoe in the early evenings on the Thames, trips that Bea loved. The canoe was a collector's item. Built of solid mahogany, it was thirty-five-feet long, seated twelve people, and was propelled by a battery-run engine. Consequently, the canoe glided over the waters without a whisper of a sound as we lounged on comfortable pillows and watched the evening approach.

Bea also loved her gardens, tended by Tony Gray, a young man who had been with her since his teens and who loved Peel Fold as much as Bea did. Gladys Cooper, who was a short distance from Bea, prided herself on her prize rose garden. Once when Cooper was in the States she was notified that the Garden Club would be judging her efforts for an annual prize given for the most beautiful garden in England. She called Bea long-distance and begged her to water the roses before the judging. Bea and Tony drove to the house, where Bea, hose in hand, attended to the matter by aiming straight at the blossoms instead of the dirt until there were rose petals everywhere. "I haven't seen Gladys since," said Bea, when she told the story. From then on she allowed Tony to tend the flowers but he did teach her how to water correctly.

Early in 1960 Bea appeared on NBC Television in a special called *The Four of Us*. The four included Bea, Ethel Merman, Ray Bolger, and Benny Goodman. She followed this with another foursome, *Four for Tonight*, for NBC, with Cyril Ritchard, Tammy Grimes, and Tony Randall.

"One of the things we were doing was this thing in canon," recalled Ritchard. "It was very tricky musically and Bea didn't understand music, really. She can take an old tune and turn it into a screamingly funny thing but she didn't understand this at all. In the end they gave it to us written out and it was about two yards long. Bea, who is as simple as a little monkey, knew just what she was going to do. We went over it and over it and over it. Came the show and she took over. She sang in French or Latin or Greek and made up her own tune and we were supposed to come in on the count. Of course, she didn't give it to us. I walked off-camera because I thought I was going to die from laughter. I came back and joined them and she was still at it!"

The show was Bea's first professional encounter with Tammy Grimes, whom she grew to love and admire. She and Cyril were continuing their friendship of over thirty-five years. "I remember when Bea called me once from Chicago," recalled Ritchard, talking about his wife's final illness. "She got on the phone and tried to speak about it but couldn't so she just hung up the phone."

Agent Richard Astor was now in charge of Bea's television appearances, a position he assumed soon after the *Follies*. Bea liked Richard immensely, especially after their first business luncheon at 21. Bea asked Astor to order Bloody Marys for himself and for her during lunch. Dick, who knew nothing of her drinking habits, acquiesced, much to John's discomfort; but John did trust him with business matters. John had the sense to realize that he himself had no knowledge of contract negotiations. His method was to have Bea agree to appear for a stipulated amount and then as she sat, pen in hand, he would suddenly list additional demands such as color television sets or record players until eventually Bea's apartment began to look like Macy's. He also antagonized various TV producers by his tactics. Bea's professionalism endeared her to all of those she worked with and restored peace in most cases. She had a wonderful time on the Arthur Murray show as well as with Jack Paar, Merv Griffin, and Johnny Carson. She enjoyed taping with live audiences present. "Television without an audience is like doing summer stock in an iron lung," she said.

One night in May, as Bea and I were walking down Forty-sixth Street, we were caught up in a group of theatre people in front of the Edison. Some who had been in the *Follies* cast told Bea they were on their way into the hotel to attend an Equity emergency meeting. Bea walked in with the group to have a look and was immediately pounced upon by Paul Hartman, male half of the famous dance team. Before Bea was able to protest, Hartman had us seated in the first row of the meeting. Helen Hayes was on the dais and beamed happily at Bea's apparent interest in union affairs. She mouthed what seemed to be important news at Bea.

"I don't know what she said. Go and find out," Bea whispered. I crouched down and approached the dais.

"Jim had a baby boy last night," smiled the proud grandmother. I crawled back and relayed the good news.

"Ask her what his name is," hissed Bea. I crawled forward once more.

"He named it after Charlie," I was told and crept back to my seat to deliver that message.

"Ask her . . ." Bea began, but I quickly responded with a very firm, "Bea!"

"Very well, I'll call her myself tomorrow." She gathered her mink coat around her, glanced at me, and said, "Really!" and snuggled down to listen to the meeting.

SIXTEEN

Bea returned to England to attend the wedding of Princess Margaret and Antony Armstrong-Jones, a union which pleased her no end. The sad young man she visited in the hospital over ten years before was now a successful photographer and a Lord. She was soon contacted by the committee for the Red Cross Gala in Monte-Carlo and invited to appear at the Gala in midsummer. At the same time an offer came from the Edinburgh Festival to appear there in *A Late Evening With Beatrice Lillie* in September. Bea chose to do "Milady" and songs for both engagements, and she asked Rack and me to be with her. We flew over in July and went to Henley. I questioned the practicality of the "Milady" sketch for Monte-Carlo, as there was no overhead or wing space for a set, furniture, and props, but since John was assuming credit as director, I left it up to him.

We flew to Nice on July 29, and Bea and John were guests of the Hôtel de Paris in Monte-Carlo, while Rack and I had rooms at the Hermitage close by.

When we scouted the Sporting Club's great outdoors, where Lena Horne had been rained out the summer before, Bea realized immediately that "Milady" could not be done on that stage. There was no wing space and certainly nothing overhead but clouds and some sea gulls. Any attempt to put up a temporary set would have caused delays and excess work. "Milady" was therefore cancelled. Bea was to share the bill with Nat "King" Cole. Because of her performing status we were allowed to sign tabs throughout Monte-Carlo and she was assigned a cabana at the beach.

There were no June Taylor Dancers to play with that summer. Instead the casino was presenting the George Reich Dancers from Paris. Both Bea and I had worked with George, an American boy, who had become very successful in Paris as a dancer and choreographer. Bea was slightly uneasy regarding Rack's drinking. He was undergoing definite personality changes when he drank lately, becoming obstreperous and nasty. He could be sarcastic and, Bea was beginning to feel, undependable. She assumed it was his reaction to Eadie's death three years before and was willing to give him the benefit of the doubt.

Bea was delighted to discover old friends in Monte-Carlo, among them Elsa Maxwell and Dorothy (Dickie) Fellows-Gordon, Elsa's lifelong companion. Ellen Graham arrived with word that her sister Mary was not far behind. We were crossing the lobby one day, when Elsa dashed up to Bea and invited her to a small dinner party she was having for Mary Martin, who, on a brief holiday from *The Sound of Music* in New York, was the house guest of Edward Molyneux, the couturier. The party would be on the terrace of the hotel.

"I suppose that means me, too!" interjected John bluntly. Elsa, without losing a beat, answered that of course it did as though she had been pondering all afternoon whom to seat with John. I silently tipped my hat to her. Rack and I had dinner in the dining room and watched the party from afar. Bea was very fond of Mary Martin and had a fun evening. She told her story about the priest who whispered to a nun that he loved her. The nun blushed and bashfully whispered back, "That's all right, just don't get into the habit." A few days after the dinner I found Bea in her room with Dickie Gordon. She was intoxicated and sobbing her heart out that John was ruining her life, and was begging Gordon to help her get him out of it. Dickie Gordon was dismayed and unable to cope with the situation and left when I told her I would handle it. Bea fell asleep soon after, but I suddenly had a premonition that this year's Gala was a disaster looking for a place to happen. I hoped it would not happen to Bea.

The following day we were at the beach when Nat Cole arrived. His appearance at lunch touched off a near riot among the guests and employees, proving just how big a star he was all over the world. As I watched the crowds around him, it occurred to me that for the first time in a long and glorious career Bea was "opening" for a major star. Usually, when two performers appeared on the same bill, the bigger star went on last and I could not help but wonder how John had let that get by him.

Shortly after that, Bea and I were waiting for Rack to show up for rehearsal when George Reich made an entrance. He spotted Bea from the top of a flight of steps and came down in a showgirl walk as he hummed, "A Pretty Girl Is Like a Melody." Mr. Ziegfeld would have been proud. We were proud until he slipped and rolled the rest of the way and stopped at Bea's feet. During the first rehearsal, my heart sank. Bea and Rack were at a grand piano out of doors and, as Bea began her first number, I realized how tiny, almost doll-like, it seemed. There was a "concert" aura about the entire rehearsal and the numbers with fans and pearls seemed, at best, almost quaint in those surroundings. Ordinarily, it would not have been so noticeable but Bea was in Monte-Carlo and was about to face an international audience whose sophistication reached gigantic proportions. I tactfully mentioned to John that perhaps Bea should utilize the Sporting Club Orchestra but he did not seem to feel that was necessary. It was a few days later, when we heard the orchestra rehearse Cole's music, that John gave it some thought. Cole's act was up-to-date, professionally staged, and large enough for Monte-Carlo, while Bea would be working with the same arrangements that Eadie and Rack had prepared nearly a decade before and now she would be supported by only one piano. It was then that John mentioned the possibility of Mr. Berelli's taking the time to run up a few orchestrations for Bea. Mr. Berelli, the orchestra conductor, was busy at the time rehearsing Nat Cole. John also did not realize that orchestrating even one number took time and money and we were quickly running out of time.

While awaiting the big event, Bea enjoyed her vacation on the Riviera. We drove to Menton and visited Daisy Fellowes, who had once sent her yacht to stand by to rush Edward VIII and Wallis

Simpson to France in the event they wished to elope. Daisy had Bea to lunch in her spacious villa and she brought her grandson to rehearsal one afternoon.

At dinner one night, Rack asked the wine steward for a sparkling white wine. We were served a sparkling Hock from Germany. From then on we ordered it at every meal. Bea was not a champagne drinker and did not join us in our nightly Hock. Rack tested it carefully at each meal for temperature, aroma, and taste, rolling it around on his tongue like an expert.

"A little grand, isn't he?" was Bea's only comment.

Finally, one night, bored with the whole scene, Bea tasted it. She nodded approval and then turned to the waiter.

"Not bad, what do you call it?"

Snapping to attention as if Bea had begun to sing the "Marseillaise," the waiter stared disdainfully down his nose at the bottle on the table and replied, "We call it German piss!"

Rack spewed a mouthful of wine across the table and began to choke violently. When things finally calmed down, Bea smiled sweetly at both of us and said, "That'll learn yuz."

On August 5, the day of the Grand Diner de Gala Annual, a glorious sun rose over the Mediterranean and remained with us all day. Silently I prayed for the same rain which sent Lena Horne and her guests scurrying indoors the year before. I felt Bea had a better chance in a more intimate ambience. We might even be able to hear the piano and Rack. However, the weather stubbornly refused to change and we were doomed to perform under the stars.

Bob Feyte had flown in from London with props and gowns for Bea and decided to play maid. Under most circumstances, his assistance would have been a great help but as the magic hour approached, Bob proceeded to get into the beer, which worried all of us a little. Ellen's sister, Mary, was in for the Gala but neglected to bring evening clothes and after pricing a few gowns in Monte-Carlo, she decided it would be cheaper to catch a plane to Paris and pick up a simple dress from her apartment there. Obviously there was a time element involved and Ellen solved the problem by lending her sister a rather ornate shocking pink gossamer concoction trimmed in marabou.

"Why haven't I seen you in that before?" Bea asked.

"Because it's my nightgown," volunteered Ellen.

All of Bea's party arrived after drinks to find her ensconced in her dressing room with Bob, who by then was spinning around like Danilova. The table where Ellen, Mary, John, and I took up residence was encircled by Aristotle Onassis, Maria Callas, and party; Princess Saroya, long-parted from the Shah of Iran, and the Maharani of Baroda, who was sporting a 49.5-carat Indian diamond ring. Elsa Maxwell and Dickie Gordon entertained Margot Fonteyn, Tina Louise, and Lueen McGrath at their table. Flanked by a bevy of attractive young people at a nearby table was the young Aga Khan. The daughter of Francisco Franco arrived dressed, oddly enough, in bullfighter red.

Once again, the arrival of Their Serene Highnesses caused a sensation. Princess Grace was spectacular in a white satin ball gown. Her hair was pulled up in a little French twist and her minuscule gold-rimmed glasses made her all the more appealing. Vera Maxwell, the clothes designer, was with the Rainiers. After the customary photographs were taken and the royal party was relaxed, the orchestra burst into spirited dance music. The dance floor, which was on a hydraulic lift, was at its proper level but nobody moved to cut a dido.

Mary and I were deep in conversation when Henry Astric unexpectedly loomed over us.

"For God's sake, get up and start the dancing," he pleaded.

I looked at him with a blank stare. "I hardly know you," I said.

"No! You and the lady. Please, I need someone to begin dancing. Everybody's just sitting there!"

Always willing to oblige, Mary gathered her gossamer nightgown over her arm and joined me in a foxtrot. As we glided past the royal table I swore to Mary that we got the nod from the Princess. We argued for a moment whether the nod might have been for us or for the nightgown. In a matter of seconds the dance floor was jammed now that everybody was satisfied that nothing dire had happened to Mary and me. While dancing, I could hear intermittent blurbs from Bea's microphone over the loudspeakers. I took Mary back to our table and hurried backstage just in time to see a body mike being strapped to Bea. When I saw Feyte, I shuddered. He was far beyond feeling any pain as he arranged the small mike below Bea's cleavage and then attached a battery onto her thigh under her dress. He rearranged her petticoat and skirt and then she was ready. Bea strode to center stage amidst the applause, bowed, and began to sing. We could hear nothing. The mike was dead. As somebody scrambled for a standing mike, I remembered Bob Feyte with his hands up Bea's skirt. It was a reasonable assumption that he had shut off the mike by mistake.

Bea did her first few numbers with the standing mike but it was obvious that it was hampering her style and restricting her movement. The audience was polite but restless. Bea usually sang "Maude, You're Rotten to the Core" while seated with a brandy snifter at a small round table. The whole point of the song depended upon this setting. When the music began, her only recourse was to drag the standing microphone across the table in order to be heard. This limited her movement severely and ruined the number altogether.

Now the booing, clapping, and the shouting had begun. The reaction was promulgated by a group of Italians seated around the fringe of the crowd. They had come from over the border to the Gala and were not understanding one word that Bea sang. She was completely lost on them and they were letting her know it as only an Italian audience can. By the time the number ended, she knew something was terribly wrong and she made her way upstage just as I arrived there.

"What's happening? What's wrong?" she looked completely bewildered. My heart was breaking for her as I led her to the dressing room. She persisted with the questions and I carefully blamed the confusion on mike failure, which, in part, it certainly was. I stayed with Bea while she changed and then Feyte came to collect her things. Onassis and Margot Fonteyn arrived to deplore the situation and to say good night. When Bea was ready, we went straight to the hotel.

John stayed behind to catch Mr. Cole's act and later provided the only laugh of the night when he stormed into Bea's suite shrieking that somebody in the Cole party must have sabotaged Bea's mike in a fit of jealousy. It might have been funnier if Cole's accommodations had not been directly below Bea's and we were afraid they might hear John. The fact that John's name appeared on every poster in Monte-Carlo and that he had not once attended a rehearsal of Bea's did not seem to deter him from blaming everyone else. A day or two after, Mr. Cole could not have been warmer or more charming to Bea in the lobby of the hotel. If Bea was ever certain of just what did occur that night she never mentioned it and the Monte-Carlo disaster was never spoken of again except by Eugenia Sheppard, who could not wait to spread the news via her column.

Shortly after Bea returned to Henley-on-Thames, she and I resumed our walks in the country. Tony Gray supplied us with plants for Lucie's grave. We visited the little church and planted them around Lucie's plot. One day Bea grabbed my arm suddenly and pointed to a tiny mound of fresh soil not far from her mother.

"Oh, my God!" she cried out. "It's a baby! How sad. How dreadfully sad!" With that she began to plant pansies around the little grave, all the while exclaiming over the sadness of the situation. "How distraught the poor mother must be. I'm sure her husband has taken her away to get over all of this. That's probably why there is no stone!" Bea had written the entire scenario and for the next few weeks she carefully planted the little grave.

When Bea returned to the States months later, I asked her if she still tended the tiny grave.

"An eighty-five-year-old man!" she snapped, pursing her lips like an angry schoolteacher. "They finally put up a marker, and it was an eighty-five-year-old man! I dug up every goddamn plant and put them back on my mother's grave!"

The recreation room at Peel Fold was known as the "windows" room. It was a large, comfortable space with floor-to-ceiling windows looking out onto patios on two sides of the house. A grand piano and the television set, flanked by comfortable couches and chairs, were the main attraction. Here Bea and her guests gathered before and after dinner for drinks and conversation, or to watch television. The room was also the domain of Mr. Lee and his family.

One night, after dinner, Bea, Bob Feyte, and I were relaxing and listening to Rack playing the piano. Bea began talking about an incident involving Bobbie as a child, a story that made us all laugh.

Later, however, Rack was playing music from "Lady in the Dark" and I noticed that Bea was lost in her thoughts and seemed sad. I asked her what she was thinking about.

"I was just thinking the only things Gertie Lawrence and I ever had that we didn't have to go out and earn were Pamela and Bobbie. He was the only thing I never had to pay for and I don't have him any longer."

She began to cry, and Bob sat on the arm of her chair with his arm around her.

"I hated my mother, you know," she said quietly.

"Now, you know you didn't," answered Bob.

"Yes, I did. I hated her," Bea stated. The conversation ended and was not mentioned again.

Early one morning I went to the kitchen for coffee and saw Bea's breakfast tray set up. Miss Magowan was making tea and toast for Bea, and I spotted the London papers next to the tray. The front pages carried the news of the death of Oscar Hammerstein II in the States. I told Magowan I would leave the papers and take the breakfast up myself. Bea popped upright in bed when I opened the drapes and asked her usual "So what's new?"

"I have some sad news to tell you," I answered. She looked straight at me and said, "Oscar Hammerstein's dead, isn't he?" Without another sound she stared out of her window at the trees and sky outside as tears rolled down her cheeks. We remained silent for three or four minutes and then Bea poured her first cup of tea and her day began. I brought the papers and left her alone. She never explained how she knew the news before I informed her.

We drove to Edinburgh for our *Late Evening With Beatrice Lillie.* The performance was to take place in the Lyceum Theatre immediately following a new play called *The Dream of Peter Mann,* in which Hermione Baddeley was starring.

As we drove through Leeds, Bea saw a marquee advertising *Ages of Man* with John Gielgud. She ordered John to stop the car and dashed into the stage entrance. The doorman recognized her immediately, but she begged him just to announce that "Her Ladyship" wished to see Sir John. As she rounded the doorway to Gielgud's dressing room, he glanced into the mirror, shook his head and smiled as he muttered, "Oh, it's you! I wasn't sure whether it was Peggy Ashcroft or Noël Coward."

We checked into the Caledonian Hotel, and it was later discovered that there was no work permit for me because John neglected to apply for one. I was not sure how to proceed, but Bea promised that the Tower of London was only used for sightseeing, so I decided to give it a go as if nothing was amiss. Bea also reminded me that Mr. Lee was illegal as well, and I felt cozier knowing that bit of information. Then we saw the program for the Lyceum Theatre. Bea, of course, was listed, Rack's name was correctly spelled and placed and, in large letters, John Philip had given himself directorial credit, but my name was nowhere to be seen either as the Waiter or as the Stage Manager. The Caledonian Hotel received credit for the food to be used in "Milady Dines Alone," and everywhere one gazed, John Philip's name was in evidence. I discussed the matter with Bea, who understood the value of the engagement as a professional credit for me, and she insisted that inserts be printed and slipped into the programs at each performance, informing the audience that I was appearing as the Waiter in the "Milady" sketch. Rack, Bea, and I saw to the setup, hung Bea's costumes in Baddeley's dressing room, and the show went on at 10:45 each evening.

Edinburgh liked the show, although Bea did take exception to one critic who headed his column "Beatrice Lillie is still singing!" "As opposed to what?" Bea asked.

"Beatrice Lillie is dining alone. Alone, that is, except for a packed house at her late night show, an audience ready to guffaw at her slightest gesture," wrote another. Bea went to Glasgow to appear on television and flew back to London after the engagement.

On Bea's property was an old mill, an empty stone building in which Gray stored his gardening tools and the lawn mowers. When John began plans to have a swimming pool installed, Bea put her foot down about the renovations. The building would require major reconstruction, and the cost would be prohibitive. No pool was ever installed.

Bea returned to New York in time to appear for Leonard Sillman at his *Fight for Sight* benefit at Carnegie Hall. Leonard invited us all to dinner at his home a few weeks before the performance. Shirley

Booth, Gypsy Rose Lee, and Dorothy Strelsin were among the guests. As we were having cocktails, the odor of garlic floated into the room from the kitchen. Ruth, Leonard's housekeeper, was preparing leg of lamb. John was next to me in a flash.

"I smell garlic."

"We're having leg of lamb."

"Bea won't eat garlic. She hates garlic! You know that!"

"They don't know it," I replied, wondering if there was going to be a scene. Dinner was announced before John could do anything. I watched Bea during the serving, knowing full well she had smelled the garlic, and she served herself potatoes, vegetable, and salad without a murmur to anyone.

At the benefit, T. C. Jones, the well-known female impersonator and satirist, was to appear. Bea, Shirley Booth, and most of the other stars were in the green room relaxing and having coffee as the evening progressed. Bette Davis chose to pace the floor in back of the curtain as she smoked. T.C. arrived with Connie, his wife, in full costume. He had dressed at home. He ran up and said hello, and I pointed out a male friend of his who was watching from the wings. T.C. ran over and gave him a big kiss on the cheek, chatted for a moment, and ran to a dressing room. Bette Davis watched the whole scene without saying a word, and when T.C. and Connie disappeared, Davis strolled over and sat next to the man T.C. had just bussed. She stared at the man for a moment and took a long drag on her cigarette.

"You know," she said, releasing a huge cloud of smoke, "that was a boy!" Stunned, the poor man could only nod his head yes. When T.C. was performing, Bette Davis stopped pacing long enough to peek through the curtain and say, "I hope he does me!"

Bea was asked to appear at the Red Cross Ball, this time in Palm Beach and headed by Mary Sandford, a former actress, who was now queen of the Palm Beach hostesses. Rack and I agreed to go, he for a fee, and I for the fare down and back. The performance would again be "Milady" and some songs. Jack Carter was on the program with Bea. Rack and I were housed in a guest cottage on the Sandford property and Bea and John were put up at a hotel. We did the show in the Palm Beach Playhouse and afterwards prepared for the evening ball which lay ahead. Rack and I were attired in our evening clothes when we were informed that John neglected to have us invited. Rack and I sat on the porch of our little cottage and drank vodka under a southern moon while Bea and John made merry with the jet set. We flew to New York the following day with no word from John or Bea.

Ethel and George Vigouroux invited Bea and John to share their palatial home for a few days. Bea sunbathed by the pool once more and, since it was the height of the season, George and Ethel kept the social ball rolling. One week stretched into two, then two into three, and so on until Ethel began to feel the strain. Ethel's dinner parties were consistently ruined by John, who felt free to return home with Bea at any hour he chose. Ethel would politely keep her guests waiting until he and Bea wandered in to eat. Finally, Ethel buckled under the strain and marched into the center of a gathering one day and declared that she was closing up the house for the summer and returning to New York. Bea and John returned home the following day.

There had been an actors' strike which closed all of the theatres. The night it ended Bea, John, and I obtained seats for *Fiorello* and dined at Sardi's. As we left Bea called out that we would be back later but she was not heard. Forty-fourth Street was ablaze with television lights and cameras were photographing the event for the late news. When we returned to Sardi's the place was jammed and the maitre d', already in a state of shock, paled when he saw Bea and her party. Sardi's being Sardi's, however, we were squeezed into a table for two with John on the outside. The table next to us was empty until Ethel Merman and a friend were seated there. Ethel was nearly in my lap but since she and Bea were old friends she did not seem to mind. The restaurant was chaotic and throngs of people waited to get in. Leonard Lyons and Earl Wilson drifted from table to table gathering bits of data for their columns. Suddenly Ethel jabbed me in the ribs.

"Isn't that Stritch sitting over there?" she pointed to Elaine Stritch sporting a new hairdo at a table some distance away. I assured her it was Stritch and she waved frantically until Stritch noticed her and smiled back.

"I like your hair!" Ethel said under her breath as she mouthed the statement. Elaine Stritch indicated she had no idea what Merman was telling her.

"Your hair! Your hair!" Merman continued. Stritch smiled and shrugged her shoulders.

"Oh, for God's sake," muttered Ethel in disgust. "I like your hair!"

"Would you like me to go and tell her?" offered Bea but by then Stritch had gotten the message. She smiled broadly and touched her hair.

"My hair. You like it?" she mouthed at Ethel, who had had it by then.

"It stinks!" roared Ethel in full voice and went back to her vodka and tonic. Later, when Bea told her the Walthamstowe Silver Band story, Ethel retaliated with one of her own. "Did you hear about the two dancing girls who roomed together? One said to the other, 'Do you remember the minuet?' and the other one said, 'Honey, I don't remember the men I fucked!' " Bea had another drink on that one.

John wanted to do another *Evening With* type of entertainment and the title *Beography* was invented. Again it was to be a rehash of Bea's career although he and Bea talked of varying it with stories about her childhood and her family. But the songs and sketches would basically remain the same. John's plan was to pull it off without spending any money. He knew nothing about budgets or contacting set and costume designers. I suggested he consider using a company manager to advise him and put him in touch with Al Goldin, a general manager of impeccable reputation and the sort of person I thought Bea would like. Al, a quiet gentlemanly man, went to East End Avenue and met with Bea and John. Bea liked him instantly and found it easy to be animated and chatty with him. John explained the premise of the show to Al, who listened politely but John did not get to the point of Al's visit. Instead he began playing Beatrice Lillie recordings and discoursing upon the life and times of the comedienne, much of which Al already knew. Gradually, John swung around to what he had in mind and Goldin realized John was expecting him to raise the money for *Beography*. Bea, meanwhile, reminisced about her early life in London and her "extra turn" at the Camberwell Palace.

"It was an amateur show such as the ones you have in America," explained Bea.

"You were never in an amateur show, Bea," corrected John.

"An amateur show as I was saying," Bea continued.

"Bea, you were never in an amateur show." John was not going to let it pass.

"I don't know what you'd call it but to me it was an old-fashioned amateur show," Bea answered angrily.

Mr. Goldin exited on that scene and was never heard from again. Bea continued to mention *Beography* but nothing ever came of it.

Fritz De Wilde was stage-managing *A Man for All Seasons* and invited Bea to dinner to meet George Rose, who scored a great personal success in the show. They had a wonderful evening together. She and Rose were dying to meet each other. Brandon was there, a nineteen-year-old man by now and very good-looking. Genie cooked a superb meal and the wine was perfect. Bea drank heavily and went to sleep in one of the De Wilde bedrooms. More and more, Bea was imbibing with little concern for where she was or whom she was with. John's denial was certainly stronger than hers. Usually he blamed it on a particular incident and acted as though it had not happened before. It did nothing but antagonize him if anyone else mentioned Bea's drinking. He would become furious as though they were implicating him in some way. But he never faced Bea squarely with it or talked it out intelligently or sought help for her from some other quarter. If one of her friends faced Bea with it they were automatically "out of the will" from then on and not invited anymore. John continued to spend hundreds of dollars on wines at East End Avenue, in his apartment and hers, and in Henley-on-Thames. Bea would go into a rage when she signed checks for the wine, which she hardly ever touched.

"Maybe he wants it all there in case I suddenly pop off," she said angrily.

In April of 1962, Bea was signed to appear at the O'Keefe in a divertissement entitled *Beatrice Lillie at Nine O'Clock*. Alexander H. Cohen produced the show and Bea shared the bill with Roberto Iglesias and his entire company of dancers. John Philip was listed as director and Rack, once again, was on hand to support Bea. She did "Milady Dines Alone" and her songs following Iglesias' company. Bea was cooperative as she usually was but things began to look grim when John started a problem with the stagehands over a technicality. We were at a standstill in the theatre until Emanuel Azenberg, Cohen's General Manager, arrived and declared emphatically that nobody in the theatre was to listen to anyone but the stage manager. When John called Manny at one in the morning to remonstrate with him, Azenberg ordered him never to call at that hour again and hung up the phone.

Once the show opened, however, Bea enjoyed the week in her home town. Her cousin, John Lillie, and his family visited her backstage and Bert Lahr showed up unexpectedly one night on his way to the Yukon. Bea then returned to New York and appeared on "Password" which also happened to be one of her favorite television shows.

Through Bert she was invited to Dawson City to open the Dawson City Festival. "Up the Pole," laughed Bea later. "I went to Dawson City to open it. It's day and night. All night all day. I can't stay awake all day at night! When I got back to New York, I couldn't sleep when it was dark!" She saw Bert open in his show, *Foxy*, panned for gold, visited a deserted mine, and thoroughly enjoyed the adventure.

Franklin Lacey and his wife, Gladys, came into Bea's life because of a show called *Captain Isabelle* which Lacey had written. John Philip knew Lacey from *Magdalena* where Lacey acted as assistant stage manager. Franklin Lacey had also collaborated on the book of *The Music Man* with Meredith Willson. Alfred de Liagre was mentioned as producer of *Captain Isabelle*, the story of a lady steamship captain. Bea began spending most of her time with the Laceys and there were publicity releases concerning her participation in the project.

Previously Bea had recorded "Typically English," written by Leslie Bricusse and Anthony Newley for their show *Stop the World I Want to Get Off*, now a big hit on Broadway. Bea's recording made the jukeboxes in England and was a bestseller. One song she loved recording was Coward's "I Pick Up Bits of Paper with My Toes" and she sang both on television when she appeared in July with Arlene Francis and in November with Johnny Carson. In July she talked about *Captain Isabelle* being done that year but in November she said it had been postponed. De Liagre had dropped the show by then.

Actors' Equity celebrated its fiftieth anniversary in 1963 and Bea was invited to participate. "At the Equity fiftieth performance, Bea was asked to do 'March with Me,'" said Cyril Ritchard. "When she first did 'March with Me,' I was watching it but I never saw the finish because I was under the seat! She still treated it as if it were a ballad. Anyway, came this show and Bea had forgotten so much of the business that I reminded her of some of it." Ethel Martin restaged the number and after thirty-nine years it still brought down the house. Bea, dressed as Britannia, trying to retain a semblance of dignity while being jostled about by her troop of girls, was hilarious and she repeated the number later in the year at the Tappan Zee Playhouse.

Reggie Gardiner was routed out of his Beverly Hills home and decided to appear once again with Bea in an interlude called *An Evening With Highlights* at the Tappan Zee Playhouse in Nyack, New York. Just before it went into rehearsal, John Philip suffered the first of a series of heart problems and was admitted to the Veterans Hospital in New York. Bea called Michael Ellis and asked if I could be released from a contract at the Bucks County Playhouse to help out and he agreed. We commuted to Nyack every day and rehearsed in the car. Bea added "The Reading of the Play" and "Double Damask Dinner Napkins" so that she and Reggie could appear together. Ethel Martin again restaged "March with Me." I did a walk-on in "Double Damask," and the day we were to open, Helen Hayes, who lived in Nyack, came by and Bea asked if I would show her the routine and she would do it at the opening. The audience was startled to see the First Lady of the American Theatre stroll out onto the stage waving a crooked shillelagh and trading words with Beatrice Lillie. There was an elegant opening night party at the MacArthur residence, and Bea and Reggie were feted by Helen, playwright Carson McCullers, the DeWildes, Tony Newley, Joan Collins, and a host of friends from New York. John remained hospitalized for the run of the show in Nyack.

SEVENTEEN

Noël Coward approved a musical version of his *Blithe Spirit* which had been created by Hugh Martin and Timothy Gray. It was to be called *High Spirits* and Martin and Gray were responsible for the music, lyrics, and book. Lester Osterman was to produce and Bea was approached to play Madame Arcati, a role which Coward for years claimed he had written with her in mind. Bea was excited over the prospect of playing Arcati and went to lunch with Coward to talk it over. Actually, Noël was interested in Bea's mental and physical health as well as her thoughts about the part and the show. Both were pleased with the meeting and parted with high hopes. The trouble began, as it always did, with the amount of material Bea was to do in the show. John, speaking for Bea once more, asked for more songs and submitted a list of other requests as well. In the meantime, Bea appeared on a television *Salute to Noël Coward* and then prepared to go into rehearsal. Tammy Grimes, Edward Woodward, and Louise Troy were signed. Bea was delighted about Tammy but suffered a temporary setback when one of the producers called her directly to ask if she would allow Tammy to share star billing with her. Bea panicked for fear that John would find out and never gave a definite answer. Tammy was eventually billed directly under Bea's name.

Bea worked hard, harder than she had in ages, on Madame Arcati. For the first time in years she was confronted with a book show and Noël Coward at the same time. He insisted she follow his directions and learn her lines as quickly as possible. Bea did her best but was surrounded by a bevy of actors and a singing and dancing chorus. She was learning lines, blocking songs, and learning dances at the same time—at the age of seventy. Hugh Martin and Timothy Gray were helpful and gentle with her and she clung to them for support at song rehearsals and progressed easier because of their consideration. José Vega and Frank Gero, the head stage managers, bent over backwards to assist her at every opportunity and the cast in general was understanding. Bea disliked the orchestra conductor, who remained openly antagonistic toward her, but for the most part she was enjoying herself and liked the people she was working with.

Noël spoke to the actors one day when Bea was absent and told them that in the forty years he had known her she always rehearsed in her vague way and that on opening night she would be letter perfect. Danny Daniels, the choreographer, informed the dancers also that Bea, at seventy, had more energy than they. Coward carped at Bea but she knew him well enough not to allow it to upset her, especially since he treated most of his lady stars in the identical manner. On one occasion he stopped Tammy in the middle of a scene to question her pronunciation of the word *pretense*.

"You've pronounced it two ways," complained Mr. Coward.

"Well, what's the difference?" asked Tammy.

"One is British and one is definitely American," stated Noël.

"Which one is British?" Tammy wanted to know.

"The correct one!" he answered and went to the men's room, leaving Tammy and everyone else to think that one over.

New Haven was a nightmare. There was far too much scenery, and it was impossible to make scene changes smoothly. A sound problem developed, and when one of the technicians asked Noël if he wanted more microphones he called out, "I want a microphone protruding from every orifice on the set!" During one performance, he was distracted by an usher in the balcony who kept flicking his flashlight on and off in an attempt to signal another usher.

"Good God!" he pleaded. "will somebody please go up there and kill Tinker Bell!" Later, at rehearsal, Tammy paused to ask Noël if her accent was British enough.

"Darling, it's pure Druid," he assured her.

Tammy was given a day to go to New York to pose for photographs and be interviewed by *Look* magazine, a commitment she had made before rehearsals began. John found out and raised a terrible scene backstage. He insisted that the *High Spirits* press department had arranged it and felt if anyone was going to talk to *Look*, it should be Bea. When I told him that Tammy's press agent had set up the date, he demanded to know whose side I was on. John was actually angry because Tammy had gotten the best reviews in New Haven; she was good, the part was showy and exciting, and she was flying all over the stage like Peter Pan.

Bea and Tammy had spectacular first entrances in the show. The crowd loved it when Bea appeared on her bicycle peddling frantically as it moved out of the wings to center stage and then eventually out the other side. Happily the bike was on a platform and pulled along by a cable which was controlled by the stage manager for safety's sake. As Bea did her opening number on the bike, a curtain went up behind her revealing the chorus on their bicycles. One night, for no apparent reason, Bea climbed down from her bicycle. The stage managers were perplexed and Coward and the producers wondered what she had in mind. The curtain went up a moment later and the bicycle went with it. The taillight was snagged in the curtain and if Bea had been where she was supposed to be there could have been a terrible accident. Bea never knew what prompted her to leave her bike.

High Spirits opened in Boston to good reviews but everyone agreed the show needed work. Bea managed to get through the opening and the audience loved her. Tammy fared better than Bea did in the review department. John was infuriated with Tammy's notices and Bea said he was impossible to deal with. The Laceys were now in town and staying at the Ritz with Bea and John. Lacey proved a detriment to the director and the stage managers by giving Bea a running discourse on the state of the show from an audience standpoint. That coupled with John's suggestions for pieces of business did Bea a disservice. When Lacey informed her that the audience could see her crawling about in a blackout Bea became highly upset and complained to the stage managers. He neglected to remind Bea, however, that Tammy Grimes was flying twenty feet above in her first entrance and every eye in the theatre was focused on Tammy. I went out front three times to check on the problem and was swept away in the excitement of the flying in all three cases and forgot to look for Bea. For all their good intentions they were really being unkind to Bea, who was busy trying to absorb a new dance number called "Something Is Coming to Tea," which stopped the show on its first performance and from then on.

Bea worked slowly and carefully, to the annoyance of some of the cast members. A few of the younger chorus workers were condescending toward her, a bit too "tolerant" perhaps, but then they had never seen Beatrice Lillie on stage. Those of us who knew her, including Noël Coward, understood exactly what she was doing and never for a moment doubted her. When a choreographic assistant huffily ordered a stage manager to tell Miss Lillie to stay out of the way of the dancers, she was abruptly informed that it worked the opposite way around. Bea learned the blocking in her own manner and was unable to follow numbers painted on the floor.

Her private joke in the show was all of the paraphernalia she attached to her costume. Her Arcati outfit became more outlandish with each performance and Lela, her dresser, had her hands full keeping track of where everything went. She and Bea argued constantly over this since Bea switched things around every day. Knitting needles protruded from her hat and her bicycle clips ended up on her arms as they did many years before in *Tabs*.

Except for the new dance number and a few changes here and there, it became obvious to everyone that little was being done to improve the show in Boston. Noël rightfully felt that the script had been proven sound over the years, so only the musical numbers were rehearsed for the most part. Tammy felt some of the book scenes ought to be dealt with but any work done was minimal. Graham Payn, who had been assisting Noël, became ill and remained in New

York so Coward carried the burden with the aid of Cole Leslie, his secretary and friend for many years. Coward himself was not feeling well at the time due to an ulcer which was acting up.

Noël disliked open set changes intensely. As a result, a blue traveler curtain closed after every scene and, while the orchestra frantically played music from the show, everyone backstage dashed about changing the set. Unfortunately, the show was ponderous and, as one critic pointed out, "all about a blue traveler!"

Katharine Cornell arrived from her home in Martha's Vineyard to see a matinee. She went backstage to visit Bea and to pay her respects to the cast. Someone had the bad taste to ask Noël Coward how old she was. "Ninety-seven," growled the Master as he angrily strode away from the offender. He found the question rude and irrelevant. Later, in Philadelphia, when he was asked the same question regarding Lynn Fontanne, a very short "one hundred and one" was his reply. It was only a matter of time before he was asked the identical question about Beatrice Lillie and it occurred at Harvard.

Noël accepted an invitation to lunch and to address a crowd of students at Harvard. Afterwards there was a question-and-answer period. Inevitably Bea's name entered the discussion, and a student asked how old she was and what she was like. Coward answered crisply and humorously, "She's seventy-five and completely mad!" Actually Bea was seventy. As it happened, among the assembled crowd were two young men who had been pursuing Bea about Boston asking for autographs and photographs. They deemed it necessary to hasten to the Colonial Theatre and report Noël's remark to John Philip.

In the audience that night was Count Fulco, Duke di Vedura, the international jeweler, close friend of Noël, Bea, and Cole Porter. Fulco had recently been in a severe automobile accident and was on the mend. After the show, he went to Bea's dressing room to congratulate her. He had barely kissed her hand before John roared through the door shouting Noël's words at Bea.

"I don't think he'd do a thing like that," protested the Duke, whereupon John flew at him and grabbed him by the throat and scratched him badly enough to draw blood before Lela was able to summon help. Bea and Gladys Lacey fled the premises immediately. Only those actually involved knew what went on in Bea's dressing room.

There was a production meeting on stage after the show that night. Stage managers, producers, designers, and lighting technicians met with Noël Coward for notes on the production. Everyone was seated under the glow of a work light hanging overhead. Noël relaxed in an easy chair on the set. He was stating his opinion of the performance, when from the wings where it was very dark came a strange, high-pitched voice.

"That's right, Mr. Noël Peirce Coward. You tell 'em, Mr. Noël Peirce Coward." Everything halted. People looked at one another and then into the darkened wings where the peculiar voice was uttering its Noël Peirce Cowards. It was obviously not an admirer. The microphones to the dressing rooms were still live and all talking ceased as the cast tuned in to what was occurring onstage.

From out of the wings, like a Phantom of the Opera, John emerged. Those who did not know John imagined at first it was all a joke, but I knew better. John approached Noël, who remained stationary and horrified. Producers Lester Osterman and Richard Horner, company manager Leonard Soloway, and the entire group stared at him as if he had lost his mind. He was pure white and enraged. When he stopped in front of Noël, he proceeded to unleash a barrage of verbal abuse so revolting that it made some of his former performances seem tame.

"We thought he was rehearsing a scene for an acting class," said actress Margaret Hall, "and not a very good one. We all stood under the speakers and listened."

Witnesses were stupefied with shock, and I prayed no one would touch John. One move from anyone present and he would have been on top of Coward in a flash. As yet, nobody present knew of the affair at Harvard or had any idea why John was so crazed.

One of the stage managers had the presence of mind to shut off the stage microphones. Some of those in the dressing rooms slammed their doors and ran down the stairs to see what was happening. Tammy Grimes, in her room at the time, was so unnerved by the display she locked her hairdresser and herself in, while Louise Troy was nearly comatose in hers. Noël, though pale, never moved or took his eyes off John.

John's remarks were becoming more abusive by the moment. Phrases such as "old queen" and "faggot" were snarled out. He said, "You're old enough to be my mother" and then threatened to "tie your balls behind your back."

"I remember wondering at the time just how he hoped to accomplish that," recalled Margaret. The cast was offstage by then straining to see who was causing the scene. Edward Woodward was standing in front of Margaret Hall trying to look over the crowd in front of him. "I pushed him and said, 'You're the leading man, go on out there and see what it's all about.' "

Coward's demeanor in the face of the onslaught was causing John to lose ground rapidly. He then babbled something to the effect that he had been guiding Bea's career instead of his own. In the silence that followed somebody said gently, "John, why don't you go home to your hotel."

With that John began pounding his thigh wildly, and turning to the darkened auditorium, he shouted, "No, I'm going to stay here where I belong, center stage!"

Noël remained the picture of dignity and poise. John finally ran out of steam, and the attack came to an end. However, for the pièce de résistance, John Philip once again faced Noël Coward and bellowed straight at him, "Beatrice Lillie loves me!" There was silence as Noël took a long pull on his cigarette. He released the smoke and spoke quietly.

"Then she *must* be mad," he said as he left the stage. He never spoke to John again for the rest of his life.

In Noël's suite later, he told us the Harvard story while we all had drinks.

"I understand he once attacked you," he said to me. "I would not harm Beattie for anything, I think she knows that. I am terribly upset with her for inflicting him upon everyone. He has been a stumbling block ever since we began, and I warned her about it at lunch some time ago. If she can't learn the show, it's his fault, not hers. I certainly know by now what makes her tick."

I attempted to reach Bea at the Ritz. In the light of John's outrageous behavior, I wanted to know if there would be a matinee the following afternoon. Gladys Lacey answered and said Bea had heard nothing about an incident at Harvard although she was still upset over the Fulco scene. She guaranteed that Bea would be there for the matinee. When Bea finally heard John's version of the episode with Coward, she was horrified. Not for an instant would she believe he had deliberately maligned her. The tragic and thoughtless part of the whole affair was John's repeating it to Bea. The Coward-Lillie squabbles of years before had been forgotten, and the tiffs that occurred during *High Spirits* were caused by two creative geniuses attempting to do their best. Coward was strong enough to stop Bea time and time again to insist that she follow the blocking and the script. Although Bea resented it she knew Noël was right, and in the end her strict adherence to the staging aided her immensely with her own creativity by supplying her with the security she needed to allow her to characterize Arcati in her own way.

"I must say my original conception is being vindicated," Coward had said recently. "Although I, of course, loved all the others [referring to the other Madame Arcatis over the years], Bea is absolute magic as Arcati. I have been writing for her most of my professional life and I should be quite used to it by now, but I am always astonished at what she finds in a role. She always adds a certain something that cannot be captured on paper."

The day following John's scene with Noël, Lester Osterman and Leonard Soloway received a phone call at the theatre. "I just wanted to tell you there will be no repercussions regarding last night," said a jovial John Philip, implying that Miss Lillie was prepared to forget the whole thing. John was ordered to come straight to the theatre. He was confronted by a very angry producer who stated in no uncertain terms that John was free to walk from the show taking Miss Lillie with him whenever he wished to go. Osterman promised he would sign another star and keep the show on the road until she learned it if need be. Once again Bea was implicated in something she knew nothing about. It was probably the first time she ever came that close to being fired and she never knew it.

In Philadelphia, Tammy Grimes was hospitalized for exhaustion, and Noël had an ulcer attack. When it became evident that he would be unable to continue, Gower Champion, fresh from a stunning success with *Hello, Dolly!*, took over. He took on Bea first and discussed changes he thought would be helpful to her and relayed Noël's ideas for a new ending to the show. I saw Bea laugh out loud, and she adored Gower from then on.

The open changes that Coward objected to went in with him observing, and the show began to flow like magic. Gower's new ending, with Madame Arcati and Charles succumbing to poisoned brandy, allowed Bea the honor of topping the show with a huge belly laugh as the curtain came down.

High Spirits ran for over a year in New York. On opening night, as Bea rode into sight on her bicycle, the roar of welcome from the packed theatre was deafening. The younger performers stood with their mouths open as the ovation increased in volume. One of the girls was staring out, tears running down her face. I asked if she was all right, and she stammered, "I have never seen anything like this before." Those who had been impatient with Bea during rehearsals watched her romp through the show with wild abandon. Noël's early prediction came true. Miss Lillie was letter perfect all the way.

She was not a few nights later, however, when, during the seance scene, instead of asking a hovering spirit, "How's your cold, Daphne?", she created a whole new mood by saying, "How's your hole, Daphne?" Edward Woodward, Margaret Hall, Louise Troy, and Larry Keith charged through the scene like brave soldiers although the set was shaking rather badly. When I told Bea later, she did not believe a word I said.

The show was a triumph for Bea, and all the reviews were love letters to her. "It has the inestimable blessing of providing the superb Beatrice Lillie with an opportunity for displaying her magic touch"; "Beatrice Lillie's performance reaffirms her place in the recorded history of the twentieth century, along with the battle of Jutland and Salk vaccine"; "I will remember it as the musical comedy in which Beatrice Lillie killed me"; "God bless Miss Lillie, the most durable and delightful comic of our era"; these were only a few of the accolades. Lucille Ball saw the show twice, and Richard Burton and Elizabeth Taylor showed up with almost all of Actors' Equity for the Actors' Fund benefit. Tammy changed her flying gear in Bea's dressing room and we maintained a close watch lest she miss entrance cues while she and Bea gossiped. In one scene Bea rode in on a small bed that was parked offstage. Night after night Tammy, cigarette in hand, would hop onto the bed with Bea and the two ladies would giggle like college girls at a slumber party. We lived in dread that Tammy would forget and be discovered in bed with Madame Arcati when the lights came up.

Bea was very fond of Tammy's little daughter, who enjoyed visiting Bea in her room. "Will you please take me to Bill Lillie's dressing room?" she would lisp to a stage manager.

In the security of her dressing room, Bea remained as always friendly to the cast and crew. She had a problem with names in some cases but still welcomed a joke or a bit of gossip. She had time to talk to the dancers and singers as she waited to go on with her bicycle. She was easy on the stage managers, who treated her like a star, and became very fond of Leonard Soloway, who went back nightly and checked to see if everything was all right. When Michael Davis told her a Bea Lillie story concerning Winston Churchill, that he had fallen off a chair at a garden party and Bea supposedly chastised him with "That's not funny, Winston!" Bea denied it but said she wished it was true.

A dancer left the show and was replaced by Frank Derbas. Bea at one point would slide down Frank's back in a dance number. She seriously cautioned Frank against laughing when she did it. "If you laugh, I shall look like a silly old bitch!" she explained. Frank laughed quite a bit at that!

The big change was in her life away from the theatre. It no longer revolved around what she wished. Surrounded by the Laceys and John and his sister, *she* followed *them* now. There were dinners at Sardi's but she was never seen in the places where the company gathered, although she was present at the opening night party. Beatrice, her maid at 25 East End Avenue, retired, which was a great loss to her. When I asked who took care of the house she said they all did. Bea said that John and his sister cooked dinner and took care of her food. I was no longer invited to East End Avenue.

John kept her waiting after the show and cast members often found her huddled in the doorway outside the theatre waiting for John to pick her up in the car. When it rained or snowed, they invited Bea across the street to the Confucius Restaurant but she did not take them up on their invitations. Often I urged her to take a taxi and offered to see her home but she steadfastly refused and I would wait with her until John arrived.

We did have one last fight, however. Bea sang a number in which she ran behind a threefold screen and pretended to undress. The screen was pulled on by a cable attached to an iron bar, and I lived in mortal terror that Bea would one day trip on the bar and injure herself. One night she did just that, and the screen fell in the middle of the number. I went quickly to her dressing room to see if she was all right.

"The screen was put on incorrectly," Bea insisted. I argued that she had simply tripped and it fell down but she was not going to listen to it. I persisted in my explanation in order for her to realize that the screen would not move onstage if put on incorrectly. Bea became angry and ordered me from the room and would not talk to me for days. When I arrived for the next performance there was a large white envelope awaiting me. From John Philip, it was a collage of chimpanzees pasted on white paper with written slurs against the stage management of *High Spirits*. I then understood Bea's attitude from the night before. She wanted me to agree with her that the screen was at fault, so that John could not blame her for ruining the number. She had asked for my help, and I had deserted her. Bea avoided me all week and seemed so forlorn that I finally sent her two dozen Tropicana roses, her favorites. In the theatre that night no word was forthcoming from the star dressing room. Lela passed by once or twice without a word about the flowers, and the show began with no message from Bea. I gave the cue for her bike to enter. Then I heard laughter from the chorus in the wings and checked quickly to see what was wrong. There were roses pinned on every available space in Bea's hat, costume, and on the bicycle. She sang the number with a hysterical and puzzled group behind her. I was cuing when she came past me at the end of the song. Bea gave me a resounding slap on the back as she passed and yelled, "Thanks for the flowers!" The fight was over and I was back in the will.

A casting director friend of mine asked if Bea might be interested in appearing on the potato chip commercial that Bert Lahr was then doing with tremendous financial success. I put them in touch with John Philip, and one or two were filmed and one was aired. It was clear to me that Bea had no idea what she was doing and had even managed to slip in some of her *High Spirits* dialogue, which made no sense. John also insisted that Bea not touch, eat, or mention the product, thereby defeating the whole purpose of the commercial. The commercials were quickly withdrawn.

Bea was given Christmas week off and flew to London. Mr. Lee had died and John replaced him with a small black Peke called Lord Button. Without a maid or somebody responsible looking after the animal, Lord Button was never completely housebroken, and John teased him so badly he became unpleasant and unpredictable, often snapping at people with no warning, so much so that Bea never trusted him.

One night in February of 1965, Noël Coward dropped backstage to see Bea. She was delighted but apprehensive that John might show up. Coward, however, was completely relaxed, and they enjoyed a quiet talk. Up until that moment Bea was not sure of the state of their close friendship. In Philadelphia and New York they carefully avoided each other but Bea mentioned him often and asked for news of him from time to time. Noël was on his way to Jamaica, and when it came time for the show to begin, he took both of Bea's hands in his and bade her good-bye. Nothing had changed in their long and close relationship. That meeting was to be the last they ever held in private.

High Spirits closed with a rousing party given by Tammy Grimes in the lobby of the theatre. It would be Bea's final Broadway appearance. Time and illness took their toll eventually, and she never knew that among the cast members Edward Woodward became a famous television star in England and America, Beth Howland scored heavily in a television series, and Ronnie Walken changed his name to Christopher and went on to win an Academy Award. Bea never knew that teenager Altovise Gore met and married Sammy Davis, Jr., or that Tammy's daughter, using her own name, Amanda Plummer, won a Tony award. Bea did know that Carol Arthur, who played Edith, married Dom DeLuise. She visited the DeLuises in California and held their first child, Peter, in her arms but never knew that Peter, too, became an actor.

EIGHTEEN

It was evident to those who knew Bea well that she was drifting away slowly during the final months of *High Spirits*. Lela Goode, her dresser, complained to Joe Busheme, head of wardrobe, that pieces of costume jewelry were missing from the dressing room. Joe advised her to watch Bea, and Lela discovered that Bea was indeed responsible. She was hiding the objects just as she would hide her jewelry in the hotels when she traveled. Often I could see Bea across stage or sitting in the wings staring into space like a lost person. The energy and the spirit were ebbing away. She responded to Tammy Grimes as always but everyone else seemed remote to her.

The Paper Mill Playhouse in Millburn, New Jersey, asked for the show, and Lacey and John set about arranging a summer tour of *High Spirits*. Teddy Woodward returned to London by ship and was wished a warm and tearful farewell by the stage managers and some of the cast. Louise Troy was not interested in a summer version of a show in which she had received excellent notices on Broadway, and Tammy had other fish to fry. John threw obstacles in the way by insisting that Bea would do the show only if the sets were exactly as they were in New York, a near impossibility in summer theatres. Two theatres managed to comply with his demands, the Paper Mill Playhouse and Mt. Tom Playhouse in Massachusetts. Those who were holdovers from the New York company were disconcerted to learn that Franklin Lacey was to direct the summer version.

But the most difficult situation facing Bea was not the set but a new cast. During rehearsals she complained that the actor playing Dr. Bradman was reading his lines differently than he did in New York. I would then have to explain that it was not the same actor. Bea would pause time and time again after a character said a line. When I attempted to prompt her she would insist he left out something. Generally it turned out to be a minor ad lib that had crept in in New York. Staging was changed, which I found difficult to take quietly in the light of Bea's problems, and the director and I were not friendly. When John and Lacey slipped a line to Bea that read "Oh, dear, my living bra just died!" I told her to refuse to say it but she was afraid to argue. When the show opened, she would exit nearly in tears every night after saying the line moaning, "I hate that line, I can't tell you how I hate that line!" Try as I might I could not convince her to cut it, especially when she heard John at the back of the theatre laughing at the top of his lungs. Carol Arthur played her original role of Edith, which gave Bea a great deal of security. But most of the other principals were new, and only a few of the chorus remained. The whole project was anticlimactic for those who had been on Broadway with the show, and there were no tears shed when it closed after the week at the Mt. Tom Playhouse.

While *High Spirits* was still on Broadway, Bea committed herself to performing at a benefit in Houston, Texas, in the fall. She asked if I would go with her. I agreed, and then the matter was dropped. Rack was called to rehearse Bea for the benefit and discovered she was not only having difficulty remembering numbers but also lacked interest in the project. John called and asked if I would do "Milady" with her and reminded me I had promised Bea I would go to Houston. It was obviously a last-minute decision on his part because it would be money out of Bea's pocket if I went. We rehearsed two days in Houston. Bea drove us all mad by asking us to walk Lord Button every half hour all day, but she was more like herself than she had been in a while and we gladly complied.

Hotel accommodations in Houston were fine, and a car was assigned to transport Bea and company to and from the theatre. The day of the performance, we ran through the show and checked scenery and props. Bea's car did not show up to take us to the hotel for a nap. We were in the lobby of the auditorium waiting. There were tables set up everywhere with white cloths and hundreds of champagne glasses, and there were customers at the windows purchasing tickets, among them a group of nuns. Bea was joking about getting into the habit and making Rack and me laugh, when John abruptly exploded and began screaming at the box office personnel regarding the whereabouts of Bea's transportation. He became completely psychotic. I suggested that perhaps a taxi would solve the problem but he would not hear of it. He called the man in charge of our accommodations and reached apoplectic heights in his tirade against the poor man. I prayed John would not toss over the tables and champagne glasses. When Bea began to fall apart, I ignored Philip and walked her quickly outside; we were back at her room in minutes a via cab. She was shaking badly with nerves when I left her after walking Lord Button once more, and I told her to lie down and take a nap.

"Milady" led off the evening, and Bea was fine if somewhat distracted. The song portion of the performance was a disaster. Bea was unable to complete one number without looking to Rack for aid. Over and over again she stopped and asked for a lyric until the audience began getting restless. Many left. For Rack it was sheer agony, and he broke down and cried later at the hotel. There was a party immediately after the performance but, typical of John, he forgot, and once again Rack and I were not invited.

The next time I spoke with Bea she told me she had signed with Doubleday to write a book about Mr. Lee called *Take a Peke*. "You know I never will," she added. When Ellen Graham published a book later called *Suzi, A Star's Story*, a Pekingese was the heroine. The work was coincidental, although Bea was wont to believe she had supplied Ellen with the idea.

Bea joined the Laceys in California and went on to Hawaii with them. She dressed up like a Hawaiian lady and in this disguise met Mary Martin and her *Hello, Dolly* company at the plane as they passed through on their way to the mainland. For short periods she was like her old self, but there were those moments when she was totally confused. John later told friends that she was being given magnesium to aid her memory.

Bob Feyte left Peel Fold and lived in London looking after Muriel, who was in poor health and drinking badly. The house in St. John's Wood was in horrible shape. There were letters from Bobbie to Bea and Lucie, photographs and memorabilia strewn about the floors, and odd people living there from time to time as guests of Muriel. She was a complete caricature of herself. "Anybody with a bottle of gin was welcome to live there," said David Bolton, who helped in watching over Muriel. Muriel refused to pay bills, or if she did she deliberately did not sign the check. On other occasions she would phone the creditor and plead illness as the reason for her tardiness. Bea was unaware of any of this or even of Muriel's death in 1973. She was buried near Lucie in Harpsden, but Bea was not informed and did not attend the burial. Abercorn Place was broken into a number of times and eventually was sold.

Bea's final screen performance was in *Thoroughly Modern Millie*, and from the moment her boots appeared on the screen she found a new audience. Thanks mainly to director George Roy Hill, who knew Bea was right for the part, hired her, and then had the courage to stick by his guns, Bea was able to finish the film.

"She had great difficulty orienting herself," said screenwriter Richard Morris. "And enormous problems retaining the lines. George Roy Hill was infinitely kind, and Julie Andrews was awfully good to her."

Bea, in turn, had great difficulty in remembering who Julie Andrews was and repeatedly asked the name of the girl who kept singing. At one point it looked as though she might be replaced. A meeting was called and the head of production insisted that Bea was unable to go on in the part, but George Roy Hill stated that Bea could do it and would do it. Simple scenes required many, many takes. In one scene with Andrews, she was supposed to answer her request for mail by saying "There's always mail for you." Each time Julie Andrews asked her if there was any mail, Bea said "No!" instead of the correct line. Bea answered in the negative for three takes. John did make sure she was always there on time, and Bea cooperated with wardrobe and makeup, but even the simplest scene meant take after take after take. At some point John evidently put the notion in Bea's mind that she should have a song to sing. "I always have a song," she complained. Through it all was George Roy Hill staking everything on his judgment. Mary Tyler Moore, who was also in the cast, could not have been friendlier, and although she did not work with Bea as much as Andrews did, Bea invited her to tea at Peel Fold and Mary took her up on it.

"Bea was indeed wonderful," added Morris. "Nobody else could have done it. She had a certain quality that nobody else ever had or ever will have and she brought it to that picture."

As he had been doing for all those years, John avoided the issues once again where Bea was concerned. During one scene that was going into its twenty-fifth take with Bea, he turned to Morris and seriously suggested that Bea should have a television series.

Thanks to George Roy Hill, Bea will be remembered as the nefarious white slaver harassing Julie Andrews and Mary Tyler Moore in the film.

Bea went to pieces one night at the home of Eve Arden where she had gone as the guest of Kaye Ballard.

"The day the three astronauts were burned I took her to Eve Arden's house," remembered Kaye. "When the news came over she totally flipped out, remembering her son. She said, 'What do you people know? You don't know what it's like!' She really had a breakdown!"

Considering the problems with *Millie* it is surprising that John would contact me and inquire if I was available to appear in Las Vegas with Bea. "Milady and Songs," he wired. Obviously it was not to be, however, and Bea went to England. Many of her English friends were dismayed at her loss of memory. When her old friend Gladys Henson visited her in Henley, Bea was warm and receptive. But after being with Gladys for two hours, Bea asked, "Whatever happened to Gladys Gunn? You remember, she married Leslie Henson?"

Phyllis Monkman spent a weekend at Peel Fold during Bea's visit to England.

"She had a man coming down to interview her at half past four," said Phyllis. "Bea suggested we go for a drive and I told her it was too late, but she insisted. We didn't get back until quarter till six and this man was waiting. He had given up his weekend for this. We went into the room where he was waiting, and I excused myself but Bea told me not to go. They both sat there, and I reminded Bea that he was there to interview her. With that she got up and went to the piano and played and sang 'None But the Lonely Heart.' She came back, and I filled in a little bit until she told a long story about Elizabeth Taylor on a ship. Then she did talk a little. I was terrified to see the article, but he was very kind."

Possibly John felt he was aiding Bea's memory in permitting her to make public and professional appearances in New York, or perhaps he simply closed his eyes to it. Sadly, she appeared at a screening of one of her films at the Museum of Modern Art and was scheduled to say a word or two after. In front of the audience, she suddenly pulled up the front of her blouse and exposed her breasts to everyone before she was surrounded and led away. The truth of the matter was that Bea, faced with an audience, could not think of anything to say, or even remember why she was there, and needed a way out. On *What's My Line* she forgot to sign in, and after her identity was discovered she walked down and began talking to the audience. In her final television stint, on the *Johnny Carson Show*, she was completely disoriented. She forgot what they were talking about and could not remember lyrics. Her friends were upset, and livid with Huck for allowing her to be seen in that state. Billy DeWolfe dined at Sardi's one night and asked Vincent Sardi if Bea still came into the restaurant. "Oh yes," answered Vincent sadly, "but she no longer knows it's Sardi's."

I wrote to Bea in care of John Brooks to let her know I was living in the Virgin Islands, and Brooks answered with Bea's love and told her where I was. John called me in St. Thomas and told me he wished to bring Bea for a visit. Coincidentally, Grant was arriving momentarily and it seemed like a wonderful time for a reunion. I found them a lovely place high on the mountain and met the plane. Bea came down the steps slowly and I could see that age had taken its toll; she had trouble walking, and had become slumped over. Lord Button was under her arm and snarled viciously when I hugged his mistress. Bea put him on the floor in the front seat and he lunged at my hand whenever I shifted gears, which amused Bea no end. As far as everything looked, nothing had changed between us. Bea quipped about the ride up the mountain roads; she loved her apartment with the spectacular view and the pool high above the sea.

We dined that night at Café Brittany, and the organist, who adored Beatrice Lillie, played every song she had ever sung and she hummed along happily. We were halfway through dinner when Bea turned to me.

"Excuse me," she asked politely, "but what is your name?"

"Gladys Bumps!" I shouted gaily although I was fighting to hold back the tears. Bea laughed at the name.

"Bea, it's Brucie Pants! Bruce! She's having trouble seeing you because it's so dark in here," John expounded in a room so full of light one could see a fly on the wall.

Miserably, I went back to my food. I was furious with John for not warning me although I was now aware of the true reason for the sudden visit. John felt that seeing me would jar Bea's memory. I felt her hand on my arm.

"Seriously, what is your name?" she asked again. I told her and determined to make the best of it. The organist then played a medley of Noël Coward songs and once more Bea hummed along. When it was over, she asked, "What is his name?"

"Paul," I told her.

"Paul?"

"Are you talking about the man who's playing the organ?" I asked.

"No," she replied. "I meant the man who wrote all of those songs."

When I reminded her that Noël had written the tunes, she smiled and nodded her head and said, "I suppose I should visit Noël while I'm here."

"Trixie, you've got the right ocean but the wrong island," I laughed.

I made the same mistake John did by hoping that the sight of Grant would jar her memory. She responded as if she knew he was a friend but was not certain which one.

I had committed myself to a party for Bea and prayed I would not embarrass her, but she came through with flying colors. Most of the guests felt her vagueness was part of her image and when introduced to a senator and his wife, the wife was so overwhelmed she said, "I think I may faint." Bea responded in a split second with, "Good, I think I will, too!" and went straight over backwards into my arms without so much as a glance to see if anyone was behind her. I noticed that she was having Scotch once again (she told me during *High Spirits* that she was not drinking anymore). During the party, however, she kept asking over and over where her dog was but only those of us who knew her noticed. She also became anxious whenever John was not in sight. While trying on a dress in a shop the following day, she ran out of the store in her slip when John disappeared for a few minutes. She acquitted herself well in an interview for the local paper and had the writer in hysterics.

Just before she left St. Thomas, Café Brittany gave a Beatrice Lillie night. Grant went through her clothes and found the right gown, did her hair and she looked wonderful. A few days before she had gone walking with Tom Gustafson, a young artist to whom she had taken a shine, and suddenly said, "You know, I am seventy-six years old." She was indeed but it was the first time she had added back on the four years she had deducted so many years before. The alley leading to the restaurant was cobblestoned and Bea leaned heavily on my arm as we walked slowly to the entrance. Paul waited at the door excitedly. "Now come into the lobby but wait until you get the signal before you walk into the dining room." He disappeared and owner Gerry Meyer took over. The dining room was packed with government officials, the governor's wife, and St. Thomas business people whom Bea had met on the visit.

"Where are we?" Bea repeated incessantly and we explained we were at a party. Then Gerry signaled and we started forward as Paul began playing "Hail Britannia." I heard the applause as the guests rose to their feet and the cheering began but what really chilled me was Bea. I had my hand on the small of her back for support and I felt her spine begin to stiffen as her back straightened and her chin tilted up. She let go of my arm, flashed the famous smile, and, straight as a die, made her entrance, once more the funniest woman in the world.

In January of 1970, the American Film Institute was opening its theatre in Washington and they held a gala as part of the celebration. Gregory Peck, who was chairman of the board, had flown in to co-host the event with Ethel Kennedy. They opened with Mae Murray's *Merry Widow* and the next night was to be *Exit Smiling*, Bea's silent film which had disappeared. It had been brought back for the New York Film Festival the year before and everybody wondered where it had been. Nobody knew about *Exit Smiling* until the New York Film Festival presented it, as Bea's first film had not been seen since it was originally released.

John Springer, the son of Bea's childhood friend, called John to invite Bea to Washington for the screening. John impressed upon Springer that Bea must be treated as a star, which Springer would have done in any case.

"Of course she was to be treated as a great star," said Springer. "Instead of the shuttle, we flew her first class and we had a marvelous suite for her. Actually, she couldn't have cared less, it was John Philip. He was so afraid that somebody else was going to get some attention, there were so many celebrities there."

The night of a party in her honor, hosted by Ethel Kennedy and attended by celebrities such as Gregory Peck and Shirley MacLaine, Lord Button remained at the hotel and for most of the evening Bea's only concern seemed to be the whereabouts of the dog.

"John Philip got into an absolute rage because *Exit Smiling* was not the opening night film," recalled Springer. "He was stamping his foot all over the place. Ethel Kennedy was so lovely and took her around and introduced her, and Gregory Peck was so charming to her, but she could only say, 'Where is my little doggie?' "

The film was shown after the party and while it was on, Bea wandered around the theatre. John sat where he was watching the picture and John Springer followed Bea to keep an eye on her. After the showing, Gregory Peck spoke, followed by George Stevens, Jr., and just as Bea was about to be introduced, she went to the ladies' room where she remained for fifteen minutes while the speechmakers ad-libbed. John Springer finally asked Shirley MacLaine to find Bea and she was brought back into the auditorium.

"The minute she got onstage," said Springer, "she started swinging her pearls and doing her zany things. She was very funny and the audience adored her."

During the celebration after the film, Bea quickly downed some drinks and John became angry with John Springer for allowing her to have them although Springer knew nothing about Bea's drinking habits. Springer took Bea back to her hotel soon after because John wanted to remain at the party. He waited with Bea until John returned. The following day, Bea joined her old friend, Richard Coe of *The Washington Post*, and Coe wrote an article on Bea and Lord Button and the film festival. The Washington experience would be Bea's final professional appearance and the last time she and Richard Coe would see each other.

In September, John and Bea, after lengthy talks with John's friend Jerry, from the *Follies* days, met in Jerry's office to sign the papers necessary to create a trust. Bea was reluctant to sign anything and held off for forty-five minutes before she finally did.

John Springer, meanwhile, for The American Film Institute did a series of weekly movie shows in better department stores as far west as Dallas, Houston, and Minneapolis in which old films were shown for a week and personal appearances were made by the various stars of the film. In return for a large cash gift to the institute, stars such as Joan Crawford, Bette Davis, Gregory Peck, Myrna Loy, and Farley Granger appeared at the stores, which usually decorated one floor to look like old Hollywood.

"At one point I thought it would be fun to do it with Beatrice Lillie," remembered John Springer. "After the Washington experience I still felt that way. I met with John Philip, who was all excited but wanted to know how much money was in it for Bea." Springer explained the purpose was to raise money for the Film Institute. "As soon as I started mentioning the various stars who were doing it," said Springer, "he got very horsy about it and then I met her again and she was just so far out of it and he was so 'I'm going to do it my way' that I called it off."

In 1972, John began mulling over the idea of moving Bea to Connecticut. He had come into possession of a house in Old Lyme and moved some of the furniture and other household items from East End Avenue into the country place. I called him there to tell him that Grant Tyler had been murdered in the Virgin Islands, in case somebody got to Bea first and she could recall who he was. A year before, Bea reacted badly when I inquired about Lord Button and found that he was dead. John decided not to say anything to Bea, but he did ask if I would care to move in with them and take care of Bea.

"There wouldn't be much money," he apologized, "but you'd have a home and Bea loves you." Since I already had a home and also loved Bea, I declined. Bea was never to live in the Connecticut house. In November of 1974, and again in early 1975, she was struck down by strokes and hospitalized. When I went to see her in the hospital, where she was registered under her childhood stage name of Gladys Montell, she was immobile and did not know me. Later Bob Feyte and David Bolton came from England and visited her in the hospital. Bea lay still and incommunicative.

With Bea's incapacity came the realization that John had no ready cash and that everything was in a trust fund. John felt he had made a mistake in listening to his friend Jerry and allowing Bea to sign the papers that established the trust. "He conned us into doing all this in September of '71," complained John. "Well, it's been a crock of shit! He said, 'It would help you and this and that ultimately.' What it's done is all Bea's affairs which I put into savings accounts and things, we took them out and put them into investments in the trust and of course they've lost fifty or sixty thousand. They were down to about thirty or forty thousand dollars."

As a result, John, with the help of the doctor, put Bea into a "retirement" apartment on Park Avenue so that he could get to England quickly. The apartment was owned by a Mary James, and each guest was given a room with bath in her large attractive apartment. Miss James supplied meals and maid service but all medical and nursing attention was the responsibility of the guest. Nurses were hired to care for Bea, and John approached the Actors' Fund for financial support.

In the thirties Bea paid seventy-five hundred dollars for a Modigliani painting of a young boy. She never really liked it but kept it through the years, sometimes hanging it in her London dressing rooms or at 55 Park Lane.

"That was left to me in Bea's will and I sold it for a world-record price," John claimed. "I didn't have to sell it, it was out of the trust, and while it was still Bea's I went over there and sold it for $381,500. I can't touch the money. They tied it up in England. I finally had to pay it back into the trust in New York. As a result, I can't touch the money."

John consulted a lawyer about the possibility of disbanding the trust and administering Bea's money himself. When it went before a judge, speculation was rampant.

"John Philip appealed to the Actors' Fund to help take care of her medical bills at a private nursing home totaling $80,000 a year!" reported one paper. "Now the Actors' Fund has learned that Bea is said to have a trust fund left to her by the Robert Peel estate of $5,000 a week, priceless paintings (including a Modigliani that Philip sold to Sotheby's for $395,000) along with a diamond and emerald necklace and other valuable jewelry from the Peel estate. The Actors' Fund is taking the case for an open hearing before Judge Greenfield of the State Supreme Court."

"I didn't deceive the Actors' Fund," John told me on the phone. "When we were in the hospital I said, 'We're spending capital, we don't have any money.' I went to see Warren Munsell and he checked with the board and they said, 'Anything Bea Lillie wants, give it to her.' I never misled them, I said we needed ten weeks' help. That's when we came here, in March, and I said till June first. So they paid out about fourteen thousand bucks which I don't consider a charity anyhow. Bea had more than earned that by filling up their damn theatres for over twenty or thirty years! They got a little sour grapes afterwards and said they were going to continue paying half and then said, 'No, you have some stock and everything.' I would never put her in the Actors' Home or the Mary Manning Walsh because they want the money. Since June the first, I've been spending Bea's money on herself. I went over and sold that voluntarily. I don't want to appear to be a saint but I goddamn well am, who else would have done it?"

When John filed to be named conservator of Bea's estate, the judge also wondered why John was living in the apartment while Bea remained in the Park Avenue room at a substantial cost, according to John close to two thousand dollars a week.

"It's like a palace up here," said John. "The flowers I put in here, the nurses, and all these people love her. I bring her pictures in. I mean we've made a home for Bea here. Nobody's ever going to question how I'm going to take care of her. She's actually improved a bit since she's been here. I haven't made one wrong move with Bea. The only wrong move I made was in 1971 letting that shitheel talk me into getting her to sign the trust, which she did under great duress, which I can prove. I might be able to sue the trust, have it set aside because it was ill-advised."

The important concern among Bea's friends was why her own bedroom which she loved would not have been as suitable since Park Avenue was not a medical facility. John asked David Bolton's aid in moving some belongings from 25 East End Avenue to the Connecticut house and David reported that Bea's flat was unkempt and filthy. Another obvious issue was why Bea was not sent to Peel Fold.

"We can't go back to England yet because if we do she's liable to be hit with terrible taxes," stated John. "She's been over here long enough to call New York her domicile of intent even though she's a British subject." He sent his friend Jerry to England to confer with a lawyer there about the possibility of registering a company under Bea's name on the Isle of Man, which would allow Bea to be taken to Henley for visits without taxation.

John also informed the nurses that hospital and nursing care in England was prohibitive.

Clearly, the judge felt differently and Sidney Fine, a former State Supreme Court judge, was appointed conservator and the judge decided that Bea should be returned to England where she could be sustained for less expense, his prime concern being "that those who are purporting to serve Miss Lillie's interests may well be profiting therefrom."

As a result of the publicity, friends of Bea's thought she was broke. Leslie Bricusse, who was in New York at the time, received a call from Jack Haley. Haley had been on the phone since the crack of dawn rounding up celebrities such as Jack Benny and many others in order to stage a gigantic benefit for Bea. Haley asked Leslie to check out the story. He phoned Arnold Weissberger, theatrical attorney and close friend of Bea's, and Arnold assured him there was no cause for alarm.

John called me in a screaming rage one day to say that Ed Sullivan, in his column, reported that Bea was seriously ill in the hospital. I pointed out that Sullivan had always been a great admirer and friend of Bea's and in reality was printing the truth. This angered John all the more, so much so that he said he hoped that Sullivan, then in the hospital himself, would never come out alive.

For two years Bea remained at the Park Avenue address receiving cards and flowers from friends all over the world. Bea, whom Judge Greenfield described as "once a gay, scintillating and zany star who delighted audiences on both sides of the Atlantic with her antics, is now a pathetic and helpless figure, paralyzed, incapable of speech, and without family," had no knowledge of the passing of Noël Coward, Brandon De Wilde, Phyllis Monkman, or Odette Myrtil. Her friends came to see her often. Ethel Merman sang songs and massaged Bea's hands and feet for her, although she and Dorothy Strelsin were not happy being asked to pose for a photograph with Bea slumped in her chair. Mary Martin, George Vigouroux, Shannon Dean, and Carol Arthur DeLuise visited; Kaye Ballard fought back tears on her trip to Park Avenue. Marc Connelly came with flowers one day at the request of Doc, who wanted a first-hand report on Bea's condition.

Earl Wilson called me one day to say he had been to see her. He asked if I truly felt she knew me. I replied it was a wonderful thought but could not honestly believe it. When I questioned a nurse as to why Bea was not on a rehabilitation program to learn to walk once more, I was told that since she was senile at the time of the strokes it would not do any good.

Lord Snowdon asked to visit Bea and we went one Sunday morning. He held her hand and talked at great length to her and then played some of her recordings which were in the room. As he left he also asked why she was not in her home in England. John was furious that I would take Snowdon to see Bea without his permission and told the nurses I was not to be allowed in again until I spoke to him.

I explained that Lord Snowdon specifically asked that the visit not be announced and I had complied.

When Helen Hayes asked to see Bea, I dutifully called and told John. His retort was, "She wrote Bea and said 'anything I can do.' Damn right there's something she can do. She's on the board of Actors' Fund, she can tell them to stop bugging us for money every time they read about a Modigliani being sold. I'm having a hell of a time with the trust over that money, they're trying to get hold of it and that was left to me in Bea's will. I sold it for a world-record price and I'm having a hell of a fight with the bank in New York about that. I mean nobody's taking care of me, I'm getting a hundred and fifty bucks a week!"

Bea seemed to sense a friend when Helen Hayes visited. She kissed her hand, and at one point put her arm around her shoulder. John insisted upon a photograph of the two women, and later Helen remarked, "I wanted to see what sort of a place she was in and it was very nice. I know that Charlie would have wanted me to go."

"When she became sick and couldn't recognize people," recalled Dr. Prutting, who had been with her over thirty years, "I would go to the nursing home and she didn't know who I was but she would look up and know I was a pleasant thing. She would smile and make sounds of joy. It was sad toward the end, her gradually going from being vague about who I was and being able to be told, to nothing."

"Part of the reason why she had the strokes was she was worried about what was happening to me," John stated.

As time passed and Bea remained in her room on Park Avenue, I questioned the nurses about the delay in her trip. John was still insisting that the taxes would impoverish her, and then it was her health. He was waiting for the right moment to go. Finally the trust threatened to send her home without John, according to one of the nurses.

Nurse Betty Manley kindly advised me that Bea was returning to England. I went to see her for the last time the day before she left. We spent an hour alone and I spoke to her at great length, hoping she might know how I felt. I kissed her and said good-bye. As I left, she sat staring down at her lap and plucking at the mohair lap robe covering her knees. For personal reasons John cast a veil of secrecy over the departure, which was hardly necessary. I remembered that Bea had once said many years before that whenever she was told her name was in the paper she ran right out and bought one. I was determined she would not leave the city she loved without some notice. Her goings and comings for over fifty years had been chronicled by the press, and it seemed fitting that her final leave-taking should be noteworthy.

I made some phone calls, and as a result Earl Wilson wrote:

"Dear Beatrice Lillie said good-bye to New York for probably the last time and she was barely aware of it. The great comedienne was carried aboard a plane and flown to London with three nurses. She's to live out her days in her house on the Thames."

And Liz Smith in the *Daily News* wrote: "The tiny figure with three nurses boarding a British Airways jet for London yesterday was the great Beatrice Lillie, who was returning to live in Henley-on-Thames under the guardianship of a court-appointed judge."

Once in England Bea was under the protection of the Official Solicitor to the Supreme Court, and a receiver was appointed to handle her estate. He was solely responsible for the financial affairs and the management of her estate. John remained in England with her. Tony Gray and his wife were dismissed as "redundant," and John's sister went to live at Henley. For whatever reasons, John's bulletins from Peel Fold continued to announce that Bea was completely cognizant of what was happening around her, and visitors were assured their words were understood. Her friends prayed it was true.

"*Bea* is *very* well (within the framework)," Huck wrote to Leonard Soloway, "and continues in general sound health, is entirely aware inputwise, can hear the proverbial grass growing; has had a successful cataract operation on her right eye!!! She continues happily being 'pleased with what is intended to please'! As long as she continues like this, I both feel and hope she will outlive most people we know!"

Those who remembered Bea's birthdays received thank-you notes stating that the card had been given the personal attention of Beatrice Lillie, who was greatly touched and had personally asked the writer to convey Lady Peel's grateful thanks.

In the solace of her own home, Bea was given the best of care by nurses. John asked for money to produce a television documentary of her life and was awarded a small amount by the courts but it was never completed. In December of 1988, John went into the hospital for heart problems and was scheduled for a triple heart bypass operation, but it had to be postponed because of his weight.

On January 20, 1989, Bea was having difficulty breathing, and at 7:30 in the morning John called nurse Susette Mitchell, who had been at Peel Fold for eight years. Nurse Mitchell arrived shortly after 8:00 and took over. As she held Bea in her arms, John took Bea's hand and sang to her softly as she died peacefully at 8:47 A.M.

The following day, John, nurse Mitchell, and another nurse were out for a stroll, and, as they crossed the bridge near Peel Fold, Mitchell noticed John's eyes flutter. Before they were able to lead him back to the house, he slipped to the ground. Resuscitation was futile, and John died thirty-one hours after Bea.

Bea was not buried at Tamworth, with Bobby and the Peel family. John's sister chose a double ceremony on January 30 at St. Margaret's Church, Harpsden.

"It was chiefly a paean to John Huck and Bea's 'adopted family,' " noted Philippa Moore, Muriel's stepdaughter and the sole member of Bea's family to attend. "Of course, John stayed with her all through the eleven or twelve years she was so ill. But he did keep her old friends away. We never saw her during that time."

Eve Bricusse, the wife of Bea's former co-star Leslie Bricusse, and their son attended. David Bolton completed the roster of those who had known Bea in better times.

Bea and John were laid to rest side by side in the little cemetery near Peel Fold where Lucie and Muriel were buried.

The folie à deux was ended.

EPILOGUE

On March 14, 1989, a crowd gathered in front of a small building at 1115 Queen Street West in Toronto, the city where Beatrice Lillie was born. A red carpet stretched from the curbside to a raised platform against the building. A section of the structure's wall was covered by blue curtains, concealing the plaque behind it. Blue velvet ropes attached to silver stands formed a barricade along the carpet on both sides. The morning was clear, crisp, and sunny. Trucks and automobiles made their way along Queen Street interspersed with electric streetcars, a service put into practice the year Bea was born. In the distance the myriad skyscrapers reached into the sky, forming a new city that she would not have recognized.

Mayor Art Eggleton and his wife arrived, His Honor wearing his insignia of office. He was followed by Paddy Browne Robertson, former actress and friend of Beatrice Lillie. The sound system was echoing Bea's recorded voice as she sang songs she had made famous throughout her career; some of the onlookers hummed along while others reacted with smiles when a familiar number began.

There was applause when Prince Philip, Duke of Edinburgh, alighted from his car and made his way with the Mayor to the platform.

The Mayor spoke first. "Your Royal Highness, friends, family, and fans of Bea Lillie. Her formal title was Lady Peel but most knew her and watched her by another title, The Funniest Woman in the World." The Mayor went on to tell some of the history of Bea and her ties to Toronto.

"In a sense, while Bea Lillie left Toronto," continued the Mayor, "Toronto never left her. The Beatrice Lillie building will serve as a public health office for this area and will serve the city and the neighborhood in which she grew up. That is a fitting tribute and a proud statement of the gratitude of the people of her home city."

Paddy Robertson was introduced next and spoke of her friendship with Bea, and of Bea's wonderful war work. At one point she misread her notes and began to say, "When she gave a commercial once," and realizing she was not reading it correctly, she looked at the sentence again, turned to Prince Philip and said in embarrassment, "With all due respect, when she did a command performance," and drew a great laugh from the Prince and the crowd. Bea would have loved it.

The Duke of Edinburgh unveiled the plaque to prolonged applause and said a few warm words about Bea, including his opinion that "Bea Lillie was one of the reasons we won the war."

And so, Bea's memorial service, attended by royalty, close friends, fans, cousins, nephews, and nieces took place in front of a building that had at one time been a library where she most likely ran up the steps to borrow a book about the theatre. The plaque and the building, one block from where she was born, will remain as a tribute forever.

INDEX

A to Z, 52
Abbott, George, 108
Abercorn Place, Lucie's houses at, 185
Actors' Equity
    fiftieth anniversary celebration of, 245
    and Lillie/Porter dispute, 134
Actors' Fund
    assists Bea, 271–73
    benefits, 78, 256
Actors' Orphanage, 119
Actors' Orphanage Fund, 207
Adams, Bob, 36
Adams, Franklin P., 129
Adams, Roger, 36
Adams and Carmichael, 105
Adelphi Theatre, 204
Adrian, Gilbert, 211
African Star, Bea awarded, 126
"After Dinner Music" (Coward), 68, 76
Ages of Man, 238
Ahearne, Brian, 176
Aitken, Max (later Lord Beaverbrook), 59
Albert, Prince (later King George VI), 53
Alcohol, Bea's intolerance for, 98–99
Aldrich, Richard, 151
"Alexander's Ragtime Band" (Berlin), 25
Algonquin Hotel, 60
Alhambra Theatre, 25, 32, 33
All Clear, 118–19
Allen, Chesney, 110
Allen, Gracie, 101,175

Allen, Vera, 100
"Alone Together" dance, 91
Althouse, Paul, 99
Ambassador Hotel, 60
American Federation of Women's Philan-
    thropies, 154
American Film Institute, 268
An Evening With Beatrice Lillie, 151–54
    album of, 185–86
    in Florida, 187–92
    London Company of, 183–84
    in Los Angeles, 175
    road tour of, 161–71
    tours provinces, 185
An Evening With Highlights, 245–46
"And Her Mother Came Too," 52
"And They Call It Dixie Land," 33
Anderson, John Murray, 155
Anderson, Judith, 78, 79
Anderson, Maxwell, 174
Andre Charlot's London Revue of 1924, 57–62
Andrews, Bobby, 137, 148
Andrews, Julie, 264–65
Angel Street, 132
Anthony, Michael, 110
Apple Cart, The, 158
April, Elsie, 121
"April in Paris," 91
Aquitania, 59, 115
Arcati, Madame, Bea as, 247–59
Are You There?, 84

281

Arlen, Michael, 67
Arlen and Harburg, 105
Armstrong-Jones, Antony, 136, 231. *See also* Snowden, Lord
Arnold, Edward, 85
Around the World in Eighty Days, 186
Arthur, Carol, 259, 262. *See also* DeLuise, Carol
Arthur, Hartney, 203
Arthur Murray Show, 229
As You Like It, 79
Ashcroft, Dame Peggy, 214
Ashley, Lady Sylvia, 183
Astaire, Fred and Adele, 92
Astley, Philip, 58
Astor, Richard, 229
Astric, Henry, 223, 235
At Home Abroad, 99–102
"At Murray's Club," 30
Atkinson, Brooks, 113
Auntie Mame, 190
    London version, 203–205
    reviews of London show, 205
Ayre, Lawrence, 79
Azenberg, Emanuel, 244

"Baby's Best Friend (Is Its Mother), A," 77
Baclanova, Olga, 84
Baddeley, Hermione, 216, 238
Bagpipe Society Band, 67
Baird, Ethel, 36
Ball, Lucille, 256
Ballard, Kaye, 274
Band Wagon, The, 85, 92
Bank, Xenia, 152
Bankhead, Tallulah, 66, 97, 101
    and Bea, 156
    escapade of, 84
    and *Ziegfeld Follies*, 195
Barangaria, 77, 100
Barnes, Binnie, 222
Baroda, Maharani of, 224, 235
Barrymore, Ethel, 69
Barrymore, John, 83
Barrymore, Lionel, 78
Barrymores, the, 82
Barstow, Richard, 197
Barthelmess, Richard, 83
Beasop's Fables, 194
Beaton, Cecil, 194
Beatrice (Bea's maid), retirement of, 256
Beatrice Lillie at Nine O'Clock, 244
Beatrice Lillie building, dedication of, 279–80
Beaumont, Hugh "Binkie," 118
Bedford, Duke of, 204
Beebe, Lucius, 134
Belles of New York, The, 20

Bellamy, Ralph, 216
Bellita, 103
Benchley, Robert, 61, 74
    on *Oh, Please!*, 73
    on *This Year of Grace*, 81
    on *Treasure Girl*, 82
Benny, Jack, 177, 273
Beography, 242–44
Berelli, Mr., 233
Berle, Milton, 87
Berlin, Irving, 193
    and "Alexander's Ragtime Band," 25
    Bea's rendition of songs of, 35
    and "I Want to Go Back to Michigan," 30
    and *Miss Liberty*, 142–43
    and "When I Lost You," 26
Better Late, 136
Bettis, Valerie, 138
    on Bea, 144
    on John Philip, 159
    paints with Bea, 142
"Betty," 33
"Big Three, The," 59
    in Charlot's Rendezvous, 68–69
Big Top, 121–22
Billingsley, Sherman, 188
Bird Song, 122
Bittersweet (Coward), 82
Black Bottom, 82
Blanchard, Dorothy, 62. *See also* Hammerstein, Dorothy
Blanche, Marie, 33
Bland, Hubert, 144
Blithe Spirit, musical version of, 247
Blue Angel, 155
Blume, Ellen. *See* Graham, Ellen
Boaters' Loche, 37
Bogart, Humphrey, 196
Bolger, Ray, 101, 228
"Bolshies Quartette" (Coward), 61
Bolton, David, 264, 271, 273
    attends Bea's funeral, 277
Bolton, Guy, 77
Booth, Shirley, 222, 240
Booth Theatre, 154
Borden's, 97
Bran Pie, 40
Brando, Marlon, 188
Bray, Florence, 152
Brice, Billy, 99, 102
Brice, Fanny, 94, 96, 97, 101
    Bea's friendship with, 74–75, 97–98
    as Bea's hostess, 108–109, 137
    in *1936 Ziegfeld Follies*, 102
Brice, Frances, 99–100
Bricusse, Eva, 277
Bricusse, Leslie, 183, 186, 187, 245, 273–74

British European Airways, 205
Broderick, Helen, 73
Bromfield, Louis, 169
Brook, Clive, 128
Brooks, John, 138, 178, 266
Broun, Heywood, 61
"Brown Eyes," 122, 123
Brunnhilde, Bea as, 112–13
Buchanan, Jack, 28, 41
  in *A to Z*, 52
  as *Charlot's Revue* star, 62, 67
  in *Tail's Up*, 42
Burke, Patricia, 110, 121
Burke, Thomas, 52
Burnett, John Dinwoodie, 22–23
Burns, George, 101
Burton, Richard, 256
Busheme, Joe, 261
Butterworth, Charles, 117
Buzz-Buzz, 35
"By Strauss," 105
Byng, Douglas, 80
Bystander, The, 36

Café Brittany, 267, 268
Café de Paris, 104
  Bea plays, 93, 111, 116
  demolished, 119
  newly rebuilt, 148
Cafritz, Gwen, 164, 220
Caesar's Wife (Maugham), 39
Caldwell, Anne, 73
Caledonian Hotel, 239
Callas, Maria, 224, 235
Calvert, Phyllis, 205
Camberwell Empire, 26
"Camp," 98
Campbell,George, 189
Canadian National Exposition, 16–17
Cape Playhouse, 151
Capri, Bea's visit to, 183
Captain Isabelle, 244
Carleton, Billie, 33, 46
Carpenter, Constance, 62, 77, 110, 187, 189, 194, 204
  in London company, 183
  in *Third Little Show*, 85
Carpenter, Thelma, 139
Carroll, Leo G., 88
Carson, Johnny, 229, 245
Carter, Jack, 240
Carton, Audrey, 84
"Casanova," 105
Castle, Irene, 171
Ceballos, Larry, 46
  and Bea, 40
Century Theatre, 140

Cerf, Bennett, 134
Champion, Gower, 255
Chandler, Julia, 58
Chaplin, Charlie, 71
Charlot, André
  and *A Season of Variety*, 32
  early productions of, 25
  fires Lawrence, 35
  hires Bea, 26–27
  hires Gertrude Lawrence, 33–34
  and *Revue of 1924*, 57–63
Charlot's Masquerade, 83
Charlot's Rendezvous, 69
Charlot's Revue, 29
Charlot's Revue of 1926, 66
Cheep, 36
Churchill, Winston, 149
Ciro's, 42
Claridge's, 42
Clark, Bobby, 91
Club Gala, 155
Cobourg, Ontario, 20–21
  Lucie directs choir in, 21–22
Coconut Grove Playhouse, 188
Cochran, Charles (C. B.), 25, 28, 33, 39
  and *Big Top*, 121–22
  death of, 148
  and *Happy Returns*, 109
  and Noël Coward, 38
  and *Please*, 92
  and St. Martin's Theatre, 41–42
  and *This Year of Grace*, 80
Coe, Richard, 198, 270
Cohen, Abe, 180–81
Cohen, Alexander H., 244
Colbert, Claudette, 175
Cole, Nat "King," 232, 233, 236–37
Collins, Joan, 246
Colombo, Sri Lanka (Ceylon), 122
"Come Into the Garden, Maude," 152
"Come, Oh Come, to Pittsburgh," 138, 149
"Come Out, Little Boy, I'm Waiting for You," 37
Compton, Betty, 102
Compton, Fay, 32, 41, 66
  and Bea, 39
  as Bea's friend, 52
  in *Caesar's Wife*, 39
  Peace Day party of, 46
Conaway, Charles, 196
Concerto for the Left Hand (Ravel), 120
Connecticut Yankee, A, 77
Connelly, Marc, 108, 274
  on Bea in Hollywood, 71–72
  on Bea's tolerance for alcohol, 98
  on Doc McGunigle, 86
  and *Third Little Show*, 85

Conover, Harry, 134
Conservative Party, Peel founds, 42
Cook, Alton, 95
Cooke's Presbyterian Church, 15–17
Cooper, Gladys, 41, 137
  prize roses of, 228
Coote, Bert, 33
Coquette, 80
Cornell, Colonel, 21
Cornell, Katharine, 21, 67, 74, 78, 79,
  251
  and *Mary Poppins* production, 116
  in *That Lady*, 139
Coronia, 67
Courtneidge, Cecily, 101, 216
Coward, Noël, 34, 39, 41, 46, 66, 107, 148,
  149, 200
  and "After Dinner Music," 76
  and *All Clear*, 118–19
  auditions for Charlot, 38
  and Bea, 158
  and Bea's use of material, 103
  in Capri, 183
  and *Charlot's Review of 1926*, 67
  and "Clam" Tyler, 128–29
  death of, 274
  farewell to Bea, 258
  and *High Spirits*, 247–55
  and John Philip, 51–53
  and *London Morning*, 214
  at Rainbow Room, 96
  at Royal Command Performance, 149
  and *Set to Music*, 111–13
  and *Sigh No More*, 128
  and *Third Little Show*, 85
  and *This Year of Grace*, 80
Crawford, Joan, 270
Crazy Gang team, 110
Crisham, Walter, 136
Criterion Theatre, 128
Crosby, Bing, 107, 176, 187
Cugat, Xavier, 101
Cukor, George, 137
Cummings, Constance, 85

Daily Express, The, 184
Daily Graphic, The, 57
Daily News, 209, 276
Daisy, 123. *See also* Flanagan, Daisy
Dali, Salvador, 134
"Dance, Little Lady," 80, 82
Daniels, Danny, 248
Daring of Diane, The, 26
Davies, Marion, 71, 156
Davis, Bette, 196, 240, 270
Davis, Harry, 162
Davis, Michael, 256

Davis, Sammy, Jr., 259
Dawson City Festival, 244
de Frece, Lawri, 32
de Liagre, Alfred, 135, 244, 245
De Wilde, Brandon, 150–51, 153, 155–156,
  193–94, 243
  and Bea, 187–88, 200–201
  and Capt. Hook, 204
  death of, 274
  introduced to Christine Jorgensen, 199
De Wilde, Eugenia (Genie), 151, 155–56,
  243
De Wilde, Fritz, 151
  and *Man for All Seasons*, 243
De Wildes, the, 204, 246
De Wolfe, Billy, 196–97, 201, 266
  in *Ziegfeld Follies*, 197
Dean, Shannon, 152, 157, 158, 187, 202,
  274
  and Bea's "pick-me-ups," 176
DeGaulle, General, 126
DeLuise, Carol Arthur, 274. *See also* Arthur,
  Carol
DeLuise, Dom, 259
DeLuise, Peter, 259
Delysia, Alice, 41
Demerol, Bea's dependence on, 181–82
Dennis, Patrick, 190, 204
Derbas, Frank, 256
DesLys, Gaby, 29, 46
Desmond, Florence, 82, 83
Dexedrine, 176
Dickson, Dorothy, 54, 158
  on Bea, 54
  with Bea in Hollywood, 137–38
  on Bobbie Peel, 121
  on John Huck, 142
Diggs, Rene, 158, 161, 163
  and Bea's drinking, 173
  and Gardiner's party, 168–69
  sets fire to room, 181
Dillingham, Charles, 50
  produces *Oh, Please!*, 72–73
Dinah Shore Show, The, 203
Dolin, Anton (Patrick), 34, 83, 103, 128,
  131
  and Bea, 88–89, 184–85
  in *London Morning*, 214
  in Monte Carlo, 221
  reads Bea's letter, 132–33
Dollars and Sense Ball, 75
Donehue, Vincent, 135
Donohue, Jack, 92
Donohue, Jessie, 224
D'Orsay, Fifi, 87
"Double Damask Dinner Napkins," 245

Dovercourt Road, 11
Dowling, Eddie Duryea, 98, 102, 104, 125, 128, 129, 188
  as Bea's manager, 105, 141–42
  and *An Evening With Beatrice Lillie,* 151–55
  stages *Happy Returns,* 109
Dr. Rhythm, 107, 187
Draper, Doris, 97
Draper, Ruth, 85
Drayton Advocate, The, 21
Drayton Manor, 47–48
  PM entertains at, 42–43
  remains of, 93
Dream of Peter Mann, 238
Du Bois, Raoul Pene, 197, 221, 222
Duke, Vernon, 91
Dunne, Irene, 77, 78
Durand, Diana, 39

Eadie, 164, 185
  argues with John, 165
  death of, 202
  in London company, 183
Eadie and Rack, 155, 159, 194
Ebb, Fred, 194
Echols, Whalen, 78
Eddy, Nelson, 163
Eden, Anthony, 137
Edinburgh Festival, 231, 238–39
Ediss, Connie, 27
Edna Wallace Hopper facelift, 223
Edward VII, King, 42
Edward VIII, King, and friendship with Bea, 106. *See also* Wales, Prince of; Windsor, Duke of
Eggleton, Mayor Art, 279–80
Eisenhower, General Dwight D., 126
El Patio Club, 92
Electric canoe, 228
Elizabeth II, Queen, coronation of, 158
Elliot, Madge, 121, 129
Ellis, John, 120–21
Ellis, Michael, 188, 245
Ellman, Mischa, 195
Embassy Club, 111
Emney, Fred, 118
ENSA (Entertainment National Service Association), 120
  Bea joins, 125–26
Epstein, Louis, 162, 165
  death of, 180
Equity emergency meeting, 229–30
Eton Crop, 68
Evans, Edith, 216
"Every Little Movement Has a Meaning All Its Own," 203

Exit Smiling, 72, 269
  reviews of, 75–76
Extra Turn, 26

Fadiman, Clifton, 129
Fain, Maude, 44, 110
Fairbanks, Douglas, 71, 204
  on G. Lawrence's talent, 39
Fallen Angels (Coward), 68
"Fallen Babies," 68
Falmouth Playhouse, 152
Fan Mail, Bea's, 97
Far East, Bea's trip to, 182–83
Farjeon, Herbert, 122
Farley, James, 134
Farnum, Franklyn, 78
Fay, Frank, 83
Fazenda, Louise, 83
Fearnley, John, 111–12
Feldon, Barbara, 197
Fellowes, Daisy, 233
Fellows-Gordon, Dorothy (Dickie), 232, 235
Fetter and Duke, 105
Feyte, Robert, 199, 201, 205, 271
  as Bea's confidante, 237–38
  cares for Muriel, 264
  at Henley, 215–16
  at Monte-Carlo, 234–35
  and Mr. Lee, 204, 206, 227
Fields, Gracie, 183, 204
Fields, Herbert and Dorothy, 188
Fine, Sidney, 273
Finocchio's, 177
Fiorello, 241
Fishing, success at, 191
Fitzgerald, Geraldine, 77
Fitzgerald, Julia (Fitzy), 140, 181
5064 Gerard, 29
Flanagan, Bud, 110
Flanagan, Daisy, 110
Flying Colors, 91
Foley, Charlotte (Chotzi), 197
Fontanne, Lynn, 73, 97, 251
Fonteyn, Margot, 204, 224, 235, 236
Fortune Theatre, 128
Fouquette's, 218
Four for Tonight, 228
Four of Us, The, 228
Foxy, 244
Foy, Eddie, Jr., 100
Francis, Arlene, 138, 245
Francis Trio, 20. *See also* Lillie Trio
Frawley, William, 77
Freedman, David, 105–06
Freedman, Harold, 190
French, Harold, 118–19
French, Hugh, 118

Freymann, Dr. Robert, 125
Front Page, The (MacArthur and Hecht), 79–80, 82
Fryer, Bobby, 203
Fulco, Count, Duke di Vedura, 251–52
Fulton Theatre, 72–73

Gable, Clark, 125, 175
  wife of, 183
Galt Reformer, The, 21
Gambling, Peel's penchant for, 49
Garbo, Greta, 72
Garden, Mary, 175
Gardiner, James, 135, 141
Gardiner, Nadia
  and Bea, 174–75
  gives party, 175–77
Gardiner, Peter, 176
Gardiner, Reginald, 89, 99, 100, 106, 107, 108, 158, 162, 164, 183, 187
  American career of, 101
  in An Evening With Beatrice Lillie, 151, 155
  in An Evening With Highlights, 245, 246
  gives party, 168–69
  on Information Please, 129
  as peacemaker, 166–67
Garland, Robert, on This Year of Grace, 81
Garlic, Bea's aversion to, 219, 240
Garrick, John, 84
Garson, Greer, 203
Gaston, Pat, 197
Gatti-Casazza, Giulio, 99
Gay, Maisie, 41, 66
  and The New Edition of A to Z, 52
  in This Year of Grace, 80
  and Up in Mabel's Room, 51
Gaynor, Janet, 211
"Geisha" idea, Bea's, 101
Genn, Leo, 205
George VI, King, 126
Gérard, Rolf, 98, 136–37, 139
  and An Evening With Beatrice Lillie, 152
  an Evening With Beatrice Lillie album, 185–86
  in Monte-Carlo, 220–21
Gerard, Teddie, 27, 52, 54
Gero, Frank, 248
Gerrard, Gene, 33
Gershwin, George and Ira, 105
  and Treasure Girl, 82
Gershwin, Ira, 101
Get Smart, 197
Geva, Tamara, 91
Gielgud, John, 216, 238–39
  on Bea's childlike view, 51

knighted, 158
  performs with Bea, 120
Gilbert, John, 71, 72
Gilbert, Olive, 148
Girl From Cook's, The, 40
"Girls of the Old Brigade, The," 56, 73
Gish, Dorothy, 193
Gish, Lillian, 108, 193
Gladke, Peter, 220
Gladstone Avenue High School, 19
Globe Theatre, 118
Going Up, 44
Goldin, Al, 242–43
Goldstein, Bob, 125, 139, 140, 141, 175
Goode, Lela, 250, 252
  on Bea's forgetfulness, 261
Goodman, Benny, 96, 128, 228
Gordon, Hal, 39
Gore, Altovise, 259
Grace, Princess, 221, 223, 224–25, 235. See also Kelly, Grace
Graham, Ellen, 149, 155, 158, 163, 177, 183, 187, 189, 232, 234–35
  and Bea, 205, 209
  and "Milady Dines Alone," 194–95
  in Monte-Carlo, 220, 232
  writes book, 263
Grand Street Follies, 63
Granger, Farley, 270
Grant, Cary, 175
Gray, Timothy, 247, 248
Gray, Tony, 237
  and Bea's gardens, 228
Great Ziegfeld, The, 111
Green Hat, The (Arlen), 67
Grenfell, Joyce, 129
Grey, Lita, 71
Griffin, Merv, 229
Grimes, Tammy, 228
  and Bea, 229, 256
  in High Spirits, 247–59
Grist Mill Playhouse, 195
Grosjean, Alice, 22
Grossmith, George, 27, 84
  as producer, 39
Guinan, Texas, 75
Guinness, Alec, 214–15
Gunn, Gladys. See Henson, Gladys
Gustafson, Tom, 268
Gypsy, 197

Haakon, Paul, 100, 106
Hackforth, Norman, 136, 148
Hague, Albert, 188
Hale, Robert, 29
Hale, Sonnie, 80
Haley, Flo, 142, 147

Haley, Jack, 138, 147
  aids Bea, 273–74
Haley, Jack, Jr. (Fig Newton), 142
Half Past Eight, 41
Hall, Barbara, *See* Feldon, Barbara
Hall, Margaret, 252, 253, 255
Halliday, Richard, 211
Hammerstein, Dorothy, 134
Hammerstein, Oscar, 63, 134, 193
  death of, 238
Hammerstein, William (Bill), 188, 190, 194
Hamilton Close, Muriel at, 185
Hamilton, Nancy
  and Bea's Brünnhilde, 112–13
  on Bea's family, 96–97
  on Bea's intolerance for alcohol, 98
  as Bea's radio writer, 102–03
  on Doc McGunigle, 86
  and *Mary Poppins*, 116, 135, 137
  and *Water Gypsies*, 94
Hammond, Percy, 67
Hampshire House, 140
Hanna, Len, 75, 109, 112
"Hang Down Your Head, Tom Dooley," 219
Happy Returns, 109, 110
Harbach, Otto, 73
Hare, Channing, 189–90, 196, 204
Harper's Bazaar, 200
Harrison, Rex, 148
Harrow, 43, 94
  and Bobbie's near expulsion, 109
Hart, Lorenz, 101
Hart, Moss, 105, 133
Hartford, Huntington, 222, 224–25
Hartman, Paul, 229
Harvard, Noël Coward at, 251
"Have You Seen the Ducks Go By?" 34
Hawtrey, Sir Charles, 51
Haydn, Dickie, 126
Hayes, Helen, 78, 97, 108, 193, 229
  at *An Evening With Highlights*, 245–46
  final visit to Bea, 275
  marries Charles MacArthur, 77, 80
  in *Mrs. McThing*, 150
Hayton, Lennie, 102, 225
Hearst, William Randolph, 71
Hecht, Ben, 82, 193
Hello, Dolly!, 255
Henley-on-Thames. *See also* Peel Fold
  Bea vacations at, 216, 237
Henley Regatta, 214
Henson, Gladys, 98
  in *All Clear*, 118
  on Bea, 40
  on Bea's grief, 124
  on Bea and her mother, 32
  as Bea's friend, 52, 53–54

on Bea's memory loss, 265
  in *Set to Music*, 111, 112
Henson, Leslie, 126
Hepburn, Audrey, 216
Herald Tribune, The, 67
Herbert, A. P., 94
Hess, Myra, 23
Hickman, Charles, 121
High and the Mighty, The, 182
High Spirits, 247–58
  summer tour of, 261–62
Hill, George Roy, 264–65
Hillman-Minx, Bea's, 150, 155, 161
Hobbs, Robert, 62
Hoey, Evelyn, 91
Hollywood, Bea's visits to, 70–71, 106–07
Holman, Libby, 134
  in *First Little Show*, 85
Homer, Louise, 99
"Hoops" dance, 92
Hooray for What, 107–08
Hope, Bob, 101
  in *1936 Ziegfeld Follies*, 102
  television debut of, 147–48
Hopper, Hedda, 176
Horne, Lena, 220, 225
Horner, Richard, 252
Hostellerie de la Poste, 218
Hotel de Paris, 223, 231
Houp-la, 41
Houston, Bea does benefit in, 262–63
"How D'you Do?", 61
Howard, Leslie, 79, 84
Howard, Nora, 111
  dinner party of, 111–12
Howard, Peter, 183
Howard, Trevor, 205
Howes, Bobby, 118
Howland, Beth, 258
Huck, John Philip, 141, 142–43, 144, 145.
  See also Philip, John
Huck family, 277
  Bea's life with, 208
  and stay at Henley, 215–16
Hughes, Alfred, 48
Hughes, Mildred, 220
Hull, Henry, 75
Hullo Ragtime, 25
Hunter, George, 135
Hupfeld, Herman, 85

"I Can't Think," 80
Iglesias, Robert, 244
"I'm the Fool of the Family," 41
In Which We Serve, 121
"Incredible Happenings," 61
Information Please, 129

INDEX

Inside U.S.A., 138, 140
  on tour, 147
Inverclyde, Lady, 89
"I Pick Up Bits of Paper with My Toes," 245
Irish Corn Laws, 42
Irma La Douce, 220
"I've Been to a Marvelous Party," 111
Ivy, the, 41–42
"I Want a Toy Soldier," 27
"I Want to Go Back to Michigan" (Berlin), 30

Jamaica, Bea's Christmas in, 148
Janis, Elsie, as America's "Sweetheart of the Armed Forces," 36
Jenkins, Gordon, 106
Jerry, and Bea's trust, 270–71
Jessel, George, 78
Jewelry, as Bea's wedding gift, 47–48
Johnny Carson Show, 266
Jolson, Al, 78, 108
  and Louis Epstein, 180
Jones, Al, 135
Jones, Connie, 240
Jones, T.C., 240
Jorgensen, Christine, 155–56, 177–79, 183, 193–94
Juliana, Queen, 149
June Taylor Dancers, 220, 224, 225

Kabuki number, Bea's, 197
Kahn, Otto, 73
Kalmer, Bert, 77
Kander, John, 187, 189, 194
Kaufman, Beatrice, 82
Kaufman, George, 82, 134
Keating, Fred, 187
Keaton, Buster, 71
"Keep the Home Fires Burning," 36
Keith, Larry, 255
Kelly, Grace, 176, 220. *See also* Grace, Princess
Kendall, Henry, 83
Kennedy, Ethel, 269
Kent, Duke of, 53
Khan, Aga, 235
Kind Lady, 207, 216
King, Walter Wolfe, 102
Kingsway Theatre, 39
Kokic, Kazimir, 143
Kristy, Gloria, 220
Kroll, Mark, 196

Lacey, Franklin, 244, 262
Lacey, Gladys, 244
Laceys, the, and Bea, 249–50, 254, 256
"Lady Fandermere's Wind," 136

"Lady in Gray, The." *See* "Wind 'Round My Heart"
Lady Pearl, 206
Lady Windermer's Fan, 136
Laffey, Bruce
  in *An Evening With Highlights*, 245–46
  and Christine Jorgensen, 177–78
  and John, 165–66, 227–28
  last fight with Bea, 257–58
  meets Bea, 157–58
  minds Bea's apartment, 182
  in Monte-Carlo, 231
  reconciled with Bea, 189
  responsibilities of, 161
  and shopping trips with Bea, 210–14
  and *Ziegfeld Follies*, 196
Lahr, Bert, 101, 106, 128, 133–34, 207, 244
  and *Seven Lively Arts*, 135
  and *Song of Woodman*, 105, 106
  in *The Show Is On*, 105
Lahr, Mildred, 207
Lane, Lupino, 92
Lang, Harold, 196
Langtry, Lillie, 42
Lanin, Lester, 192
Lantz, Robert, 139, 140, 141
Lardner, Ring, 74
Late Evening with Beatrice Lillie, A, 231, 238–39
Latin Casino, 164
Lauder, Harry, 78
Laughton, Charles, 205
Lawrence, Carol, 197, 200
Lawrence, Gertrude, 107, 112
  in *A to Z*, 52
  and Bea's age, 143
  as Bea's understudy, 33, 36, 38
  death of, 153–54
  divorces first husband, 77
  financial troubles of, 96
  friendship of with Bea, 34–35
  and "Limehouse Blues," 62
  and New York apartment with Bea, 63–64
  pranks of, 34–35
  talent of, 38–39
  tours with Bea, 65
  in *Treasure Girl*, 82
Lawrence, Pamela, 39
  on Bobbie Peel, 55
Lawton, Frank, 92
Le Fevre, Guy, 33, 37
Le Gallienne, Eva, 79
Le Ruban Bleu, 109
Lee, Gypsy Rose, 240
Leigh, Vivien, 126
Leon and Eddie's, 105
Leonard, Billy, 39

Les Joyeuses Équippées de Till L'Espiegle (Strauss), 222
Leslie, Cole, 251
Leslie, Fred, 62
Levey, Ethel, 25, 33
Lewis, Bud, 116
Life magazine, 197
Life and Times of Cleopatra, The (Weigall), 30
Lillie, Bea
  in *A to Z*, 54
  in *All Clear*, 118–19
  in *An Evening with Beatrice Lillie*, 151–58
  in *An Evening With Highlights*, 245–46
  in *Are You There?*, 84
  in *At Home Abroad*, 99–102
  in *Auntie Mame*, 203–06
  aversion to being alone, 32
  awards given to, 140
  begins to paint, 139
  as "belly-time" eater, 108
  in *Better Late*, 136
  in *Big Top*, 121–22
  bon mots of, 51–52
  and Brandon De Wilde, 150–51, 155, 156, 200–201
  as Carmen, 99
  in *Charlot's Masquerade*, 83
  in *Cheep*, 36
  and "comeback," 165
  and Cyril Ritchard, 229
  and disputes with John, 162–63
  death of, 277
  and death of son, 122–25
  and Doc, 86–87
  drinking habits of, 163
  drinking worsens, 173–86
  early musical training, 16–19
  early press notices of, 21
  at El Patio Club, 92
  and electric canoe, 228
  with ENSA, 125–26
  entertains troops, 117–18, 120–21
  in *Exit Smiling*, 72, 75–76
  and filmmaking, 84–85
  and fire in suite, 144–45
  and French language, 88
  and gardens, 228
  and Gertrude Lawrence's death, 153–54
  goiter surgery of, 94
  greatest weakness, 40
  in Hawaii, 263
  in *High Spirits*, 247–58
  hired by Charlot, 26–27
  hospitalized, 271
  at Houston benefit, 262–63
  impetuosity of, 94–95
  investments of, 196, 201–02

  and life away from theatre, 256
  loses chance at *Mary Poppins*, 135
  and loss of memory, 265–68
  and male friends, 150
  as male impersonator, 28, 39
  marriage of, 79
  and marriage, 115
  and men she loved, 139–40
  at Monte-Carlo, 217–27, 231–37
  and Nadia Gardiner, 174–75, 176
  and New York apartment, 63–64, 84
  New York press reviews, 62
  and Noël Coward, 80–81, 258
  in *Now's the Time*, 30–31
  and Odette Myrtil, 36–37
  in *Oh Joy*, 39
  in *Oh, Please!*, 72–73, 75, 76
  in *Please*, 92
  on political race, 152
  and Presidential matinee, 153–54
  radio career, 94–96
  at Rainbow Room, 96
  reserve of, 58
  restlessness of, 93–94
  and "retirement" apartment, 271–73
  and Rolf Gérard, 139, 141
  and Royal Command Performance, 149–50
  in *Set to Music*, 111–13
  in *Seven Lively Arts*, 132, 133–35
  in *She's My Baby*, 77–78
  shopping trips, 210–14
  in *The Show Is On*, 105–07
  in *The Third Little Show*, 85–87
  in *This Year of Grace*, 80–82
  in *Thoroughly Modern Millie*, 264–65
  and *Too True to Be Good*, 87–88
  in Vancouver, 179–80
  in *Walk a Little Faster*, 91–92
  as widow, 93
  working habits of, 250
  in *Ziegfeld Follies of 1957*, 199–200
Lillie, John, 11–23
  at Bea's wedding, 47
  death of, 92
  in Ireland, 80, 83
  opens boarding house, 22
  opens cigar store, 15
Lillie, John (cousin), 244
Lillie, Lucie, 72, 124, 148
  death of, 201
  increasing senility of, 135–36, 184
  jealousy of Bea, 32
  as Mumsie, 76
  rears Bobbie Peel, 50, 66–67
  sponsors musicales, 18–19

Lillie, Muriel, 12, 47
  at Abercorn Place, 148
  and Arthur Weigall, 31, 34–35, 76, 80
  death of, 264
  divorce of, 66
  drinking, 135–36, 264
  with Lillie Trio, 19–21
  marriage of, 22–23
  marries Napper Dean Paul, 110
  musical training of, 14–16
  and 1926 revue, 67
  press notices of, 22
  as problem, 201
  relations of with family, 184, 185
  and *Tabs*, 36
  and *The Nine O'Clock Revue*, 56
  as widow, 92–93
Lillie Trio, 19–21
  in England, 25–34
  uneasy home life of, 28–29
"Limehouse Blues," 54
"Limehouse Night," 52
Little Darling, The, 76. *See also She's My Baby*
"Little Old Lady," 105
"Little Slut of Six, A" (Coward), 68
Loeb, Philip, 133
London
  Lillies move to, 23
  zeppelin raids on, 31, 38
London Fever Clinic, 26
London Morning, 214
London, Paris, and New York, 54
Long, Nick, Jr., 73, 77
Look magazine, 148, 249
Lord Button, 258, 262, 266, 269, 271
Lord, Pauline, 78
Lorraine, Violet, 89
Louise, Tina, 235
"Love, Honor, and Be Gay Is the Vow the
  Modern Wife Takes," 39
Loy, Myrna, 270
Lucky. See Oh, Please
Lunt, Alfred, 74, 193
Lunts, the, 82. *See also* Fontanne, Lynn
  and "There Shall Be No Night," 131
Lux Toilet Soap, Bea's commercials for, 82
Lyons, Leonard, 241
Lyon's Tooth Paste, 97

MacArthur, Charles, 78, 82, 98, 108
  Bea's romance with, 73, 77
  death of, 193
  marries, 77, 80
MacArthur, James, 208
MacArthur, Mary, 139, 147
Mackenzie, Compton, 32
MacLaine, Shirley, 269

MacRae, Gordon, 177
Macrea, Arthur, 118
"Mad About the Boy," 111
"Mad Dogs and Englishmen," 85
Magdalena, 244
Magowan, Eileen, 138, 184, 214, 227–28
Majestic Theatre, 102, 141
Manley, Betty, 275
Manville, Tommy, 197
"March with Me," 61–62, 73, 78
  Cyril Ritchard on, 245
Margaret, Princess, 149–50
  wedding of, 231
Margaret (Bea's London maid), 195
Markova, Alicia, 128
Martin, Ethel, 245
Martin, Hugh, 247, 248
Martin, Mary, 148, 274
  on Bea, 210–11
  in *Hello Dolly*, 263
  in Monte-Carlo, 232
  in *Peter Pan*, 204
"Marvelous Party," 149
Marx, Harpo, 69, 74, 175
Mary Poppins, 128
  versions of, 116
Matheson, Murray, 136, 190
Matthews, Jessie, 37, 62
  in *This Year of Grace*, 80
"Maude, You're Rotten to the Core," 236
Maxwell, Elsa, 88, 97, 101, 108, 224, 232,
  235
Maxwell, Vera, 235
Mayfair, Mitzi, 106
McCollough, Paul, 91
McCort, Mac, 170
McCullers, Carson, 246
McGrath, Lueen, 235
McGunigle, Rupert Bloomfield (Doc), 86–
  87, 98, 274
  and Bobbie, 97
  last days of, 167–68
  leaves Bea's world, 150
  personal problems of, 141–42
  writes for theatre, 91, 92
McIntosh, Alastair, 59–60
McLean, Mrs. Evelyn Walsh, 76
McMein, Neysa, 73–74, 77, 143
McPherson, Aimee Semple, 84
Medlin, Janet (Mrs. Stern), 161, 178
Melchior, Lawritz, 99
Member of the Wedding, The, 150
Merman, Ethel, 228, 241–42, 274
Merrill, Gary, 196
Merry Widow, 269
Messel, Oliver, 136
Metropolitan Police Force, 42
Meyer, Gerry, 268
Middle East Diary (Coward), 131

"Milady Dines Alone," 195, 196, 207, 244
  in Edinburgh, 239
  staging at Monte-Carlo, 231
Millar, Gertie (later Countess of Dudley), 41
Miller, Gilbert, 134
Miller, Marilyn, 78
Miller, Woods, 100
Mills Brothers, 87
Mink coat, Bea's purchase of, 213–14
Minnelli, Vincente, 175
  and *At Home Abroad*, 100–101
  and *The Show Is On*, 105–06
Mirror, 209
Miss Liberty, 142, 144
Mississippi Flood benefits, 107
Mitchell, Susette, 277
"Moanin' Low," 85
Modigliani painting, 271–72
Molyneux, Edward, 232
Molyneux, Eileen, 27
Monkman, Phyllis, 27, 33, 66, 148, 158, 216
  and Bea, 40, 206–07
  on Bea's drinking, 185
  on Bea's interests, 51
  on Bea's memory loss, 265–66
  on Bea as mother, 124–25
  on Charlot, 28, 38
  death of, 274
  on Lawrence, 39
  and Robert Peel, 42, 44–45
  and Temple of Sun dance, 29–30
Monte-Carlo
  Bea's visit to, 217–27
  honeymoon at, 48–49
Montell, Gladys, 19, 20
  Bea hospitalized as, 271
Montgomery, General, 126
Moore, Grace, 84, 108
Moore, Mary Tyler, 265
Moore, Philippa, 148
  on Bea's funeral, 277
Moran, Polly, 109
Morehouse, Ward, 134
Morgan, Jane, 197, 198
Morley, Robert, 127, 205
Morris, Richard, 264
"Mr. Cochran's Young Ladies," 110
Mr. Lee, 193, 204
  bites, 200
  death of, 258
  journeys to Henley, 206
"Mrs. Ladapeel," 189
Mrs. McThing, 151
Mt. Tom Playhouse, 262
Mundin, Herbert, 62
Munsell, Warren, 272
Murray, Arthur, 200

Murray, Mae, 101, 269
Music Box Review of 1922, The, 91
Music Man, 244
"My Heart Stood Still," 77
"My River Girl," 37
Myrtil, Odette, 32
  and Bea, 36–37, 50–51
  on Bea's finances, 54-55
  on Bea's friends, 98
  on Bea as mother, 124
  on Bea's wedding, 47
  in *Bran Pie*, 40
  death of, 274
  in Ireland, 83
  on New York parties, 63

Nast, Condé, 108
Nathan, George Jean, 81
National Conferences of Christians and Jews,
  140
NBC, Bea's radio career with, 94–96, 138
Nelson, Portia, 209
Nesbitt, Cathleen, 78
"Nesting Time," 39
New Edition of A to Z, The, 52
New Faces of 1934, 94
New Republic, The, 72
New York Post, The, 92
New York Times, The, 62
New York Tribune, The, 62
Newley, Anthony, 186, 245, 246
Ney, Richard, 220, 224
"Night in a Turkish Bath" party, 204
"Night May Have Its Sadness," 61
Night of 100 Stars, 207, 216
Nine O'Clock Revue, The, 56, 73
1936 Ziegfeld Follies, 102
Not Likely, 27
Novello, Ivor, 36, 137
  and *A to Z*, 52
  and *All Clear*, 118
  death of, 148
  elevator apartment of, 52–53
  financial assistance of, 50
  and 1926 revue, 67
"Now," 105
Now's the Time, 30–31

Observer, The, 205
Oh, Boy. See Oh, Joy
Oh, Joy, 39
Oh, Kay!, 73, 96
"Oh, Leo," 101
Oh, Please!
  Bea in, 72–73, 75
  on tour, 76
O'Keefe, Walter, 85

O'Keefe (theatre), 244
Oliver, Vic, 119
Olivier, Lawrence, 207, 216
Olympic, 66
On Approval, 127–28
"On the Western Plains," 85
Onassis, Aristotle, 224, 235, 236
"One Dozen Double Damask Dinner Napkins," 101. *See also* "Dozen Double Damask Dinner Napkins"
One for the Money, 112, 116
Opium, addiction to, 33
Orchestre National de l'Opera de Monte-Carlo, 221
Osborn, E. V., 81
Osborne, John, 204
Osterman, Lester, 247, 252, 254
Ouverture des Noces Figaro, 221
Over the Page, 89

Paar, Jack, 229
Palace Theatre, Bea's appearance at, 83, 85, 87
Palladium, 79, 83
Palm Beach Night, 75
Palm Beach Playhouse, 241
Palmer, Hilde, 141
Palmer, Lilli, 148
Paper Mill Playhouse, 261
Parker, Dorothy, 61, 63
Parker, Lew, 147
Parsons, Louella, 175–76
Parsons, Schuyler, 60
"Password," 244
Pasternak, Dorothy, 224
Paul, Brenda Dean, 110
Paul, Lady Dean, 110
Paul, Napper Dean, 110
Pavillion, 26
Payn, Graham, 250
"Pearl Necklace, The," 29
Pearl trick, 149
Peck, Gregory, 269, 270
Peel, Lady Emily, 43, 64
Peel, Robert, first Baronet, 42
Peel, Robert, second Baronet, 42–43
Peel, Robert, third Baronet, 43
Peel, Robert, fourth Baronet, 44
Peel, Robert, fifth Baronet, 43, 81
   in Australia, 44, 64
   courts Bea, 45–46
   forms orchestra, 75
   joins Bea in Hollywood, 72
   manages theater, 50, 55–56
   marries Bea, 47–50
   and Phyllis Monkman, 44–45
   visits America, 76

Peel, Bobbie (sixth Baronet), childhood of, 50
   and first sports car, 117
   letter on death of, 132–33
   and Lucie, 97
   missing in Ceylon, 122–23
   vacations of with Bea, 99–100, 102, 103–04
Peel Fold. *See also* Henley-on-Thames
   final bulletins from, 276–77
Pekingese puppy, Bea's, 192
Pelham, David, 203, 205, 207
Pelissier, Anthony, 32, 47, 111
Pelissier, Henry, 32
Perelman, S. J., 85
Peter Pan, 204
Philip, Prince, Duke of Edinburgh, 117
   and Bea's final tribute, 279–80
Philip, John, 147, 195–96. *See also* Huck, John Philip
   accompanies Bea, 147, 149, 150, 155, 157, 159
   and Actors' fund, 271–72
   in *An Evening With Beatrice Lillie*, 152
   battles with creative staff, 198
   and Bea, 209
   and Bea's charge accounts, 188
   and Bea's drinking, 173, 181, 185
   and Bea's family, 149
   and Bea's Far East trip, 182–83
   and Bea's final departure, 275–76
   and Bea's final illness, 276–77
   and Bea's investments, 201–02
   and Bea's trust, 270–71
   and *Beography*, 242–43
   and Christine Jorgensen, 179
   and Connecticut move, 270–71
   and Count Fulco, 251–52
   dates another, 184
   and David Pelham, 207
   death of, 277
   and denial of Bea's drinking, 242–43
   as director, 244
   and disputes with Bea, 162–63
   and fight with Bruce, 165–66
   heart problems of, 245
   jealousy of, 191, 215, 249
   and Maxwell Anderson, 174
   and Mr. Lee's journey to Henley, 206
   at Nadia's party, 176–77
   and Noël Coward, 252–53
   own apartment, 208
   and Rene, 180
   and renovation program, 206, 239
   side trip to Spain, 227
   and Thames Conservancy, 207
   treatment of Bea, 257
   unprofessional behavior of, 199–200

Phony War, 117
Pickford, Jack, 72
Pickford, Mary, 19
"Pick-me-up," 176
Pilcer, Harry, 29
Pillbox hats, Bea's, 68
Pins and Needles, 107
Pippen, Donald, 187, 194
Please, 92
Plummer, Amanda, 259
Pons, Lily, 99
Pope & Bradley, 30
Porter, Cole, 133–34
Powell, Eleanor, 100
Powers, Tom, 39
Power, Tyrone, 148, 164
"Pretty Girl Is Like a Melody, A," 233
Pride and Prejudice, 102
"Prisoner's Song, The," 75
Prutting, Dr., 140, 275
Purcell, Charles, 73

Queen Elizabeth, 137, 138
Queen Mary, 107
Queen's Theatre, 118

Rack, 164, 166–67
    accompanies Bea, 238, 239, 240, 244
    drinking of, 232
    and Eadie's death, 202
    at Houston benefit, 262–63
    in London company, 183
    in Monte-Carlo, 231–33
Radio, Bea Lillie and, 94, 96, 102–03
Rainbow Room, 96
Rainier, Prince, 221, 223, 224–26
Rains, Claude, 88
Randall, Carl, 85
Raye, Martha, 108
"Reading of the Play, The," 245
Rebla, 33
Red Cross Ball, Palm Beach's, 240–41
Red Cross Gala, 220–25, 231–37
Redhead, 194
Reeves-Smith, Sir, 117
"References" sketch, 83
Reich, George, 232, 233
Reinheimer, Howard, 152, 188, 194, 203
    and Bea's will, 182
Renee, Ida, 33
Reserve Officers' Association, 140
"Retirement" apartment, Bea's, 271
Reuben's, 75, 213
Revue de Paree radio series, Bea in, 107
Rhodes, Eric, 190
"Rhythm," 105, 106, 110
Rich, Harry W., 18

Rich Concert and Entertainment Bureau, 18
Richardson, Ralph, 216
Ritchard, Cyril
    on Bea's grief, 122–23
    on Bea in *Four for Tonight*, 228–29
    on Bea's male friends, 116
    in *Big Top*, 121
    on Bobby Peel, 44
    as Capt. Hook, 204
    and *Nine Sharp*, 110
    in *Sigh No More*, 129
Robertson, Paddy Browne, 229, 280
Robeson, Paul, 216
Robey, George, 41
Robinson, Robert, 205
Robinson, Airman, 37–38
Rockwell, Doc, 85
Rodgers, Richard, 193
Rodgers and Hart, 105
    and *The Little Darling*, 76
    and *She's My Baby*, 76
"Room with a View, A," 80
Rose, Billy, 74, 131
    and Cole Porter revue, 128
    and Lillie/Porter dispute, 134
Rose, George, 243
Ross, Harold, 78
Ross, June, 117
Round Table group, 61, 82
Royal Court Theatre, 122
Ruby, Harry, 77
Rule's, as trysting place, 42
Russell, Anna, 177
Russell, Mabel, 33, 41
Russell, Rosalind, 203
Rutherford, Margaret, 216

St. Agnes College, 21–22
St. James Theatre, 92
St. Patrick's Cathedral, 211–12
St. Paul, Drayton Bassett, church of, 47
Sally, 54
Salute to Noël Coward, 247
"Sammy," 36
Samples, 33
San Simeon, 71
Sandford, Mary, 240–41
Sardi, Vincent, 266
Sardi's restaurant, 105, 108
Saroya, Princess, 235
Savoy, The, 42, 117
Savoy Plaza, 212
Scapa Flow, Bea entertains troops at, 117–18
Schlee, George, 108
Schwartz, Arthur, 63, 85
Schwartz and Dietz, 138
Season of Variety, A, 32

Sellers, Peter, 216
Selwyn, Arch, sponsors Charlot's *Revue*, 57–61
Sentinel Star, The, 22
"Serenade" (Schubert), 195
Set to Music, 111–13
Seven Lively Arts, 132–35
Shakespeare, Bea plays, 78–79
Shaw, G. B., and *Too True to Be Good*, 87–88
Shaw, Lucy Ann, 11–12. *See also* Lillie, Lucy (Lucie)
Sheen, Fulton, J., 212
Sheppard, Eugenia, 237
Sherbourne Street, 15
She's My Baby, 77–79
  special matinee of, 78
Shore, Dinah, 203
Show Is On, The, 63, 105
  moon number from, 197
Show of Shows, 82–83, 87
Shriner, Herb, 139
Shubert, John, 102, 152
  and *Ziegfeld Follies*, 195
Shubert, Lee, 101
  death of, 170
Sigh No More, 128–29
Sillman, Leonard, 94, 107
  and Huntington Hartford, 222, 224–25
  and *Fight for Sight* benefit, 239–40
Simpson, Wallis Warfield, 106, 192
Simpson's on Strand, 42
Sinatra, Frank, 155
Sissle, Noble, 85
Smith, Clay
  and "America Answers the Call," 35
  in *5064 Gerard*, 29
  return to States, 41
  in *Some*, 33
Smith, Liz, 276
"Snoops the Lawyer," 66
Snowden, Lord, 274–75. *See also* Armstrong-Jones, Antony
Soloway, Leonard, 252, 254, 256, 276
Some, Bea Lillie in, 33–34
"Something Is Coming to Tea," 250
"Song of the Woodman," 105, 106
Sound of Music, The, 232
Spiegel, Sam, 183
Spring Party, 126
Springer, John, 103, 269–70
Sporting Club, 220
  orchestra of, 225
Stall, Sir Osgood, 25
Stanley, Phyllis, 110
"Stay-sober," 176
Steele, Marjorie, 222
Stephens, W. Ray, 128

Stern, Milton, 152, 157, 158, 161, 163
  and John Philip, 198
  and *Ziegfeld Follies*, 196
Stern, Victoria "Old Vic," 161, 165
  and Pekingese puppy, 193
Stevens, George, Jr., 269
Stewart, Donald Ogden, 108
Stewart, William Rhinelander, 60, 134
Stock Managers' Association, 152
Stop That Clock, 91–92. *See also Walk a Little Faster*
Stop the World I Want to Get Off, 186, 245
Stork Club, 105
"Stormy Weather," 222
Stravinsky, Igor, 133
"Strawberry Girl," 18
Strelsin, Al, 222, 224
Strelsin, Dorothy, 222, 224, 240, 274
Striptease, Bea's, 143
Stritch, Elaine, 242
Summer Stock, Bea and Reggie in, 153
Sunday Graphic, The, 205
Sunday Times, The (London), 205
Sunny, 54
"Susannah's Squeaking Shoes," 56, 68
Sutton Club, 87
Suzi, A Star's Story (Graham), 263
Swaffer, Hannan, 58
Swarthout, Galdys, 108

Tabs, 36–38, 250
Tail's Up, 42
Take a Peke, 263
Talmadge, Constance, 60
Tappan Zee Playhouse, 245
Taylor, Albert, 179
Taylor, Elizabeth, 30, 176, 256
Taylor, Sam, 72
Temple, Dot, 39
"Temple of the Sun, The" (dance), 29–30
Terry Twins, 33
That Lady, 139
Theatre Guild, and Shaw's *Too True to Be Good*, 87–88
Theatre Royal, 33
Theatre World, 152
"There Are Fairies at the Bottom of our Garden," 85
"There Are Prairies at the Bottom of Our Garden," 164
"There Are Times" (Novello), 61, 68
"There's Life in the Old Girl Yet" (Coward), 61, 66
Third Little Show, The, 85–87
This Year of Grace, 80–82
Thoroughly Modern Millie, 264–65
Tibbett, Lawrence, 99

Tiffany's, 212
Tiller line of girls, 78
Times, The (London), 205
Times Square Theatre, 61, 80
Titheradge, Dion, 89
  and *Please*, 92
Tonight at 8:30, 119
Tony Award, 158, 194
Tony's, 105
Too True to Be Good (Shaw), 87–88
Toots Shor's restaurant, 105
Toronto, Canada
  Bea's life in, 11–23
  Bea receives keys to, 103
  Beatrice Lillie building in, 279–80
Toronto Conservatory of Music, 17, 21
Toronto Globe, The, 21
Touring, Bea and, 20, 76
"Transatlantiveness," Bea's, 96
Travers, Pamela, 116, 135
Treuman, Paula, 63
Trevor, Claire, 196
Trix Sisters, 52
Troy, Louise, 247, 253, 255, 261
Truex, Ernest, 85, 86
Trust, arranged for Bea, 270–71
Tucker, Sophie, 34, 54, 101
Turgeon, Peter, 141, 143
21 Club, 105
Two Bobs, The, 36
Tyler, James Grant ("Clam"), 127, 128–29,
    136, 137, 163, 168, 208, 266, 267
  as Bea's "nephew," 150
  on Bea's sleeping pills, 149
  and Ellen Graham, 155
  murdered, 271
  and Portia, 209
Tynan, Kenneth, 205
"Typically English," 245

Ulric, Leonore, 75
Under-dressing technique, 26
Up in Mabel's Room, 51, 52
Ure, Mary, 204

Valentino, Rudolph, 71, 72
Vallee, Rudy, 94, 168
Van, Gus, 85
Van Cleef & Arpels, 223
Van Druten, John, 135
Variety, 62, 79
Vega, José, 248
Verdon, Gwen, 194
Victor, Eric, 138
Vigouroux, Ethel, 190, 201, 204, 241
Vigouroux, George, 77, 190, 201, 204, 241,
    274

Virgin Islands, Bea visits, 266–68
Voile, Gladys, 33
Vortex, The (Coward), 67

Wales, Prince of. *See also* Edward VIII;
    Windsor, Duke of
  in theatre crowd, 53
  visits Bea, 55–56
Walk a Little Faster, 91
Walken, Ronnie (Christopher), 258
Walker, Mayor Jimmy, 102
Walsh, Sam, 83, 92, 96
Walthamstowe Silver Band, 225–26
Warner Brothers
  Bea's work for, 82, 87
  suit against, 87, 94
Washington Post, The, 270
Watch Your Step, 33, 171
Water Gypsies, The, 94
Waters, Ethel, 99
Waters, Ronnie, 148
Watts, Richard, 154
"Weary of It All," 111
Weatherly, Tom, 85
Webb, Clifton, 77, 78, 91
  entertains Bea, 138
  in *First Little Show*, 85
Weissberger, Arnold, 274
Weigall, Alured, 92–93
  on *An Evening With Beatrice Lillie*, 183–84
  on Bea's intolerance for alcohol, 98
  on Bea's presence, 111
  cares for Lucie and Muriel, 135–36, 148
Weigall, Arthur, 30
  and *Bran Pie*, 40
  death of, 92
  divorce of, 66
  and Muriel Lillie, 31, 35–36, 76, 80
  and *1926 Revue*, 67
  and *Tabs*, 36
  and *The Nine O'Clock Revue*, 56
Welch's grape juice, 102
West Side Story, 195
Whalen, Tim, 72
What's My Line, 266
"When I Lost You" (Berlin), 26
"When I Said Goodbye to You," 36
"When Yuba Plays the Rumba on His
    Tuba," 85
"Where Did That One Go, Herbert?" 31
Whistler, Rex, 121–22
White, Lee
  in *5064 Gerard*, 29
  return to States, 41
  in *Some*, 33
Whiting, Jack, 77
Whiting, Richard, 33

INDEX

Whoopee Sisters, The, 96
Wilder, Thornton, 82
Wilding, Michael, 176, 204
Williams, Herb, 99
Williams, Hope, 88, 108
  and Bea's hairstyle, 68
  teaches Bea to skate, 91–92
Williams, Rosemary, 220
Williams, Walter, 36
Wilson, Earl, 241, 274
  on Bea's goodbye, 276
Wilson, John C., 111
Willson, Meredith, 244
Wiman, Dwight Deere
  and *Information Please*, 129
  and *The Third Little Show*, 85–87
"Wind 'Round My Heart," 122
Windsor, Duke and Duchess of, 156, 191. *See also* Edward VIII
Winninger, Charles, 73
Winter Garden Theatre, 100
Winwood, Estelle, 170–71
Withers, Iva, 123, 143
Wolfington, Iggie, 190
Wolin, Don, 196
"Woman's Morals, A," 84
Wood, Peggy, 79

Woodward, Edward (Teddy), 247, 253, 255, 258, 261
Wooley, Monte, 92
Woollcott, Alexander, 67
  on *Oh, Please!* 73
  on *She's My Baby*, 78
  Sunday get togethers of, 82
Words and Music (Coward), 111
Works, The, 188, 190, 194
World Telegram, The, 95
"World Weary," 80
World's Fair, 116
Wright, Cobina, Sr., 99, 101, 117, 192
  gives party, 109
Wright, Cobina, Jr., 99–100, 102, 117
Wynn, Ed, 78
  and Bea, 108
Wynyard, Diana, 128

Youmens, Vincent, 73
Young Idea, The (Coward), 38
Young, Loretta, 83

Zanuck, Darryl F., 176
Zeppelin raids, 31, 38
Ziegfeld, Billie Burke, 199
Ziegfeld, Florenz, 25, 50
Ziegfeld Follies of 1957, 199–200